(Continued)

Out
of This World

WHY LITERATURE MATTERS
TO GIRLS

Holly Virginia Blackford

Foreword by Carol Christ

TEACHERS
COLLEGE
PRESS

Teachers College, Columbia University
New York and London

Published by Teachers College Press, 1234 Amsterdam Avenue, New York, NY 10027

Library of Congress Cataloging-in-Publication Data

Blackford, Holly Virginia
    Out of this world : why literature matters to girls / Holly Virginia Blackford ; foreword by Carol Christ.
        p.   cm. — (Language and literacy series)
    Includes bibliographical references and index.
    ISBN 0-8077-4467-0 (acid-free paper)—ISBN 0-8077-4466-2 (pbk. : acid-free paper)
        1. Girls—Books and reading—United States. 2. Girls—United States—Interviews.
    3. Reader-response criticism—United States. I. Title. II. Language and literacy
    series (New York, N.Y.)

    Z1039.G57B58 2004
    028.5'5—dc22   2003068699

ISBN 0-8077-4466-2 (paper)
ISBN 0-8077-4467-0 (cloth)

Printed on acid-free paper
Manufactured in the United States of America

11   10   09   08   07   06   05   04   8   7   6   5   4   3   2   1

To Todd

———————————

My partner in all things great and small

Contents

Foreword

WE ALL FEEL that books take us out of ourselves; they transport us to imaginary lives that transfigure our own. Despite the common agreement that fiction enlarges our experience by inviting us to contemplate its characters, few scholars have tried to investigate in a rigorous way the nature of our relationship to fictional characters in the process of reading. Many assume that we inhabit a book by identifying with its protagonist. When we read *Alice in Wonderland*, we are Alice; when we read *Pride and Prejudice*, we are Elizabeth Bennet. On the basis of this theory of reading, those interested in developing a sense of power and independence in groups of people whom society has traditionally constrained—women, for example, or African Americans—assume that fiction is a powerful tool. By reading stories about strong, feisty, courageous characters of our own gender or ethnicity, we more easily incorporate those traits in our own characters. We identify with Jo in *Little Women* and imagine the possibilities in our own lives differently.

In Holly Blackford's remarkable book, OUT OF THIS WORLD: WHY LITERATURE MATTERS TO GIRLS, she has subjected these assumptions to empirical testing. For all the talk among literary critics about reader responses, there has been remarkably little study of actual readers. How do they reflect on their experiences? How do they describe the perspective from which they inhabit a book? Professor Blackford has designed a study in which she has interviewed a group of girls, ages eight to sixteen, from a variety of backgrounds, about their experiences of reading. Her findings challenge conventional assumptions. The girls that she interviewed do not describe reading a book as inhabiting a single point of view. They enjoy moving among points of view, taking pleasure from the entire design of the fiction. If there is a position that they inhabit, it is the position of the author.

The voices of girls are vivid in this study: "Actually I haven't read too many stories about girls. I like traveling through magical places" (eight-year-old Wendy). "Even though Harry Potter is a boy, it's like you're in the story" (nine-year-old Jessie). Professor Blackford's conclusions take shape from interviews as vividly recounted as the stories that the girls relish. She has used the tools and methods of social science research to test assumptions in literary theory; her book is methodologically bold. Her conclusions are important for several fields—for literary criticism, where they challenge assumptions that are common in literary theory about reader response; for women's studies, where they question an identity politics of reading; and for education, where they encourage a more generous, playful, and literary understanding of the uses of children's books. In working with young readers, Professor Blackford has constructed an empirically based argument for the enabling power and pleasure of literary form.

Carol Christ
President, Smith College

Acknowledgments

A BOOK IS a silent record of many lively conversations in the immediacy of the oral mode. My continual conversations with my colleagues and friends Diane Matlock and Katie Vulic were invaluable. In the throes of interviewing, I showed Katie the transcripts of the eight- and nine-year-old respondents, and she, noting their denial of pretending to be the female characters of stories, immediately said, "That means they are identifying with the narrator." With this sentence, she opened for me a world of possibility. Diane was the first to express astonishment at the girls' disregard of female role models in fiction, which is precisely when I knew that I had to dig further into the issue.

From the inception of the project, I had encouragement and feedback from Julia Bader, Kamilla Elliott, Carol Christ, Barrie Thorne, Sam Otter, Dori Hale, Carol Singley, and Carol Collins. Kamilla Elliott was a particularly sharp reader of an initial draft, encouraging me to consider form beyond genre. Julia kept me going with her warm spirit and guidance. Cindy Clark saw the value of the project in its very early stages and awarded me pilot funds from her Rainbow Foundation for Children's Research. She also gave me the rare opportunity to learn her phenomenal techniques for interviewing children and made me change careers from market research to higher education after she noticed that my face lit up when I discussed children's literature. The English department at the University of California, Berkeley, was generous with awarding me fellowships and giving me a beautiful teaching schedule during the years of the research and writing. Thanks also to Cathy Karmilowicz, Public Information Coordinator at Rutgers, Camden, who patiently listened to the results of this project at Barnes & Noble's "Cappuccino Academy," after which she calmly titled this book.

Various scholars, whether they know it or not, have influenced the direction of the project, particularly at annual meetings of the Children's Literature Association. Even an offhand comment can make such a difference to a researcher trying to put together a puzzle. Karen Coats, chairing a panel at which I presented the contrast of girls' reactions to human and animal social worlds in texts, noted that attention to form would be the postmodern approach to fiction, and identification with animals a remnant of an older pastoral narrative. After I presented the girls' responses to *Harry Potter* at an MLA conference, Roberta Trites said to me, "This kind of close narrative analysis of what kids say about reading is *so* important. Please do more." With those words, she rekindled my enthusiasm for putting together this final analysis, even after a reviewer for a journal had decided that "it just doesn't make sense" that girls would not find of primary interest stories about growing up female. I thank the numerous listeners at panels, many of whom asked for copies of my papers and said that they, too, had engaged in reading practices similar to those of the girls, and thought that their child-selves were "just different" from everyone else. I hope that this book will trigger many more conversations about the value of literature.

I am lucky to have had the support of my immediate family. Unlike the girls of this study, who read when "the real work" of the day is done or when their structured activities are canceled, I grew up free to read anything and everything, anytime. My mother kept me out of school on certain Wednesdays to take me to discount matinees; in an era when the arts were not supported in schools, she ensured that I grew up with an aesthetic education. She gave me books and she took me to her favorite films. Few other children had seen *Agnes of God* and *Witness* by the age of twelve, read *Little Women* by nine. Few other children knew so intimately that art has something to say; few grew up hearing a parent say, "Art is what distinguishes us from animals."

My greatest supporter of all is my husband, Todd Wadhams, without whom I would be completely lost. The synergy of our lives and this project seems most evident in the fact that we welcomed two daughters of our own during this research. Jade and Cassie, thank you for your patience as Mommy shooed your hands away from her laptop. And how quickly you both learned that those three magic words, "read to me," would mean the laptop was turned off and your bedtime delayed until the moon was out in full!

Literature: Vive la Différence

> Most of the books I read have nothing to do with my life and that's the reason that I read them. It's kind of like something new.
> —Twelve-year-old Tae

> I live [being a girl] every day so I know everything like me, so I want to know about something else.
> —Fourteen-year-old Hope

> I like reading different things, about people who are different from me, and not going through the same things I'm going through. I like that. It's just a change from, you know, you get so accustomed to your own life, that reading something's totally different, I like that change. I like that better.
> —Fifteen-year-old Ruth

AS WE ENTER the twenty-first century, with all the changes and mysteries it holds in store for us, people like me, who love to read and talk about stories, are challenged to articulate why literature matters to the future of our citizenry. The girls whom I interviewed for this book taught me that literature matters because it teaches how perspective can be brought to bear on experience. It makes people see and experience worlds they would not normally see, experience, and think about in their everyday lives. Like all art, it is a vehicle for reflection. But literature is a particularly accessible art. Very few storytelling media both entertain and make people think about how reflective experience can be given vision and form.

I did not fully understand this until I interviewed racially, socioeconomically, and geographically diverse girls, ages eight to sixteen, about their experiences with stories in books and other media. I was used to thinking about literature as a form for understanding self, particularly the politics of identity—for example, how a young girl learns about who she can be from seeing girls and women represented in stories. Proponents of multicultural literature, including myself, have tended to feel that all children deserve to have their identity category dignified by seeing the experiences of people like themselves represented in literature. However, the thirty-three girls of this study have a very different story to tell. They have sophisticated ways of engaging with literature that does *not* represent female experience, and indeed they quest for texts that display a vision of difference. In their view, literature is an invitation to move beyond the self, beyond the politics of identity, within which we live our everyday lives. Believing that they open themselves to the vision of life that a text presents, the girls journey out of this world, a world that, they feel, limits them to one subjective point of view and one realm of experience. By departing and returning anew, they experience pleasure and epiphany: in both secular and spiritual senses of the term, literary experience is "out of this world."

I present these girls to those who are interested in the complexities of the narrative imagination. These girls read to enjoy an aesthetic realm of experience. They led me to intense contemplation of genre, form, and media, a shifting emphasis among some scholars of reading and writing: "What seems clearly necessary is a shift of emphasis from language as representation (i.e., what words say) to discourse as action (i.e., what words do). The significance of what an utterance or text says should be understood in relation to what it does" (Coe, Lingard, and Teslenko 5). While many educators carefully select literature for children based upon the values and experiences represented by content, the words of these girls demonstrate that the way in which literature formally *structures* different values and experiences—through literary conventions and genres—defines the content of literature and the experience of reading as a journey.

WHY STUDY CHILDREN?

From the perspective of identity politics and the question of canon diversity, children are a crucial group to study, because the reading and identity-formation processes of children display the negotiations by which a culture reproduces. Many scholars of literature interpret texts and either implicitly or explicitly make claims about the ways in which literature shapes and reflects culture. In today's critical environment, it would be considered inadequate to interpret or teach literature by formalist principles alone, because we have become more attuned to gender and racial politics in stories. For example, *The Adventures of Huckleberry Finn* (Twain) is a text at the forefront of racial controversy. In *Playing in the Dark: Whiteness and the Literary Imagination*, Toni Morrison argues that Mark Twain's novel represents the way in which an American vision of freedom could only be understood through the drama of the "not-free"—the African American slave. In his criticism of those who defend the novel, Jonathan Arac asserts that White critics have identified with the character Huck, who always feels right toward Jim in his heart (19–20) even though the social context for their relationship creates and perpetuates racism. Some parents take the issue of identity politics to the extreme, wishing to censor texts such as *Huck Finn* because they believe them to influence children's and teen's perceptions of themselves and of value systems. I believe that studies of how children actually construct meaning from texts have much to say to all professionals in English studies.

In her study of children reading fairy tales, Bronwyn Davies argues that many disciplines now attend to the role of language in shaping people's understanding of themselves and their worlds and that this interdisciplinary attention to language allows researchers to make sense of how discourses shape people yet allow people to shape themselves:

> Poststructuralist theory undoes the boundaries between the disciplines of sociology, psychology, history and studies of literature. It demonstrates that we need to look not just at the work that collectivities collaboratively do to construct gendered worlds but also to look at the work the language does to limit, shape, make possible, one kind of world or another. . . . The individual subject is understood at one and the same time to be constituted through social structures and through language, and becomes a speaking subject, one who can continue to speak/write into existence those same structures through those same discourses. But, as a speaking subject, they can also invent, invert and break old structures and patterns and discourses and thus speak/write into existence other ways of being. (Davies xviii)

The study of children can revolutionize knowledge, because it can lay bare the intersection of child and adult cultures, clarifying the linguistic embeddedness of individuals. I believe that we have focused more on the ways in which literature "limits" children's worlds than on how reading expands their worlds.

Many scholars of children's literature come to a particular understanding of children's books by interpreting the texts themselves.[1] How children themselves produce meaning is a particularly crucial area of study because child readers are, by definition, colonial subjects of a genre that is controlled by layers of adults and adult institutions (writers, publishers, marketers, critics, bookstores, libraries, educators, parents, and producers and marketers of commercial products and multimedia adaptations), although Eliza Dresang sees the powerlessness of children changing, with the advent of the digital age. Several critics have noted the problematic nature of children's-literature critics who presume to know what "the child" is like and what is good for the child to read (Rose; Lesnik-Oberstein; Shavit), and many scholars and teachers have made efforts to capture the child's point of view on reading and particular texts (Applebee; Benton, *Secondary*; Hubler; Davies; Cherland; Wilhelm; Smith and Wilhelm). My in-depth interviews with girls continues the latter tradition, seeking to advance the conversation between professional and lay readers.

WHY STUDY GIRLS?

I chose to study girls because, for years, I have understood stories of female experience as sites of negotiating female identity:

> The act of reading is one of the modes by which we acquire our social—indeed, gendered—orientations to or identification with the world, as a form of cultural contact. . . . If, in fact, "One never reads except by identification" as Catherine Clément and Hélène Cixous debate in "Exchange," then this identification engenders (reinforces gender difference) at the same time that the act of reading reveals gender. (Bauer 672)

Not only do girls read more fiction than boys (Smith and Wilhelm), but girls also represent a crucial and problematic site of socialization. Psychologists Carol Gilligan and Mary Pipher argue that girls are at risk for losing self-esteem, a theme endlessly repeated in novels by women writers who reflect upon growing up female (see B. White for a survey). Peggy Orenstein, Judy Mann, and the American Association of University Women, in its report *Short-changing Girls, Shortchanging America*, suggest that educational practices privilege male points of view and stories, which my own secondary education in literature echoes. In school, for example, I read William Golding's *Lord of the Flies*, F. Scott Fitzgerald's *The Great Gatsby*, Nathaniel Hawthorne's *The Scarlet Letter*, Ernest Hemingway's *The Old Man and the Sea*, and Robert Louis Stevenson's *Dr. Jekyll and Mr. Hyde*; I also read *Beowulf*, *Oedipus Rex*, and *Hamlet*; at home, I read and appreciated the Laura Ingalls Wilder's *Little House* series; Louisa May Alcott's *Little Women*; Emily Brontë's *Wuthering Heights*; Charlotte Brontë's *Jane Eyre*; Harper Lee's *To Kill a Mockingbird*; Judy Blume's *Are You There, God? It's Me, Margaret*; Johanna Spyri's *Heidi*; countless novels by Danielle Steele; biographies of Harriet Tubman, Judy Garland, and Margot Fonteyn; and my high school favorite—William Styron's *Sophie's Choice*. It was not until my senior year of college, when I enrolled in Julia Stern's American women's writing course, that I understood *Little Women* to have literary value and rich symbolism.

The past thirty years have shifted matters, I reasoned. The contemporary scene of children's and adolescent literature has seen a blossoming of women writers and intriguing female characters. The National Council of

Teachers of English advocates the inclusion of multicultural female characters on syllabi. And numerous guides to selecting and promoting books with strong female characters exist (see Allen; Dodson; Odean; Bauermeister and Smith; Newman; Feminists on Children's Media). Children's-literature scholars Marsha Sprague and Kara Keeling recommend that girls' struggle for self in a patriarchal world be authenticated through the assignment of literature with this theme, suggesting that female characters function as role models, just as women do in girls' lives (Taylor, Gilligan, and Sullivan).

Thus, I set out to interview a diverse group of girls, looking for evidence of girls' performance of and resistance to dominant discourses of growing up female, as articulated in literary stories and other narratives they encounter in life. I organized my research questions around three topics of inquiry:

1. How do girls use narratives about girls and women to interpret their own experiences of growing up female?
2. What are girls' own stories of growing up female and how do girls reflect, construct, or resist available discourses about growing up as an experience of gender's intersecting with race and class?
3. How are the sites of their struggles and joys (in relation to their bodies, for example) structured by narrative texts?

I was particularly interested in their narrations of growing up in a female body, which Joan Brumberg, Susan Bordo, Karin Martin, Emily Martin, and Kim Chernin insist becomes the representation of the female self, a representation fraught with cultural meanings.

Although I pursued an open interviewing style, I kept the order of topics consistent. I first asked the girls to tell me the stories of themselves and their lives. I then introduced the topic of stories and asked them to tell me about stories that engaged them, probing the intersections between stories and their lives. Finally, I asked them imaginative questions that would allow me to analyze how they understood girlhood and womanhood as cultural categories and how those understandings framed their own experiences. My methodology stems from current trends in qualitative research, namely "the interpretive turn" (Lightfoot 38–66), and from close readings of the interview transcripts, which yielded more than two thousand pages of data. For a discussion of methodological issues, see the Appendix.

SO, WHY DOES LITERATURE MATTER?

The reading material that the girls mentioned was as diverse as their lives, with one consistent underlying theme: the literature they most appreciated actually had little to do with their own experiences, leaving all the precious data that I collected about their lives meaningless in an analysis of their reading practices. Despite differences in race, class, age, family circumstances, reading preferences, and reading abilities, the girls' reading practices reveal a consistent pattern. They read for a good story, and a good story means one that they are *not* living—that actually looks *nothing* like the life they know.

In fact, a good story makes them think about the conventions of storytelling, and this consideration of form—the craft of storytelling—is the subject of this book. While it sounds simple, even intuitive, to the many lay readers who ask about my book, it actually raises complex theoretical implications. The reading practices and materials of the girls in this project go against the grain of thirty years, or more, of teacher wisdom: the belief that readers are engaged by stories with characters and social worlds that they can relate to themselves and their own experiences. I found that the girls wish to read or see fiction in order to experience something radically different from their everyday lives. In fact, even when I found that girls appreciate stories that seem reminiscent of the lives they live as girls, upon discussion I found that the girls deny this connection and construct the text's difference from their own lives. They actually voice a philosophy of literature as an aesthetic realm of experience and hunger for encounters with an aesthetic imagination, which they believe removes them from the social role they inhabit in life.

Not only are the stories they appreciate radically disjointed from their personal experiences and life-narrations, but their narrated lives and preferred fictional texts are also distinct in terms of narrative form. The narrations of their lives take the form of the novel of manners, in which plots are developed through an understanding of how shifts in social relations redefine the self and social world through time. They narrate their lives in the comic style of a Jane Austen, intriguingly linked with the "tear-jerking" conventions of the female bildungsroman, a belief in growth through social experience (in the mode of Brontë's *Jane Eyre*, L. M. Montgomery's *Anne of Green Gables*, or Wilder's *Little House*), fused with observations of social nuances that an adult might find in the literature of nineteenth-century masters George Eliot and Anthony Trollope. The narrations of the girls' lives model and perform the fact that girls think of themselves as "relational selves," the term coined by psychologist Carol Gilligan to describe the way in which the female self exists as a self-in-relation-to-others.

When asked, "What makes you *you*?" and when urged to "tell me the story of your life as you've grown up so far," the girls spin rich and engaging narratives about their relationship with family and friends (usually a shift from one circle to the other), their teammates and activities in the community. They display sophisticated understandings of how to read people's body language, meaning, and social intent, and they comprehend the implications of these elements in terms of who stays friends with whom; who moves on and bonds with a different social set; who defies girl networks by beginning to date; how two best friends change alliances, come back together, and shift in many different social circles. Continually "reading" and rereading the situations of family, friends, and community, the girls made me feel as though I were reading *Little Women*. Their stories, like Alcott's novel, combine the interpretation of social details with maintenance of an individual bildungsroman. The girls' bildungsromans follow pastoral narrative: the belief that for the self, things were a little simpler and safer when the girls were younger. Once upon a time, the self was perhaps more authentic and less self-conscious but infinitely more interesting as time went by.

Yet the girls do not emphasize engagement with characters and social worlds in the written fiction they choose to appreciate. My initial research question, "Tell me all the stories you know about girls and women," quickly shut down conversation as the girls struggled to answer. I quickly learned to say, "Tell me stories that matter to you," triggering discussion of a variety of stories, some of which included girls and women and many of which did not. It was the very principle of thinking of a story as "about girls and women" that dampened their conversations of fictional engagement, because the very suggestion of stories about people like themselves, or communities like their own, conflicts with how they grant attention to, and build meaning from, fictional literature.

WHAT WAS WRONG WITH MY RESEARCH QUESTIONS?

I soon came to the realization that my research questions were deeply flawed and revealed my own presumptions, not theirs, about the kinds of literature girls would find meaningful and the way in which literature shapes readers' self-understandings. The girls embraced a different phenomenology of reading and theory of literature from those that I did. This project then became an interrogation of my assumptions and the assumptions of the critics who shaped my training in literary study. Indeed, my understanding of the very processes of reading was shaken at its core. My question "Who would you want to be in that story?" was continually critiqued by the girls, who replaced my assumptions with their own philosophies. They do not experience the "relational self" (Gilligan) of life when engaging with stories in books, films, and plays. Rather, they feel "lost in a book"—the term used by Victor Nell, in his empirical research with adults who are ludic readers, to describe pleasure reading. The girls welcome this loss of self and feel that a powerful piece of fiction both "grabs" them and gives them the power to create a cinema in the mind, demonstrating a continuum of response to literature and film.

In effect, the girls experience narrative literature as immersion in a virtual world, theorized by Marie-Laure Ryan as a phenomenology of reading that is both immersive and interactive, and thus indicative of the sophisticated mental capabilities of all readers to imagine the temporal, spatial, and emotional plane of novels (16). In Ryan's book *Narrative as Virtual Reality*, immersion is the very principle by which both written and visual narrative (other than the avant-garde) operates. She argues that the narrative strategies and techniques developed by nineteenth-century realists and continued by popular fiction in the twentieth century perfect the reader's immersive experience by creating a storyworld that the reader feels to be "real"—not so much in the terms of "lifelikeness," but in the structure of a belief that the spatial and temporal dimensions of the novel (setting and time) continue beyond what the reader sees; that the characters "there" are simulated human beings; and that the descriptions denote not backdrops and props but real scenery and objects (158–59). Although the reader's view of the narrative world is partial, the reader gleans an independent sense of the textual world, apart from the perspective or unfolding (temporal) plain through which the reader discovers the world (90–92). A narrative text creates the feeling that the reader can see a distinct world in which characters live and act. In describing the various paradoxes involved in reading literature, Michael Benton argues that the reader is both a spectator and participant (*Secondary* 15) in the textual world, citing the work of Donald Harding, who argues that experiences described as identification or vicarious experience are not adequate to describe the spectator role; readers react to, not as, characters. Using Harding's insights into the reader's double role as spectator and participant, Benton asserts that detached evaluation (spectating) and imaginative sharing (participating) are connected rather than mutually exclusive processes. See his *Studies in the Spectator Role: Literature, Painting and Pedagogy*, 16–17.

Although the girls emphasize their spectator role and use that role to critique my assumptions about identifying or vicariously experiencing self in fiction, the girls actually define this phenomenology of reading through engaging with aesthetic form. Their understanding of form determines their "horizon of expectations" (Jauss). They feel that a piece of fiction invokes a structure of storytelling through narrative voice, genre and genre combinations, intertext, narrative structure, plot, archetype and symbol, thematic unity, shifting points of view, and authorial design. They seldom have all the terms for these formal elements—their understanding of genre stems from the ways in which films are marketed—but they, for example, describe the interest of characters in terms of formal relationships (hero/villain); they describe the plot according to generic precedents in their minds ("world ending" or "apocalyptic" story); and they maintain interest in the structure of even a verisimilar text ("I like [Flora Schreiber's] *Sybil* because at the end, she's all one," emphasizing quest).

To the girls, then, texts materialize the process of a storytelling imagination and the conventions by which an alternative world can be constructed. Just as Ryan argues, the experience of immersion in narrative is not, as is often thought, an experience of the text as transparent, and thus an inactive reading experience. The girls' rich engagement with form demonstrates the sophistication of experiencing and reflecting upon immersion, because the girls are always aware of the forms by which the narrative allows them to experience immersion. This book is a response to their desire for discussing *their* phenomenology of reading rather than emphasizing transparent aspects of literature—for example, whether female characters and stories empower girls, what lessons or values literature teaches, or how social and diversity issues are represented in children's reading.

THE CHAPTERS

In Chapter 1, "Seeing and Imagining the Text," and Chapter 2, "Going 'Off-World' for Insight," I explore how the girls construct a text as an aesthetic object with spatial and temporal boundaries, which they describe as a world and which we can understand as both a product of the novel's narrative strategies and the girls' propensity to be proficient with narrative strategies, used in both literature and film. The act of witnessing narrative in film pervades the girls' metaphors for the action of reading literature. The girls articulate an omniscient presence that they establish "in" the literary text, as readers and "inside" participants. Girls construct a literary text as both an aesthetic object and an alternative world, separate from life and their social worlds. By forging a relationship with the presumed spectator of a text, they experience a welcome diffusion of identity, bifurcating themselves into a "seeing and imagining" agent "in" the text and differentiating this omniscient, reading self from the self that exists in life. Inhabiting this reader position allows them to feel that they "see" the conventions by which a literary world is made and the vision of the world that the text presents. Thus the text comes to stand for the materialization of imagination and vision as well as the nature of thought and perspective.

In Chapter 3, "'It's Like a Fantasy World': Gender and Form," and Chapter 4, "The Genre of Identity: Suspense, Action, Quest, and Gothic Form," I scrutinize the means by which the girls both identify with the formal elements of fictional texts and trace those elements to generic storytelling traditions, with which they develop proficiency in both literature and film— both narrative forms because of their temporal dimensions. The girls discuss each text as a unique presentation of formal elements, a blend of distinct generic strands. By virtue of presenting narrative genres, literary and cinematic texts embody not only alterity from the girls' social selves and worlds, but also alterity from generic traditions. The girls place themselves within a tradition of reader/viewership and authorship/production based upon their accruing narrative experience. Characters are only important insofar as they embody such dialectical forms as hero and villain, character and foil, and so on. Close readings of the girls' responses reveal that they conflate identity with literary traditions—"I'm not a romance person; I'm more action"—and that they feel particular value in reading and viewing forms they know well, forms that I historicize to suggest that there are important connections between gender and genre.

In Chapter 5, "Cherchez la Femme: The Problem of Verisimilitude," I analyze the rhetoric of alienation that girls voice when they discuss texts that depict complex female characters and social worlds. Because many of the fictional texts that girls appreciate feature predominantly male universes, power structures, and social worlds, I first worried that my findings suggested that the girls view male experiences as more universal and significant, or more worthy of aesthetic form. Importantly, girls' quest for aesthetic realms does not preclude the possibility that they will find stories about girls and women meaningful, but they only do so if they themselves can create an aesthetic distance and thematic unity. Texts that they perceive as verisimilar—as "like" the social worlds that they know in life—pose a problem of "invisible" form; thus they try various formal approaches to verisimilar literature, measuring plot and narrative structure against traditional forms, such as quest and mystery.

The girls are much more likely to seek out stories about girls in films, which I discuss in Chapter 6, "Film and 'Reelism.'" Although girls discuss their experiences of written and viewed fiction as spectator-response, film is also a symbol for adaptation of text into the viewer's real social world. It is a more popular social form and thus has social implications in girls' real lives. Because films organize social events and serve as social currency, films signify the "real" space of adolescence. They believe and wish film to have more mimetic qualities than literature.

In Chapter 7, "Beauty in the Beast: The Power of Metamorphosis," I discuss the ways in which the girls contrast reading literature with the role-playing they do in pretend play, in which they imagine themselves as other people, and animal pretend, in which girls *do* identify with the animal character, feeling a truly embodied identification with all kinds of animals in all kinds of animal narratives. When encountering animal characters in both literary stories and other life-narratives, girls desire to role-play the animal, stressing the bodily power, movement, and revenge plot that they enjoy in such fantasy. In this fascinating embrace of the narrative plot of meta-morphosis, they demonstrate that their pleasure in "losing themselves" in a book is complemented by a longing to pretend "just being" (eleven-year-old Vanessa) in the material, animal body, as if they have both a postmodern and pastoral consciousness.

WHERE ARE THEIR HUMAN ROLE MODELS?

Lest we feel that the girls are just not conscious of how literature affects their identities, we have to note that they self-consciously identify with role models in what they perceive as real life. They crave stories about and told by the women in their lives. They hang posters around their mirrors and imagine themselves becoming the women of those posters: sports figures such as Mia Hamm, titled "woman hero" on a poster in a ten-year-old's bedroom; or singers such as Monica, whose song about menstruation "makes you feel less alone" (fourteen-year-old Alevay); or actresses such as Sarah Michelle Geller, Drew Barrymore, and Katie Holmes:

> My role model is Katie Holmes. I love her acting. The way she deals with things on the show—I like to sort of do that. [In *Dawson's Creek*] they have problems in school that I will have. I feel what they feel. Sometimes when I get into a problem I look at myself and I'm doing what she would probably do. The way she deals with things, it helps. (Fourteen-year-old Alex)

Many girls feel television and magazines to be models of information for problem solving in their lives, taking an efferent stance (Rosenblatt) toward discourses that they perceive as "windows" onto the contemporary scene.[2]

The girls' mothers and friends lead them to self-help books about being a girl or a teen, books such as *How I Survived Being a Girl* (Van Draanen), *Chicken Soup for the Teenage Soul* (Canfield, Hansen, and Kirberger), *Reviving Ophelia* (Pipher), and *Girltalk* (Weston):

> [*Girltalk*] gets me through so much. If I have a problem I just look it up. My question's answered. She [the author] was talking to me. I feel exactly that way! I know a lot of girls do! It matters to me because now I know that other people are thinking it too and there's nothing wrong with me! (Twelve-year-old Randi)

These books "tell you what your life can be" (fourteen-year-old Margaret) and connect the girls to an "imagined community" (Anderson) of girls-becoming-women, the friends with whom they discuss the situations of *Chicken Soup*, and the mothers who, through giving them these books, show how much they care about them. The girls constitute memory and life itself as a constantly evolving autobiographical narrative: "My life is just one big story. Like it's all one big story put together. When you think about it, it's just like one big story complete and so everything leads to another thing" (twelve-year-old Margaret). This big story is not the story they appreciate in fiction, however. The adolescent or coming-of-age novel has become less relevant in a world featuring a plethora of information on growing up.

WHY ARE FEMALE CHARACTERS OF FICTION NOT ROLE MODELS?

The more direct role-playing experiences that the girls describe in their accounts of "real life" narratives and animal stories exemplify the responses that I thought I would find in their accounts of reading about girls and women in fictional literature, in which female characters struggle for or achieve self, agency, power, or social and self-awareness. But the respondents perceive literature as a vision of difference from self and life. This need to experience difference is perhaps why the girls read at all, when they have so many other things to do. Although not avid readers, the girls in this study read at bedtime, on the bus between sporting events, in waiting rooms—in other words, when "the work of the day" is done or suspended, demonstrating the predominant idea in our culture that reading fiction is actually not an activity in itself, but something to be done after dinner and dishes. For the girls in this study, reading is a special time and not "real life" at all; it is something to do after the chores of real life are complete. Adults view it as relaxing, while the girls view it as a deeply satisfying immersion in imagination, even authorship.

My research with these contemporary girls demonstrates that even when encountering the text in which the respondents' category of identity *is* represented, the respondents still seek a primary relationship with aesthetic form. Feminist debates about *Harry Potter* (Rowling) often revolve around the question of whether Hermione is a strong female character or not (in, for example, the discussion at the panel "The Poetics and Politics of *Harry Potter*," MLA, New Orleans, 2002). While the feminist in me agreed with Roberta Trites's critique that "Hermione spends most of the second book as a stone," rich narratives of formal concerns among my respondents who discuss *Harry Potter* suggest that in their reading strategies, they move beyond identity politics and into philosophies of aesthetics. I am not suggesting that we should not be happy that, for example, the female character Jane of Disney's *Return to Never Land* is a much more assertive and modern character than Wendy. But Jane became my daughter's "friend," just as Peter always had been. Neither character actually gives her unique access to the fantasy of Neverland, because an active imagination builds and owns the fantasy in a mental landscape.

Colleagues who have been kind enough to listen to the results of this study have pressed me to consider "why" I found what I found. That is, why do these girls primarily engage with theme and form, rather than character, when they read? There are at least seven possible explanations, and all of them are probably interacting to produce the aesthetic stance (Rosenblatt) that troubled my feminist perspective on how women's writing might engage girls.

1. *Is it something about reading?* Certainly Ryan, Benton, and Nell would say yes, and both Ryan and Nell would emphasize the effects of popular literature, which tends to be less experimental and more formulaic.
2. *Is it something about children?* Young readers have always read or been encouraged to read more fantasy and are often considered to be less "fixed" in their identity. Is it only in looking back at our child-selves that we more fully consider the socializing effects of the stories we read? In fact, the girls themselves consider their younger selves as more fully engaged with female characters. But they also think that "other people" relate to same-gender characters because of "the gender thing."
3. *Is it something about girls?* The traditional wisdom of marketers and publishers is that male characters will more readily engage both male and female readers. In *You Gotta BE The Book*, Jeffrey Wilhelm finds that girls engage with characters and boys with action, replicating our assumptions that there are "girl-books" and "boy-books." However, in their recent book, Michael Smith and Wilhelm argue that boys forge relationships with characters, and the authors thus critique the presumption that girls are more oriented toward the social world than are boys. Feminist critics assert that female characters are important to female readers (Hubler; Davies; Cherland; Brownstein). I had also anticipated the possibility that girls might identify with male characters, who often embody possibilities for action, power, and agency. But the respondents of OUT OF THIS WORLD prefer to identify with omniscience and genre, which does not preclude engagement with character but which problematizes unmediated connections with characters.
4. *Is it something about American readers?* The concept of detached viewing is an established nineteenth-century concept in American letters, so probably the answer to this question is yes.

5. *Is it something about our cultural moment?* Eliza Dresang finds that today's children more casually cross the race and gender of characters in books because they are more open to diversity and do not view identity category as a ruling principle of story engagement, whereas their parents would (70). Is it something about today's changing book market? We see increasing attention to aesthetics and new narrative strategies in children's books, Dresang demonstrates, and any trip to Barnes & Noble reveals an immense display of fantasy, science fiction, and mystery for children and adults, suggesting an interaction of factors. Fantasy is enjoying a revitalization, and just as the advent of film in the early twentieth century pushed the novel in a more interior and psychological direction, argues Kamilla Elliott in her lectures at the University of California, Berkeley, the plethora of information and visual entertainment available today may be driving literature—and people's use of literature—in directions not satisfied by visual media. (See Sherry Turkle and Dan Tapscott's books for accounts of the Internet generation. See Neil Postman for a discussion of the way in which electronic media is eroding the lines between childhood and adulthood itself.)

6. *Are children taught to read in a detached manner?* I tried to gather a diverse array of responses to avoid capturing any particular teaching style. But however much Benton ("Reader-Response") claims that today's secondary school practices are influenced by reader-response principles, New Critical principles may still inform classroom instruction. To respond to this issue, I would argue that the way in which girls apply film genres to literature suggests that they have not mastered literary genres and narrative techniques, if it has been taught to them. High schoolers, at least, feel that they are only taught the relevance of literature to history. So perhaps the answer is no. We can certainly say that the genres these girls most appreciate are not typically included in the high school curriculum and that the teen girls in this study seek to appreciate form nonetheless. In fact, it would seem that the genres marketed by publishers, bookstores, and film marketers are controlling literary experience more than teachers are, a fact that is neither surprising nor enlightening.

7. *Is it something about less avid readers?* I do have some evidence to suggest that the children of academics, included in my following project, pay greater attention to character and empowerment through character, so maybe. My intent in this project was to capture children who are *not* academic children, a population that I would like to engage more fully in reading. And however well versed academic children are in the discourse of identity politics, they still carefully explain to me the generic categories with which they divide types of literature in their minds. It seems simply obvious to the girls of today that genre is the main principle of

understanding literature. And the girls do not mean the basic genres of poetry, play, and prose, but the publisher categories of fantasy, mystery, science fiction, myth and legend, and "young adult"—perceived as "chick lit," which is "you know, girls who discover their inner female being," states a sixteen-year-old with biting irony.

Last, some scholars resist viewing my findings as positive, interpreting the girls' sense of visualizing the literary world and form as disengagement. I have been surprised that my results even disturb some scholars. I grew to value these responses, and I hope you will too. I find them incredibly sophisticated and indicative of a beautiful impulse to think about how language can shape an experience beyond self. I feel that my results have implications for engaging young readers, and I reflect on those implications in a coda at the end of the book.

These girls have changed the way that I teach literature at the college level, where many of my students are future teachers of English. I reflect upon these changes and gesture toward curricular implications in the coda, "Tapping Girls' Responses to Reading." Whereas I formerly represented multicultural literature to my students as embodiments of diverse identity-struggles and experiences, I now focus more on form, realizing that it is a disservice to writers to present their stories as instantiation of specific identities, rather than art. When you think about it, *all* children should be able to "see" worlds that are distinct from their own through appreciating storytelling forms. Literature uses form to bridge author and audience, and that bridge becomes a way for children to imagine and tell stories. I hope that this book will encourage a new understanding of why literature matters and open up possibilities for all of us to appreciate how literature continues to structure the creative imagination.

Seeing and Imagining the Text

Even though Harry Potter is a boy, it's like you're in the story. The words
make you feel like you're in the story and you're there.

—Nine-year-old Jesse

WHAT IS THE NATURE of this reader's presence? How is she "in the story"
and what is that experience like? Is her presence dependent upon "whom"
the story is about? Is it accurate for children's-literature critics to equate her
presence with Hermione, or a female character in the story?

Without readers, literature has no life. Before I answer the questions I raise,
I have to describe my point of entry into the study of "formative" literature.
Literary critics working to historicize texts and readers, whose strategies vary
with cultural circumstance, have lent invaluable insights to the project of interpretation by answering Fredric Jameson's call to restore the political unconscious of texts: "All literature, no matter how weakly, must be informed
by what we have called a political unconscious, . . . all literature must be read
as a symbolic meditation on the destiny of community" (70). I embarked upon
this reader-response project to "read" the ways in which narratives that girls
find meaningful reflect upon their destiny as women. I assumed that the content of the literature that girls discuss would reflect their sense of self, based
on a critical assumption that literature expresses how a culture thinks of itself (Tompkins, *Sensational* i). During the past twenty-five years, the field of
literary studies has responded to the perceptive criticisms of feminist and
multicultural-studies scholars who voice the need for us to diversify the canon
and represent diverse voices, students, and experiences in the literature we
choose to teach, research, and publish. Despite this critical environment, training, and belief system, I was astonished to find that in the accounts of reading
voiced by thirty-three racially and socioeconomically diverse girls, formal rather
than sociological characteristics of texts take precedence. Form "makes" the
reader "feel" an impersonal presence, and the phenomenon that we would call
imagination unhinges these readers from "who they are" in life, allowing them
to experience and appreciate mental worlds in an aesthetic fashion.

HOW CRITICS BELIEVE THAT IDEAS INFLUENCE PEOPLE

Literary texts—particularly popular novels—are often imagined to have the power to exclude or include particular people, and even to import ideology (Baym; Davidson; Armstrong; Miller; Brodhead). Our tendency to view literature as powerfully shaping people's identities stems from the influential theories of Michel Foucault, a historian who argues that in the nineteenth century, *ideas* became a form of discipline and that ideas are a more effective way of controlling behavior than is physical coercion. Ideas, imported through discourse, shape people's self-understandings. Critics who study how gender roles are reproduced within the family, such as Valerie Walkerdine, who studies the impact of *Little Orphan Annie* on a working-class family, often feel that popular stories help shape who people understand themselves to be.

Judith Fetterley asserts that to be a reader of texts representing male experience is to identify as male: "To read the canon of what is currently considered classic American literature is perforce to identify as male. . . . [T]he female reader is co-opted into participation in an experience from which she is explicitly excluded; she is asked to identify with a selfhood that defines itself in opposition to her; she is required to identify against herself" (492–93). Similar points are made by Elaine Showalter ("Toward"), Jonathan Culler, and Patrocinio Schweickart, who argues that although the female reader is invited to identify with the male self at the center of a text, she is always simultaneously implicated in the representation of the female character (535). Toni Morrison and Barbara Christian suggest that it is an inherently different process for a woman or African American reader to read the "great" American male classics than for a White man to read them.

I mention these pioneering critics because they have helped to shape the contemporary sensibility of the university. As more women and minorities have entered literary studies in the university, they have demanded inclusion of female and minority writers in curriculum and syllabi; the signifying practices of women writers (Showalter, *Literature*) and African American writers (Gates), for example, have enlightened institutions to the fact that all American students should see their identity categories represented in their intellectual and cultural heritage. In a recent *PMLA* article, Stephen Greenblatt argues that identity politics has been institutionalized by English departments, which expect applicants with an ethnic surname to have an interest in the corresponding ethnic literature. This view has become common among children's writers and publishers. Despite the continuing power of folktales and fairy-based stories or classics with characters of all ages, many publishers insist that child readers need a hero or heroine only a few years older than they are for a full identification. Apparently, few have noticed, for example, that many of the most cherished stories and nursery rhymes of our culture neither necessarily reflect age-related concerns of contemporary children nor the values with which we regard our children.

The pressure to provide literature that mirrors real life is particularly poignant in visual media. Recently, artist John Blackford (also my brother) was designing a fantastic image of a boy on a subway for New York City's Metropolitan Transportation Authority, when a discussion arose about whether the child in the ad should be wearing a seatbelt. The very idea of aesthetic fantasy has been continually assaulted in American culture (Avery), and if childhood as an idea is currently being undone by the electronic age (Postman), it is certainly the case that today there is little faith in the value of imaginative realms that are not subject to the same laws as everyday life. In his preface to the new edition of *The Disappearance of Childhood*, Postman comments on the letters that he has received from children, letters suggesting that children themselves may be keeping childhood alive. The conflict that I have detected here, between adult-critical views of what children's stories should do and children's own views of what stories should do, suggests that through literature, the girls in my study are claiming spaces in which to fly without seatbelts. To the aesthetic perception, seatbelts are irrelevant and pedestrian. In nonvisual media, the adult tendency to measure textual worlds against everyday universes imposes worldviews that may not be important in the context of an artistic world.

THE RELATIONSHIP BETWEEN LITERATURE AND LIFE

As meaningful as it is to include all perspectives in literature for contemporary children, historians such as Marilyn Yalom argue that it is hard to determine and assert the relationship between literature and culture. A scholar can never be sure if a popular story or literary scene expresses a cultural reality or an idealized fantasy. In "Gender as a Personal and Cultural Construction," Nancy Chodorow cautions critics about overgeneralizing claims about how culture influences gender. "When an object, experience, thought, or category of meaning is particularly important to us, we may experience it as a transitional phenomenon, as both personally created and presented from without" (520), she writes. For ideas in literature to influence individuals, the stories need to matter enough to be granted personal meaning. The meaning of a text for a lay reader may be quite different from the literary critics' understanding of the literature's cultural role, as Janice Radway shows in her interviews with romance readers. Although Radway's literary-critical lens allows her to deconstruct the romance novel and conclude that the form and content seek to produce women who wish to define themselves through men and (inadvertently) become wives and mothers, she also determines through interviews that romance readers use the novels to remove themselves from their daily social roles as wives and mothers. They grant the act of reading a meaning in defiance of the genre's glorification of romantic desire for men.

After interviewing the thirty-three girls about their narrations of their lives and stories that had meaning for them, I detected a similar disjunction between how the girls view literature and the critical fact that the way they produce meaning from literature would be impossible to understand from a content analysis of the works that they appreciate. Although the predominant life themes of my respondents include defining the relational self by stressing relationships and communities, the literature they wish to discuss looks nothing like their life—formally, stylistically, socially, or thematically. The patterns that I trace in this chapter concern the girls' desire for literature to be an aesthetic realm of experience. They deny identification with character, male or female, and instead, embrace a formal self-construction through taking on the role of impersonal reader, identifying with an omniscient narrator, and emphasizing the mental activities of "seeing" and "imagining" a storytelling world, which includes seeing the shifting points of view of characters and narrator within a text.

FLOATING ABOVE THE STORY

The girls construct a piece of literature as an aesthetic object, separate from life. They claim a presence "in" the text, not as a character or a specific identity, but as an omniscient gaze, which they distinguish from the self of life. When reading literature, they deliberately put aside their social context for identity and ask that the literary text give them an experience that transcends their own lives, reading not to learn about themselves or who they can and cannot be, but to encounter alterity, or a radically different experience and world. The girls' narrations emphasize that their reading is a process that mirrors the illusions of art. For them, art aspires to transcend historical context and stand alone. The girls ask that literary texts reconstitute them as a formal, impersonal presence and remove them from the "myself" they are outside the text, in life. The aesthetic act is itself ideological (Jameson). It allows the girls to imagine that they take a break from and move beyond themselves.

When choosing to become a reader, girls rupture the self from frames of reference for identity, time, environmental context, and the body:

> [Reading *Harry Potter*] I felt like I was in the audience. I don't picture myself like seeing myself. I just think I'm in the story, like

floating above them or something. Watching what they're doing. In
Harry Potter I think I'm just watching them. But in, I have this Spice
Girls video and it's them singing their songs. And I picture me
walking beside them. But when I watch [*Harry Potter*] I don't picture
me right there. I just think I'm there. Just I don't see myself. And
they're friends with me and stuff, just they don't care how I look or
anything. (Eleven-year-old Vanessa)

Vanessa feels that the text establishes her presence as a formal construct of
impersonal audience, which is neither her identified self of life nor a male
perspective. She experiences this presence as an out-of-body experience, in
which she is floating above the field of action and characters but lacking a
social picture of herself. Although the characters are her "friends," she does
not connect them to relationships in terms of body or appearance, as in social
life. She struggles to define her presence "in the text," an impossible presence, given its status of disembodiment and invisibility.

This insistence that textual presence is not embodied or visual recurs in
the girls' descriptions of reading. In everyday life, we feel present but have
no picture of our whole bodies from our own gaze, yet a social idea of us
creates a conceptual "picture" of ourselves in social life. But in the literary
text this picture is diffused, for texts refuse to "picture" a specific social reader.
The effect is to create a desocialized reader, through whom the text transcends the social constructs of its making. The watcher of the text is beyond
social pictures of the self, beyond referential "how I look," beyond communal identity, since the characters cannot "see" or define this watcher, and
beyond membership in a community that makes Vanessa *Vanessa*.

Vanessa discerns reading as a movement beyond identity and yet she
performs feminine identity with the Spice Girls video, demonstrating that in
a video she identifies with the act of performance and in a book she identifies with the act of omniscient reading. The performance that she enjoys with
the Spice Girls video operates by the principle of identity politics; she both
sees women acting in a particular way and imagines herself as Vanessa performing the actions of the Spice Girls. In that imaginative experience, she is
both Vanessa the girl and Vanessa the possible Spice Girl, two identities fused
in imaginative role-playing.[3] The impersonal reader of Vanessa's descriptions
parallels the text's third-person narrator more than a person in the story.
Like the reader, the narrator is always present but has no social "picture,"
no human form. And, in Vanessa's words, the narrative establishes intimacy
with the characters ("friends") since the characters "don't care how [the
narrator] looks" either. The narrator also "floats above" the characters,
"watching what they're doing."

THE IMPORTANCE OF THE NARRATOR

Girls identify with and establish a relationship between themselves as readers and the storytelling narrator, and this identification supercedes their relationships with characters:

> I don't really put myself in the story. I like the whole bizarre fantasy thing [of King's *The Stand*]. I just kind of like "wow," what if that ever did happen. The narrator tells you everything, that's just what I think it is. Having the story told to you by the narrator of the story. I just think of it more as like watching it happen, like hearing it happen. It's the whole better understanding thing. I like that in stories. (Fifteen-year-old Ruth)

Ruth replaces "herself" with the constructed nature of the narrative. She defines her reading self as bifurcated by the language, as revealed by her awareness that a person *could* put themselves *in* a story, but *she* does not appear in the text as "myself." She replaces the active voice of the first sentence with the passive construction, "having the story told to you," both participating in and allowing the text to happen (Benton, *Secondary* 18). The formal device of the omniscient narrator allows the "whole bizarre fantasy" that part of the self is left outside the story and the self as pure eye and ear, or as abstract sensory experience, comes into being. She highlights narration as a process with the present participle *having*, showing that the text achieves its possibility and imaginative reality ("what if") by pushing aside her social reality and remaking her into perpetually present senses without a body, just as the narrator is a perpetually present voice without a body in the text. The disembodied voice needs a disembodied ear, for the narrative voice constructs the illusion that someone is being spoken to. By becoming conscious of narrative process, Ruth links the craft of storytelling to its action upon the reader—its ability to invoke a rhetoric of wonder and the illusion that a fantasy has come to life through the narrator-reader relationship.

The distinct role of the narrator has been an element of novel theory in the work of many critics (W. Martin). Critics such as Henry James, Percy Lubbock, and Mikhail Bakhtin tend to separate the narrator from characters and regard the characters as independent entities, Dorothy Hale observes. By distinguishing reading from role-playing actual people, my research subjects suggest that this separation between narrator and characters is crucial to the process by which they become a reader and thus view the field of action "with" the narrator rather than central protagonist(s). Girls separate who is speaking from who is seeing in the novel in a process that mirrors narrative focalization, theorized by Gerard Genette and Mieke Bal. The narrator focalizes the narrative through a character or particular point of view, and, importantly, narrative involves shifts in focalizations. The idea of shifting focalization accounts for the girls' separations between narrative voice and ways of seeing the field of action.

The various points of views and social consciousnesses in the novel are more commonly thought of as dialogic voices, given the popularity of Bakhtin's novel theory. To Bakhtin, the novel embodies the social heteroglossia of life by representing the social discourses that real individuals use in different social settings. Characters are allowed to dialogue in their own voices, independent of narrator and author. This allows the novel to include a fascinating array of voices and the reader to feel she has perspective on many voices, wandering from one perspective to another while reading. The idea that engaged readers *hear* the language of literature should be familiar to those who advocate reading aloud to children, believing that oral qualities inform children's later success in silent reading.

Ryan identifies the aesthetics of the nineteenth-century novel as pivotal in allowing readers to experience immersion in a storytelling world. While earlier narrative style simulated nonfictional narrative modes, the nineteenth-century novel changed fiction:

> High realism effaced the narrator and the narrative act, penetrated the mind of characters, transported the reader into a virtual body located on the scene of the action, and turned her into the direct witness of events, both mental and physical, that seemed to be telling themselves. Readers not only developed strong emotional ties to the characters, they were held in constant suspense by the development of the plot. The immersive quality of nineteenth-century narrative techniques appealed to such a wide segment of the public that there was no sharp distinction between "popular" and "high" literature: wide strata of society wept for Little Nell or waited anxiously for the next installment of Dickens's serial novels. (4)

The evolution of the twentieth-century novel "split literature into an intellectual avant-garde committed to the new aesthetics and a popular branch that remained faithful to the immersive ideals and narrative techniques of the nineteenth century" (5), the storytelling forms dominating the literature mentioned by the girls. However, the term *immersion of the reader* "implies transparency of the medium" (4), while the girls are fascinated with the process of immersion and the activation of immersion by both reader and text. Immersion allows the reader to imagine that she is "lost in a book" (Nell) yet "there" as the addressee of the narrator.

READING WITH MULTIPLE SELVES

Feeling that immersion in a literary text allows the reader to see a world in its entirety, which Ruth (above) expresses as a "whole understanding" because the narrator reveals "everything," the girls reveal that to experience this whole they have to split the self into two, the referential and textual self. A self exists outside the text, in life, and a discursive self floats, hears, sees, or reads the text, as nine-year-old Sam insists: "I read it [the story] to myself." The girl is the agent and receptor, a doubled self of both imaginative involvement and aesthetic detachment (Benton, *Studies* 16–17; Ryan 98).

Many girls voice this sense of being doubled when reading, even when the narrator of the text has a human form, as in J. D. Salinger's *The Catcher in the Rye*. In fact, when sixteen-year-old Olive describes her experience with *The Catcher in the Rye*, she splits herself into not two but three parts: the "I" who imagines, reads, and sees the text; the "I" who imagines and sees herself outside the text, as she exists in life; and a "myself" independent of both the text and the socially identified self:

> I can imagine myself in [Holden's] position, sort of taking on some of his characteristics but not really exactly being him. I just saw myself making those same kind of choices, you know, seeing that person the same way he did. (Sixteen-year-old Olive)

In reading, Olive not only sees *through* the narrator Holden ("seeing in the same way")—which she describes as a "teenage perspective"—but also sees apart from him, "not exactly being Holden." She identifies on one level with the narrator's voice, but also on another level with a reader construct, a reader who is aware that a self-presence exists in the text *and* outside the text. She sees a further self (her referential self) outside the text and measures Holden's character, ways of seeing, and choices against that self. The self outside the text is then both the self she compares Holden to and the imaginal agent beside Holden in the text: "I can imagine myself seeing." She layers the "I" as imaginal agency over the self whom she can imagine sharing Holden's viewpoint.

Olive establishes a relationship with the narrator, and that relationship alienates and dissociates the reading "I" from the referential self, doubled by formally identifying with the act of reading *and* with the act of seeing through Holden. By reading, she separates herself from the social self that exists in life, and that social self becomes visible to her, in a vision seldom possible in life. Reading thus creates a nonsocial space for identity, diminishing the importance and totality of her socially identified self, and provides a vantage point from which the social self can be evaluated. Olive's category of identity is othered by her experience of the text. She achieves a new sense of herself when constituted in Holden's point of view; and she obtains a reading self, imagining and seeing these other senses of self at the same time that she sees through Holden's eyes ("I"). The textual presence she creates is a construct of literary narrative but is not limited to the narrator.

SEEING AND IMAGINING AT THE SAME TIME

The girls emphasize that literature gives them a way of seeing and imagining, thus standing for the materialization of vision. The key terms of seeing and imagining proliferate through the girls' descriptions of literary experience, and they often combine these two terms to define the process of reading as "imagining seeing" (Olive, above). They contrast these actions of seeing and imagining with the concept of being a person or character, embodying a human person or role in the story:

> [I'm not imagining I am Martin the Warrior when I'm reading the *Redwall* series by Brian Jacques]. I'm more just watching him. I'm just watching him do this, or I could be like the little mice-maid, I think that's what she says, but at the time I'm just more watching it going on, or I could just be there battling, or I'm more imagining that I'm just watching this whole thing going on. It's kind of like a movie, an exciting movie. (Thirteen-year-old Jessica)

Like Vanessa when she describes her floating presence in *Harry Potter*, Jessica defines the reader as a hovering presence in the text, a presence distinct from the possibilities of who she could "be" if she had to choose a person in the text. To ask her who she could be would force her to reconsider the female-identified "myself" of life; as such, she would have to choose "the little mice-maid," the insignificant female role in the text. Outside questions of being, she achieves an abstract textual presence and critiques the identity politics questions I had been asking as the wrong kinds of questions for literary experience. Rather, the seeing presence established by the text emphasizes the uniqueness of the text as a formal subjectivity, a way of visualizing a world, rather than a limited character subjectivity.

To "imagine watching" (Jessica, above) is both to imagine the text in the mind (its boundaries and its quality as an alternative world) and the mind in the text (presence as imaginal agent and the gaze). It is to stress the possession of a roving point of view (Ryan 53), which accompanies the reader's sense of entering the novel and being surrounded with depth. This rhetoric

of presence—being there—characterizes virtual immersion (48) and the embodied nature of cognition (69). Steven Johnson suggests that an ideal of
"visual thinking" has come into vogue with the advent of hyperspace, but it
is also a very old concept of structuring ideas. For example, missionaries in
the seventeenth century would use "a spatialized rendition of the Bible" (12)
to apply the visual tool of "memory palace" to those unfamiliar with written text. Many teachers know that students retain information more readily
when they visualize concepts in spatial terms, which is why we use charts
and images as much as oral discourse when we teach.

The respondents' emphasis on mental imaging of place, which the mind
must fill in, demonstrates that they regard literature as not just thought but
the very structure of thought. They construct a sense of the novel's spatial,
temporal, and social dimensions independently from the temporal experience of the actual reading, but in their rhetoric they emphasize the process
of imagining—thus interacting and producing—the novel in their own mind.
Through the idea of mental imaging, explored by Ellen Esrock as reader response, they create and remember their presence as a reader in a particular
(fictional) space. None of the critics whom I mention in this and the preced-
ing paragraph are explicitly discussing young readers, suggesting that there
may be more similarities than differences between child and adult reading
processes.

WRITTEN TEXT AS CINEMATIC IN THE MIND

The dialogical constitutions between text and reader represent a circulating
power in that the text and reader mutually constitute each other in narrative
time. Reader-response critics often differ on the question of which has the
power—the text or the reader[4]—but in this study, girls use the metaphor of
film to suggest that they give tremendous power to a text in order to appreciate its ability to come to life in the mind. Like Jessica, above, many girls
describe textual experience as watching a movie and thus draw attention to
the construction of their formal presence in narrative time. The text contains
its own narrative time, defining the girl as a reader within that time, and the
girl defines her "seeing," "watching," "imagining" presence as the perpetually present (participle) of that time. The metaphor of the text as a film demonstrates the girls' conceptualization of narrative time and space as the formal
elements that construct them in a nonsocial space, outside their historical
time and social space. The girls' invocation of film as a metaphor for reading demonstrates the influence of film and both visual and virtual culture on
their conception of how storyworlds can materialize. For the film industry
has designed the movie theater as a space in which the viewer leaves his/her

world, walks through the liminal space of the ticket booth and candy counter, and enters the dark world to be an invisible spectator of the story in the light. Christian Metz argues that neither identification with character nor identification with actor is a sufficient explanation for the viewing process (46–47). Actually, the viewer of film identifies with the possibility of transcendent spectatorship in the self (49), an identification we see in the girls' rhetoric of spectatorship. The metaphor of watching a film for reading implies that the conjunction of narrative time and space constructs the reader's presence in the fictional world, all the while giving the reader the illusion that the reader is seeing rather than participating (as a human embodied being) in the social relations of the text.

The feeling that they are immersed in a text through the text's motion and narrative time explains why girls feel they become disembodied presences in texts, always approximate presences, because they imagine that they leave their social selves outside narrative time and enter a material space "of" that time:

> Even though Harry Potter is a boy, it's like you're in the story.
> The words make you feel like you're in the story and you're there.
> (Nine-year-old Jesse)

Jesse accords to the text a spatial, material existence. The text embodies a place to go by means of "words." The words are the action of the sentence when Jesse voices her experience, making "you" the reader. They produce *you* as a textual presence ("you're there") by paradoxically rupturing all the frames of reference of your usual sense of presence (body, environment, community, etc.). Jesse prefaces her discursive presence with the idea that she transgresses her female "space" in the real world, saying that she is *in* the story "even though Harry Potter is a boy." She transgresses by virtue of experiencing presence as a simile, not as an actuality. She does not identify with the male hero and extract an extralinguistic identity from the "words"; but, in her description, the words make her feel approximate and outside her identity. The use of simile suggests that "being there" in the text is always approximate presence, shifting because it exists only within narrative time and space. Many girls construct this rhetoric of the text as a powerful formal object that diffuses and bifurcates them into an abstract formal presence. They explain this experience of reading by proliferating similes and metaphors to describe reading, metaphors ranging from racing downhill on a bicycle to floating on a raft in the middle of the ocean. The metaphors always involve an alternative sense of time, accelerated or decelerated experiences that stand apart from everyday life and heighten or arouse the senses.

SHIFTING POINTS OF VIEW

Nevertheless, in literature it's "the words" that construct presence and point of view. In order to fully appreciate the complexity of a text as a formal object that offers ways of seeing, we have to fuse Mikhail Bakhtin's idea of a text's voices with Wolfgang Iser's theory of the text as shifting points of view.[5] Bakhtin's insights help us understand the novel as a social form (Hale); although narrative theorists distinguish voice and viewpoint (Nikolajeva 11–12), Iser helps us understand that points of view occur through imagining that voices represent points of view:

> If the function of the different perspectives is to initiate the production of the aesthetic object (i.e., the meaning of the text), it follows that this object cannot be totally represented by any *one* of those perspectives. And while each perspective offers a particular view of the intended object, it also opens up a view on the other perspectives. The interaction between perspectives is continuous, because they are not separated distinctly from one another, and they do not run parallel either: authorial comment, dialogue between characters, developments of plot, and the positions marked out for the reader—all these are interwoven in the text and offer a constantly shifting constellation of views. These, then, are the "inner" perspectives of the text—to be distinguished from the "outer" perspective, which links text to outside reality. (Iser 96)

What Iser terms *perspectives* Bakhtin calls "voices of the novel," both of which express the ideological positions and social consciousnesses that define the novel as a formal subjectivity and an aesthetic. While some films employ multiple points of view, the traditional storytelling form of the omniscient narrator characterizes most nonexperimental films, which, ironically, may increase the girls' perceptions of "voiced views" in literature. The way in which the narration is focalized through different characters/narrative views at different times (Genette, Bal), most effectively allows the girls to shift from seeing one character's consciousness to another, all the while dialoguing these perspectives with the girl's self as both formal presence and "myself" outside the text.

Sixteen-year-old African American Shereen's discussion of *Black Girl Lost*, by Donald Goines, demonstrates the reader's cocreation of narrative focalizations. After she retells the plot, she demonstrates how plot revelation allows her to shift between the consciousnesses of characters and omniscient reader. The African American female character represents only one of the many points of views that she takes in the text:

> *Black Girl Lost* was about a girl. It's by this guy but he always makes the bad people, like the criminals, you feel sorry for them like you want them to get away with what they do.

It just really got to me, something about it really got to me. Would I have killed him? What could have happened if she didn't? Like could he have gone back to jail and then got out later or something? I don't think I would have killed him because then she didn't die so she still has to live without him so there was really no point in him breaking out of jail. I could put myself in [his position] because he didn't really want to go back to jail so I think I would have told her to kill me too but I don't think I would have killed him.

It was just a really dramatic ending. It left you. There was an ending but there wasn't really an ending because you don't know what happens to the girl. It just ends and I think about what I would have did. Since it's not real in your head you make it go any way you really want to because in reality the book ended and in the book nothing's going to happen to the girl because she's not real but you can always think. When you think about it you don't really think about it as being fake, you think about it as being real. So you're like "what happened to the girl?" But you can always came back and realize it's not real so she's OK. The story was more about him though. I guess they were trying to say if she wouldn't have been with him or whatever she would have never got raped and if she wasn't with him she would have stayed with her mother and not him because he was selling drugs and stuff but they had a lot of money and they were getting along fine but with the mother she was always hungry and she had to steal to live basically. I guess I felt bad for her throughout the whole story because it started out bad, then in the middle she was OK and at the end back where she started basically. I felt bad for her. I mean I feel sorry for her but he just went and killed a whole bunch of people and he was in jail for selling drugs. In that part [where he killed the rapists] I was kind of rooting for him but I shouldn't have been because I was like they didn't really kill her, they just raped her so he didn't have to go kill them but when you're actually leaving the story you don't think of it that way.

It grabs your attention from the first sentence. You felt bad and you wanted to know what was going to happen to her. I guess I was angry at her mother because she was an alcoholic and she would just beat her for no reason and she just made me angry. Even though it wasn't real I was really mad at her mom.

Shereen hovers between a sense of the author's design and the moral problems within the text, depending on whether she inhabits the position of the female or of the male character. But her responses frequently shift to the fictionality of the world and the way the text positions her and constructs her as a reader. She begins with a statement about the author's style and storytelling design; she knows that sympathy for the criminal will be evoked. She then shifts to comparing herself to the female character: "Would I have killed him?" But quickly she draws back, looking at the moral problem of the character as a "she." Shereen then shifts to the philosophical quandary of experiencing fiction, a quandary she has narratively enacted. Thus her experience as "reader" ↔ "character" returns her to consideration of literature as a form, her role as a reader, and both the text's and her role in materializing the unreal. She fluidly becomes the male character, the female character, a transcendent reader (grabbed by the text, desiring knowledge), a transcendent narrator (indicting the mother), and a critic of the author's project. With all these shifting possibilities, Shereen demonstrates the impulse to rewrite the story in different ways and determine the consequences of that rewriting. The text has different meanings depending on where your point of view rests, and it never rests.

Although she produces an understanding of the text as an aesthetic design, Shereen does not "fix" the text as an already written object and thus continues to tell the story—"what if" the character had not killed her boyfriend. The production of an aesthetic object does not foreclose but enables the possibility for imagining sequels or different paths that the narrative could have taken. Shereen vacillates between moral discomfort and a forlorn feeling at being "left" by the text. She turns toward trying to guess authorial intent, but that guess then gives way to the more interesting question of how the unreal can be made so real through pure discourse. How can the reader remind herself that this is an imaginary world, to feel better about being left? The power of the text lies in its formal invocation of imagination as a material place; while Shereen constitutes the text as a place and her role as reader in that time and place, this constitution does not foreclose the possibilities of moving in and out of characters, as controlled by the text. She can simultaneously consider the referential content and the design of signification. When she turns to the realization that she was rooting for the criminal and that that was part of the narrative design, she then resists this feeling, turning away from it and ultimately turning away from identifying with the female character. Shereen's statement "They just raped her, they didn't kill her" minimizes what in the text is a horribly graphic representation of brutality against girls and women. Ironically, the title *Black Girl Lost* comes to describe the experience of the reader, who, in life or in visual media, would probably more fully empathize with someone in the situation of the protagonist. In literature, form moves the reader's attention between concrete story and abstract ideas. This is mind over matter, for better or worse.

Going "Off-World" for Insight

I think it's a little bit healthier . . . to be able to relate to something that far
away. . . . With a different story you have to think. . . . When you can't really
be a man in the Mafia, then you can sort of figure out where you fit in.
—Sixteen-year-old Olive

How do texts take readers far away from themselves? What is to be gained
from the journey?

The girls maintain that a literary text opens their eyes and engenders
ways of seeing because the text is radically different from them and thus from
life as they know it. They assert that their constitution of the text as a vision
allows them illumination and philosophical thought that moves beyond the
specific situation depicted by the story. The text presupposes an impersonal
reader who will see it and see through its ways of seeing, and the reader steps
into that role and imagines herself as a seeing agent "in" and "of" the text.
Ironically, girls voice an active project of imagination, through which the
reader becomes passive ("having the story told to you") or open to receiving
the vision of the text. Ultimately, their belief in the transcendent power of
artistic form and theme mirrors Romantic ideals of art as transcendence.
Believing fiction to transcend both writer and reader, they differentiate a
storytelling world from life, revel in how the craft of storytelling in literature helps them gain perspective on themselves and their own lives, and suggest that the values of a storyworld can unproblematically conflict with their
own. Going "off-world," as one girl puts it, keeps them healthy.

GRASPING THEME

The girls ultimately describe each text's meaning by constructing its thematic
unity, which they define as a vision of life. Some examples include the precious,
precarious nature of life, in reference to *The Strange Adventures of Dr. Jekyll
and Mr. Hyde*; the theme "if you stick together, you can get through anything,"

in reference to *Little Women*; the sadness of "not being able to go back" once you are grown, in reference to J. M. Barrie's *Peter Pan*; our continual quest for magical places in C. S. Lewis's *The Lion, The Witch, and the Wardrobe*; the "love, life, and loss" of Susan Kay's *Phantom*; and the mysterious and continual search for truth in Alexander Dumas's *The Count of Monte Cristo*.

The respondents identify with theme across media, based on their understanding of how to read literature for theme. For example, the girls cite the words of some narrative songs as poetry they distill into theme.[6] Twelve-year-old Randi appreciates the lyrics presented in TuPac Shakur's song "Changes," identifying the theme of racism. Although she is neither African American nor male, she identifies with the song's meaning by deciding that "people can be racist about the color of your eyes, or the clothes you wear." She feels that the theme applies to her situation, for classmates often make fun of her clothing. Sixteen-year-old Shereen appreciates Aretha Franklin's "A Rose Is Just a Rose" for its message, "Do not change who you are for a man," because she feels that many of her friends are changing as they date more.

Sixteen-year-old Zoe discusses the powerful experience of seeing the musical *Rent*, stressing her role as a disembodied agent encountering alterity and vision, through which she achieves an understanding of the "whole theme" and which "opens her eyes" to something more than self:

> I don't think I imagine myself as a character. I imagine myself as there. I wouldn't be the person having AIDS but I would be kind of like a fly on the wall sort of thing. I'm there but not a person in it. I don't know. It's kind of like I've never said, "Oh, I'm Mimi," or whatever. I'm like, "Oh, I'd love to play her," but I've never really thought of myself as that person. It's just, say, maybe my friend or something. I'm just like, how could someone live a life like that, you know? I don't really know. I don't think I ever imagine myself as her because I guess I can't really think of myself as having AIDS. It's not so much "oh my gosh, I have AIDS"–type thinking, or like what would I do if I had AIDS? It's the whole cherishing-life thing. One of the main themes through the whole musical is that there's no day but today, and to live each day to its fullest and everything. It made me realize about real life. Because the whole theme was about people dying of AIDS and living poor on the streets of New York and things like that. It just kind of opened my eyes and to have life so, it's just kind of opened my eyes more.

Even when the aesthetic involves a public musical, at which the audience is literally "there," the girl construes her presence as a disembodied, imaginative presence—eyes opening onto experience. She takes the posture of the fourth wall beyond its referential meaning, referring to the actual audience witnessing the event, to denote a posture outside personhood. Zoe begins by articulating presence ("I'm there"), then she denies that presence as a "human being" ("there" but "not a person"). She moves to a construction of the text as alterity, which allows her to express wonder. She then discusses the text as a complete "whole" or unified world vision, voicing from this vantage point "theme" and its significance to her. She returns to a sense of the text's power: "It opened my eyes." She feels that the text enacts the interpretive process upon her by diminishing her, so that she feels like a fly in the wall, and expanding her vision, making her small to "see large." To constitute the text as a powerful object that creates and defines its viewer is to enjoy a self-transformation by taking pleasure in the decentering of subjectivity that radically "opens" up the reader to aesthetic experience.

Sixteen-year-old Olive describes a similar process of vision and growth through a piece of literature that she constitutes as a radically different perspective, to enjoy an eye-opening experience of alterity. She further suggests that fiction specifically about girls "like" her (in age) prohibits the decentering of identity that she requires to open herself to the text:

> The story about the Mafia [Mario Puzo's *The Godfather*] was really really fascinating because first of all it's really far off from where I am at this point, or probably where I ever will be. There's certain things about it that are just sort of like, wow, you know? That's really sort of amazing how they can live their life like that, something in a weird sort of ironic way admirable.
>
> I think it's a little bit healthier or a little bit better to be able to relate to something that far away to what I'm doing as opposed to relating something close to me, because it's easy to become what that is. It's easy to become the other girl, the sixteen-year-old in the story because she's so like you and with a few little changes you could be her, you know? But with a different kind of story you have to think. You have to really think about it but you can't be that. And so it still leads you to become your own person and it still leads you to making your own choices and being who you are, instead of becoming something so easy to become, you know? When you can't really be a man in the Mafia, then you can sort of figure out where you fit in, or what that has to do with you but at the same time what it doesn't have to do with you. It's hard to explain.

Both Olive and Zoe employ the same narration to describe aesthetic process. Fascination compels them to look, suggesting the text as exhibitionist or seducer; the text opens their eyes by engendering amazement and revelation; they construct the text as alterity through distance and objectification; they recognize conventions and appreciate devices such as irony, devices that separate textual worlds from the moral standards of their own lives (the text invites regard for the Mafia with literary conventions); the text constructs a unique vision, which the girl instantiates as her vision of the text; the social self is alienated and diffused by aesthetic response ("Who am I if this admirable, ironic world is so far away from me?" Olive says); the girl affirms the text as powerful and constituting her ("It leads you"); the girl resynthesizes the experience with self ("It leads you to making your own choices and figuring out what the text has to do with you").

Thus the girls create the storyworlds into alternative universes as if those universes were completely distinct from the real world, even though both Zoe and Olive live in urban communities visibly suffering from AIDS and violence. Olive has perspective on the intricacies of politics, powers, rules, and social obligations that are present in *The Godfather*, but does not in her own world. Forging a connection with an experience "far off from where I am," which she conceives as a "faraway" place, gives her a sense that she sees how the characters live and views them through the literary devices of irony and heroism. She thus prefers a text in which she cannot "be," because it "others" her category of identity. She can then other herself and gain some perspective on "where she fits in," what her own choices might be. This experience of "wonder" and "amazement" she contrasts with an "easy" model of becoming a young female character. She resists "easy" identification and demonstrates the fact that fiction in which the reader's identity category is *not* represented gives the reader, paradoxically, the opportunity for considering self-possibilities.

The girls create for themselves a rhetoric of the text as a powerful object in order to experience wonder ("like, wow") at both the text and the self outside the text, which the reading self then wants to integrate into the experience. This rhetoric of the text as a powerful exhibitionist, compelling the reader to look, parallels the process of reading described by Georges Poulet in his essay "Criticism and the Experience of Interiority." In his view, the text embodies the author's mind or consciousness and completely takes over the reader's consciousness. My respondents similarly experience the text as a "takeover" of self, yet their rhetoric implies that the power is given to a text rather than seized by it.

SEEING AND TRANSCENDENCE: THE AMERICAN VIEW

Girls do not view the world of the text as embodying the mind of one writer, but they do regard the text as a formal subjectivity, a way of seeing as well as a particular vision of the world. On one level, their translation of the words to voice and then to sight suggests the influence of visual culture, yet the application of terms from the visual arts to literature is an older, established tradition (W. T. J. Mitchell), invoked even in Aristotle's *Poetics*, in which Aristotle recommends that a poet "place the scene, as far as possible, before his eyes. . . . as if he were a spectator of the action" (87). The girls focus on the spectacle of a novel as if it were a play or film unfolding before their eyes, parallel to the poet's play of which Aristotle writes. In many ways, the girls of this project regard texts in the same way that writers do, indeed using reading to stimulate imagining or writing their own stories and utopian visions of their futures. To further this finding that attention to form allows a writerly perspective to develop, the girls' focus on structure and unity is quite separate from hero: "Unity of plot does not, as some persons think, consist in the unity of the hero. For infinitely various are the incidents in one man's life which cannot be reduced to unity; and so, too, there are many actions of one man out of which we cannot make one action" (Aristotle 67). The beauty of form that Aristotle cites is also the love of form that Benton cites (*Secondary* 20); writers and reader share this love, finding a "delight" in the very *meditation* of mimesis through an aesthetic view.

The idea that a text instantiates a particular way of seeing invokes Henry James's conceptualization of the novel, suggesting that American sentiments may inform writers and readers across time. In his preface to the New York edition of *The Portrait of a Lady*, he argues that artists see what other people cannot—although they look upon the same human scene—and the artist then articulates that vision in the novel. What is particularly useful about Jamesian novel theory is James's assertion that literature presents a combination of authorial consciousness and literary form: "The spreading field, the human scene, is the 'choice of subject': the pierced aperture, either broad or balconied or slit-like and low-browed, is the 'literary form'; but they are, singly or together, as nothing without the posted presence of the watcher—without, in other words, the consciousness of the artist" (7). The novel registers posted presence not only by virtue of the artist's vision but also by the vision implied by "literary form." To complement James's view of the posted presence of the artist, girls present the idea of the posted presence of the impersonal reader, a formal component that defines for them literature as vision. For the girls, novelistic form calls attention to itself as not just "a human scene" but also a way of seeing the human scene, a form foregrounding processes of vision in addition to the content actually seen.

The girls' use of the term *seeing* for experiencing literature denotes a particular philosophy of aesthetic experience in that their imaginations of seeing through fiction elides the idea of seeing, which involves distance, with the idea of thinking, which involves active creation of the mind. As W. T. J.

Mitchell observes, *idea* and *image* share a root word; thinking is seeing, as revealed by our terms for thought—*insight*, *sight*, and *sense*: "I see." Seeing and alterity are interrelated concepts among American writers, Carolyn Porter argues in *Seeing and Being*.[7] In major American works, Porter asserts, figures "struggle to 'be and see being at the same time'" (xii), or to disappear yet see all. The participant observer Porter describes in American fiction, in her view, is an indication of alienation suffered under capitalist culture. For the purposes of this study, we can note that by emphasizing reading as disappearing and yet seeing "the whole," the girls alienate the real social self from the reading self, which becomes a mode for experiencing literature. The ways in which the girls describe the reading process closely resemble the philosophical stance of American transcendentalism, which suggests shifts of power between see-er and seen. To Emerson, about whom Porter writes, the self goes out into Nature to become a transparent eyeball. What one "sees" circulates back to the self to define a sense of the self's potential transcendence. Thus even though the respondents use contemporary visual media as a frame of reference for the experience of reading and appreciating themes of fiction, they continue an established American belief system which values transcendence and the idea that for democracy to be effective, people must feel that they have the power to appreciate something greater than themselves.

TRANSCENDENCE OF ARTISTIC LINES

The girls' theories of art thus parallel Romantic concepts of art as a liberating force that lifts people to a higher plane of contemplation. The respondents expect literature to transcend the cultural situation of production and reception. They expect literature to maintain an illusion of completeness and universality through transcendence, which by implication points out the narrowness of one's everyday perspective. Fifteen-year-old Ellie, for example, defines the power of passages by their ability to apply to new situations:

> If one of my friends had a bad day, I'd quote *Cabaret*, like "Life is disappointing, forget it. In here, life is beautiful." And it's just kind of like, I don't want to say inspirational, but sometimes it is and sometimes it's just tactless; it's like the wrong time and wrong place to say something like that but still it has to do with it. For example the line from *Cabaret*, it had to do with the Holocaust and the strip club actually. But it can, it can be, I don't know how to say this but it could be put to so many different, not descriptions but like so many different people and so many different problems and opportunities and stuff. It kind of brings you that much away. So it's kind of like putting yourself

in that character but not totally and completely, but just knowing that you can relate to a fictional story is kind of like a sign that "oh you know, I don't have to deal with that right now." I can live in the now. Like in [*Cabaret*] that's what they did, because that's what the line was from. So you just take the line and then go with it, like, "Oh I don't have to deal with that homework right now. I can go off and talk with my friends," because that's what the line was in the movie. It kind of gives them ideas. It kind of gives us ideas of like . . . People can escape from realities outside.

She uses the line to both voice and escape anxieties in other contexts, yet she recognizes the text as an escape and her consciousness of escape as illusion denotes her experience as only a partial escape, over which she has control and through which she empowers herself. The line always bears the resonance of its textual context. She speaks the line like a maestro and alludes to the cabaret's function as an escape, a space pretending to avoid historical events. Universal pretense frames the desirability of stories and art, in which the specific setting combines with form and theme. The line itself alludes to transcendence by its form *and* content; it thematizes the existence of a space outside politics and referential identity, yet that space is never innocent. That space is framed by and universalizes particular responses to sociological context. This line is in some sense the perfect demonstration of the girls' expectations for an aesthetic space, because Ellie both uses the line (formally) as a means of transcendence and uses the content of the line to thematize art as transcendence, showing that the ideal of transcendence is an important illusion of art and of girls' engagement with art.

A SEPARATE MORAL VISION

Because they desire aesthetic fiction to stand apart from the lives they live and the identities they inhabit, the girls separate the moral universe of the text from the moral code of their lives. Unlike the adults whose interests mediate the literature to which children and teens are exposed, the girls do not see a problem when a text represents that which they would define as immoral in their lives, desiring in texts not mimesis but the instantiation of a particular artistic vision in which everyday moral rules are temporarily suspended:

> There's a lot of homosexual stuff [in *Rent*] and I don't like that because you know it says in the Bible you know homosexuality is not a good thing, but the thing to look for [in *Rent*] like love, life, and

loss, is pretty much what it's all about. I listen to everything they talk about, the love, life, and loss, and I can relate to that. That's just my interpretation of it. You get a better understanding, like a better feeling to like what they're trying to say in the whole thing. I don't really put myself in that situation. That's pretty much what life is about, you know, it's like living it, and loving and losing things. That's what I see life as. (Fifteen-year-old Ruth)

Ruth differentiates the specific subject matter from her selective apprecia-tion of, in her view, "the whole thing," or her interpretation of the text's meaning. When Olive speaks of the Mafia as ironically admirable, she, like Ruth, maintains the distinction between textual theme and personal moral reference. By encountering a text with a moral code that differs from that of the reader, the girls make the text conform to an imaginative alterity, and the girls can easily remain outside the characters for an appreciation of a broader theme. Although Ruth's personal moral ground remains stable, the artistic text temporarily brackets her philosophy of life, which adults who wish to censor *Harry Potter* for witchcraft or *Huck Finn* for racism believe young readers cannot do. For Ruth, *Rent* does not present a vision of life as a society in trouble by virtue of its disregard for artists and for people dying of AIDS, which would probably drive her away from the text, but it pre-sents a vision of "what life is all about." She identifies with a generic mes-sage of love, life, and loss, and imagines that the message is separable from the specific social situation represented in the story.

The idea that art is not fully subject to the girls' official moral frame-work cannot be overemphasized. The creation of a discursive imaginative space, outside their "reality," means that they understand their (referential) reality as *one* specific reality, as neither universal nor morally absolute. And they imagine that they can suspend this referential reality in order to appre-ciate a transcendent philosophy of and in art. This reverses the predominant logic of many parents who feel (who fear) that children get ideas from fic-tion and that those ideas evolve into the moral fabric of children's lives. As an example of how a central confusion exists within "where the moral lies" in aesthetic fiction, I quote eight-year-old Wendy's love of Greek myth:

Oh "The Golden Fleece." That is a Greek legend. Greek legends, you never ever know what's going to happen and so you know, the Greeks were really good storytellers, but these they believed actually happened and they're such good storytellers. If they just told the stories and didn't believe they were real and they were just Christians, they'd do fine. I mean of the stories, because we have these Greek books and I read them over and over and over and over and I really know about the Greek stories. D'Aulaire's book gave me a riddle. And the riddle is, I will see if you can figure it, the riddle is what walks at four feet in the morning, two feet in the middle of the day and three feet at the end of the day . . . Man! Because when he's a baby he's on four feet and then he gets up on two feet and then he's an old man with a stick and he has three feet. And that one there's this lion lady, it's a lion lady head and she's like, "Oh no!" because she had like this fate and if anybody said she could she'd tear them in two pieces if they couldn't answer the riddle and then she was to have her doom if they did. And then she's like, "Ah!" and she had her doom.

Wendy differentiates the storytelling world from the moral universe she inhabits, the latter informed by the biblical text she views as "true." The definition of a text as aesthetic rather than "real" determines her response. She enjoys the craft of storytelling that D'Aulaire's collection presents to her, and her reenactment of the unfolding riddle shows her appreciation of storytelling structure, suspense, and narrative situation—the idea of fate and doom. The intent of the myths as creation stories bothers her for a moment, because she cannot, nor does she want to, reconcile the world of storytelling with her own reality. Pausing with the thought that the myths are not Christian perspectives, Wendy quickly continues and brings to life the riddle of the Sphinx. Concepts of fate and doom, and constructions of reality for teller and reader, conflict with her perspective on religion, but that irreconcilability can exist when Wendy approaches art. Like fifteen-year-old Ruth, she brackets the fictional world and is then free to enjoy and immerse herself in it.

My respondents contrast the power of a storytelling text that calls attention to the aesthetic act of storytelling with religious stories that claim to represent "what really happened," concerned more with reference than story:

> There isn't anything in that [my favorite biblical passage about Christ]. It's just because I'm thinking of what has happened so you don't really need to feel like I'm in it or anything. I just know that it has happened, and so I like it because that's what happened and it helps me think about what Jesus could have done, and what Jesus did. And it's a lot in just that little sentence, and that's why I like it so much and I feel very good when I read it. It's totally different [from how I feel about the *Redwall* series]. I feel this nice feeling like somebody has done something really nice for me. And it helps me think that he has really done that for me. I don't feel like I'm acting it. I don't feel like I'm seeing it. I feel like I'm just, that it has happened, you know? (Eight-year-old Wendy)

Wendy is moved and religiously inspired by the passage, but the societal definition of the text as referential history prevents identification and immersion. Little relationship with the text is possible for her when the text is not aesthetic. A text defined as realism invokes a response to "what is," invoking social identification and everyday social roles. The idea of the aesthetic invokes a fantasy identification, defined by the powers of imagination. Many of the religious girls in this study contrast their experiences of fiction with those of religious writings, one fourteen-year-old Mormon girl even saying that the life of Christ "is just an ordinary life, not like a story or something" (fourteen-year-old Hope).

VOYAGES OFF-WORLD: HEALTHY?

If literature embodies a philosophy of quasi-transcendental possibilities for the girls, then girls' aesthetic response entails a quest for an ideal of transformation, of the pleasurable power accompanying the ability to remain above the people whom the story is about and transcend historical moment, social identity ("You get so accustomed to your own life," says fifteen-year-old Ruth); the everyday incapacity to glimpse a whole world; and their everyday struggles as girls. Critics often ask me if I believe that a "pure" aesthetic space "beyond" identity exists, a situation that would confuse my report of how the girls feel and how I interpret their responses. In my view, they are so conscious of their quest for alternative universes, and how alternative perspectives can be appreciated, that, I believe, they blend an Emersonian belief in the self's transcendence with a contemporary, even postmodern, sensibility that all perspectives are inherently different and that their own everyday point of view on life is very limited—by being only one point of view. Literature gives them something more.

A tremendous variety of literature is available, to be appreciated in different ways. I feel that the girls' persistent belief in literature as a different perspective that opens their eyes is ideal and should not be limited to fantasy, which seems the sine qua non of alternative universes to these respondents. Fantasy depends upon your point of view, of course. *The Catcher in the Rye* is an immersion in fantasy to me, a mother and teacher who is not particularly interested in indulging adolescence and stopping time. *The Godfather* is fantasy for Olive, as it also is to me. *Harry Potter* has a less fantastic effect on me, since the politics of school and learning constitute my everyday life. For Shereen, a middle-class African American girl, the world of *Black Girl Lost* is an "alternative universe" of abandoned children, drugs, intrigue, criminals, and rape.

The girls prefer literature to take them "off-world" rather than embed them in what they feel to be their real world:

Anne McCaffrey, she writes, well like I have this *Crystal Singer*, a lot
of her stuff is off-world. She wrote some about psychics and the one
about like their planet was called *Crystal Singer* and they get the
crystal off the ranges and they forget if they go off too much. And it's
kind of romantic. And she has the *Dragonriders*, about dragons and
stuff like that, which I like a lot. I think those are more like [helpful
for me]. You know, I'm not the only one with problems [social
problems, worrying about appearance, peer pressure, drugs, etc.] and
I kinda know how to handle it. But these [books] help me more.
(Thirteen-year-old Jessica)

Rather than confront them, Jessica temporarily escapes from social problems through fiction. She was not the only girl to compare her use of aesthetic experience to other kids' use of drugs, surely a healthy alternative. But
the reading is more complex than escape, because her reasoning involves the
desire to encounter spaces in which she is not specifically framed as a young
girl, and she identifies that space by genre ("romantic"), which means she
attends to the literary structure by which she can shed her self and "center
world" (Ryan).

The girls are quite conscious of the pervasive nonfiction rhetoric that
describes girls as lacking in self and needing representation and role models.
An environment full of discourses "about girls" was symbolized by the fact
that *Reviving Ophelia* lay on Jessica's bookshelf. *Reviving Ophelia* is psychologist Mary Pipher's depiction of girls she has seen in counseling, girls
engaging in self-deprecating behaviors. Many responses to *Reviving Ophelia*
have been published (S. Shandler; Dellasega; Sprague and Keeling). Although
Reviving Ophelia is a narrative work, structured similarly to a collection of
short stories, Pipher claims to represent girls, and the book's narrative is
announced as "real life" discourse, not fiction. Works such as *Reviving
Ophelia* embody the kinds of discourses about "female character" that the
girls seek escape from, a didactic rather than aesthetic approach to story.
Jesse thus feels compelled to go off-world for more radical encounters with
texts that do not claim to know her. For these girls, vision and radical alterity
are both more desirable than representation and more empowering in that
they give them perspective on their social role, paradoxically, because the
female role is *not* specifically scripted in or by the text.

"Going off-world" thus serves as a metaphor for the reader's process
of embarking into a storytelling world in order to diffuse the totality of
the female social role. This diffusion results in a very unexpected kind of
social transformation as girls claim the right to imagine and fantasize in a
manner that questions all that critics mean when they say literature is representation. Berenstein argues a similar point in *Attack of the Leading*

Ladies. She, like Jacquelyn Stacey in *Star Gazing*, draws attention to the female spectator of film and asserts that spectators derive pleasure from the text's separateness:

> The theories that dominate the field describe viewing pleasures via similarities (e.g., women identify with heroines on the basis of shared biological sex), and sexual drives (e.g., straight women are romantically invested in heroes due to heterosexual desire). This scenario overlooks the possibility that spectators also identify *against* themselves. Viewing patterns depend as much upon the dissolution of a one-to-one viewing-character relationship as they do on its perpetuation, as Mayne notes of cinema's safe zone. Identification-in-opposition may be one of the medium's primary pleasures—viewers may relish the ability to escape their everyday social, racial, sexual, and economic roles. It is crucial to remember that narrative cinema is a fantasy scenario, a confirmation of, and temporary release from, the subjectivities engaged in by spectators in their everyday lives. (47)

Berenstein's description of the dominant model of identification in film criticism describes the paradigm of many literary critics as well.[8] I agree with her critique of this model. In Berenstein's account of "identifying against the self," the viewer of film fiction does not necessarily identify with male experience or the gaze that some film critics have described as male (Mulvey). Rather, film provides a form by means of which the female spectator can imagine that she transcends her social categories of identity.

The link between girls' responses to film and to literature needs further explication, for they inform and invigorate each other. Film gives the girls a model for seeing rather than being in the textual imagination, which has made them conscious of the novel's narrator's role in making them experience temporal, spatial, and emotional immersion. Film also provides generic intersections with literature in the girls' minds, such that they ultimately define aesthetic form by genre, the issue to which I turn in Chapters 3 and 4. The girls look to genres of films, terms marketed by the film industry, to elucidate the question of a book's fictional genre, which in turn determines response.

"It's Like a Fantasy World": Gender and Form

Romance stories, they're OK, but sometimes they're really boring. See, I like adventure stories, like when I read, I like sci-fi and stuff like that.
—Thirteen-year-old Jessica

HOW CAN WE understand this zest for particular forms? What is "stuff like that"? Why is genre so important and how do girls pay exquisite attention to generic traditions?

Although many literary critics focus on the constitution of identities in, through, and by literary texts, the girls' discussions of literary texts stress the formal conventions through which literary texts materialize imaginary worlds. They understand their role of impersonal reader as a function of genre, shaping their response to a text differently depending on their definition of the text's genre. The girls' narrations of their reading practices focus on the generic tradition(s) that, they believe, each text embodies and makes unique, a tradition made up of intertexts, literary conventions, narrative structures, and archetypal characters, symbols, and plots. Not only does a literary text embody alterity from the girls' social worlds, then, but it also embodies alterity from literary tradition by uniquely combining genres, in the girls' view. Thus girls experience alterity not only through the act of reading, but also through their diagnosis of the text's generic deployment. Their discussions source the text's power over the reader to its ability to control reader response through genre. Knowing that genres are equated with categories of identity such as gender, the girls conflate genre and identity and define people as, for example, "romance people" or "action people," defining identity as a function of genre and thus a product of a storytelling system of meaning.

The girls distinguish the generic traditions of fictional books, films, plays, and some narrative songs from other narrative discourses by attending to the craft of story across media. Their proficiency with viewing film and understanding genres of films gives them a language of genre to describe the craft of story in books. For example, their understandings of fantasy, romance, comedy, horror, mystery, and history (autobiography and documentary) stem from both popular movies and widely read literary genres such as fantasy, science fiction, detective fiction, and nonfiction. The content of films that exemplify particular genres provides intertexts for literature, intertexts that the girls compare with the content of fictional books.

By foregrounding their attention to narrative form rather than medium, the girls define both literary and filmic texts as aesthetic materializations of the structure of thought and imagination. They use their knowledge of these structures to reauthor, revise, invent, and imagine their own secondary worlds, enabled by their identification of self with genre. Thus they not only use aesthetic texts to escape their social identities and worlds, but also transport the text's use of storytelling conventions to their own lives and reintegrate the aesthetic realm into social space such that aesthetic form transforms their perceptions of how the social world could be. Examples are numerous. Many girls fantasize or write about environmental utopias for the future (desire for "world peace" is more than a trope for Miss Congeniality); many have personal pastoral visions of where they might find happiness in the future, ranging from small women's colleges in the mountains; the wilderness, in which they might be lone photographers for *National Geographic* magazine; or the jungle, where they could be lone zoologists studying the animals. Later in this chapter I give just one example of a teen girl who authors her own animal utopias, along with the multifaceted meanings of her fantasies. The girls find particular value in how literary worlds display power dynamics, applying such conventions to their understanding of life.

The ideology underlying the girls' use of form in self-understanding is more important to understanding girls' engagements with literature than is ideology determined by content analysis. Although the conventions of the literary system are internal to literature, certain forms tend to flourish at certain times, Northrop Frye's comprehensive theory of modes suggests. An example is the rise of the novel in the eighteenth and nineteenth centuries, as historicized by Ian Watt. The artistic use of form, including revisions of established conventions, reveals particular social and historical moments, Jameson suggests. In responding to historical conditions, then, each text also responds to a history of literary tradition by engaging with the forms of past texts. Jameson calls this "ideology of form," and T. S. Eliot describes this process as "tradition and individual talent," defining the dynamic canon of literature as a continuum of reader response, each artist reading and responding to another's work with his/her own production. The girls' integration of film into their continuum of reader response is consonant with academic treatments of film as a high-art as well as popular-culture medium. Film also calls attention to the craft of story through its manipulation of point of view, special effects, and elaborately staged settings and imaginative theater spaces, which viewers are trained to appreciate at the earliest ages (both animation and picture books train the youngest viewers to appreciate image and the art that produces it, deemphasizing the mimetic qualities of stories). The girls in my study use form to establish their role as a reader of literary aesthetics and they define their preferred reading by genre, yet they define each text as a compilation of genres. Their attention to genre proves Jauss's supposition that readers manage their horizon of expectations with the consistent ability to revise expectations based upon the text's revelations. The following discussion of girls' immersion in forms of high romance, especially fantasy and adventure, gendered forms that I historicize, reveals that an identity politics approach to texts is insufficient, because it ignores aesthetic form, through which the impersonal and real reader are defined.

GENRE AS FOCALIZER, ADVENTURE QUEST AS FREEDOM

Fifteen-year-old Ruth cites generic forms to construct the text's alterity from both herself and distinct literary traditions, thus revealing that she identifies with the uniqueness of a text's use of convention. The text's difference from her is mirrored by its difference from her mental conceptions of specific genres:

> [Ken Follett's *Pillars of the Earth*] takes place in either the 15 or 1600s and it's kind of hard to explain. It's a really different story. A whole different time. It was different from anything I've ever read before. It's not a romance specifically, or it's not you know, a history story. It's not you know a science [story] or anything. It's just really different, you know a combination of everything. And I liked that. It's a little love, life, and loss, but not as much as everything else is [*Rent, Phantom*]. That's just, you know, kind of a small role. It has more love, life, and loss than *The Stand* does and it does focus on that quite a bit, but not as much as most other things do. It's different.

She defines the text as a compilation of impurities, measured against pure generic conventions in her mind—romantic, historical, science fiction, and the "love, life, and loss" theme of "most other things." She approaches each text intertextually, with unspoken intertextualities informing her reading. The way a text refocuses its generic strands and thematics (love, life, and loss take a smaller role here, she says) becomes an important part of her self-constitution as a reader, for she views the text as revising the always impure traditions that precede it and developing her expertise as a reader. Because Ruth's engagement with *Pillars of the Earth* embodies and makes visible her prior experience of reading different traditions, Ruth's discussion culminates in her claim to love the act of reading.

Jameson's assertion that literature articulates its own context is particularly provocative for understanding how it is that aesthetic texts, for the girls in my study, transcend the moment of their making such that the girls imagine that their reading selves mirror the text and transcend who they are in life. "Genres can be defined as patterns/forms/styles/structures which transcend individual art products, and which supervise both their construction by artist and their reading by audiences" (Ryall 28, qtd. in Lacey 132). As Nick Lacey describes in his excellent introduction to the way in which literature, film, and television employ genre in different but related ways, "Genre exists in the space between artists, audiences and the text itself" (133). The girls suggest that each text articulates its context (Jameson) as a context of form. They differentiate their responses to texts based upon how they define the text's announcement of its generic conventions. For sixteen-year-old Zoe, the film *Titanic* is not so much a love story as a historical story, although she recognizes the text as generically multifaceted, one that changes from history to romance upon reviewing. Ten-year-old Becky says *Sabrina, the Teenage Witch* makes her laugh not because it is funny, but "well, because it's a comedy."

The text's genre "combinations" define the extent to which the girl engages in aesthetic appreciation or attends to the referent world, which they do not appreciate:

> Romance stories, they're OK, but sometimes they're really boring. See, I like adventure stories, like when I read, I like sci-fi and stuff like that. When I watch movies, sometimes I like romance stuff and other times I just like adventure stuff much better. It's more exciting. Because like love songs, they always have like all "Oh I love you," "I love you too," I don't like that. The *Redwall* series by Brian Jacques is like these little mice basically and it's like this fantasy world. And they have to save their abbey and battle against guys and stuff like that. It's funner because you just actually [are there]; and when I'm reading science fiction I can imagine I'm there but romance you can't because there's like people there. Sometimes reading romance makes me sad, or my friend sad, because if we watch romance, because they don't have a boyfriend and they want a boyfriend. See, I don't really care if I have a boyfriend; I'm glad I don't because all the guys at our school are really jerks.
>
> The *Redwall* series it's just fantasy more. It's more of a fantasy. These animals live in this big abbey and they have to solve these riddles to save the abbey and stuff. And then there's always this little

warrior mouse, Martin. He's like this ghost, and he's the savior of
Redwall. And there's all these little warrior mice and it's really neat.
Because he gets to go off on adventures and stuff like that.

[Reading romance] keys into school-type situations. It just gives
me more worries to think about. And I don't want to think about
[that]; I want to think about different stuff. Take my mind off of it
instead of battle another day maybe. I just like adventure books better
I guess. Girls, some girls want to fly and be like Amelia Earharts,
because women, some of them are pilots, or like on a boat and they
want to go off and do adventures and stuff like that. Like being free.
(Thirteen-year-old Jessica)

Jessica discusses her response by invoking generic conventions, which cross
the boundaries of medium. She groups science fiction and adventure with
one type of response, and romance in books, films, and songs with another.
When she says "romance," she means the particular type of heterosexual
romance novel serialized in Harlequins and romantic comedy films. She
does not mean high Romance, the literary term for the older medieval structure of Romance, which informs fantasy and science fiction in both today's
literature and film. Because we can easily confuse the two kinds of romance
as they are used today, I use the uppercase *R* to designate high Romance
(which critics and writers such as Hawthorne distinguish from the novel
and its realism) and the lowercase *r* for heterosexual romance novels.

Jessica's engagement with genre displays her knowledge of fantasy
adventure's structural elements, central tropes, symbols, and devices. She
contrasts fantasy with heterosexual romance. For her, the latter foregrounds
realistic human characters and the former foregrounds the alternative world,
while it backgrounds issues of character. She instinctively understands the
distinction between novel and Romance, as defined by Leslie Fiedler. She
regards fantasy as more "free" from sociological markers of human identity
and reveals the fact that her "center world" (Ryan) in life is one of complex
characters and relationships. She prefers the recentering of her world that
she can enjoy in fantasy. Fantasy foregrounds the logic and knowledge required for the reader to navigate a storytelling world in an imaginative environment, while heterosexual romance, Jessica states, is about "people"; she
chooses not to develop a reading presence in heterosexual romance because
she feels that real "people" already inhabit the world of the text and because
the alternative world does not require her cocreation. More in line with her
center world, the "realistic" social world (to her) within heterosexual romance
texts grounds her in her socially identified female self, forcing her to shift
her response to consideration of her own life—to the fact that she lacks a

boyfriend. To the extent that genre and aesthetics are less visible to her, she feels "outside" rather than "inside" the storyworld.

Conversely, the symbolic structures defined by the tropes of fantasy give Jessica the means by which to structure herself as an imaginal agent "in" the text. As the imagining reader, she recognizes the intertextual relationships between fantasy, adventure, science fiction, and the Gothic, weaving an intricate understanding of *Redwall* in terms of its compilation of literary traditions. She sites the form of adventure; the structure of an archetypal battle between good and evil; the convention of the hero/"savior," which is "always" present; central tropes of medievalism; and logical puzzles or riddles that involve word- or book-knowledge. Gothic elements such as ghosts, legends, and types of ancient knowledge inform the fantasy world and denote that world as a kind of past despite its fictionality. By detailing a relationship between the Gothic and Romance adventure, both of which stem from the medieval Romance structure, she enjoys a presence as a highly developed reading self that is separate from her everyday self and refuses to worry about her everyday "feminine" concerns. She ends her discussion by invoking the desire incited by the adventure form, the desire to transcend limits by questing and being "free." Thus she uses the form to suggest an ideology she can appreciate—the production of a free agent, questing for more.

WHY GIRLS APPRECIATE *HARRY POTTER* AND SECONDARY WORLDS OF FANTASY

What does it mean to appreciate a text that is "like a fantasy world"? This sense of a world approximate to the real world, totally imagined yet dependent on literary conventions, evoking the past but the never-existed, defines for the girls literature as a whole and their role as readers within it. Fantasy literature asks the reader to cocreate a coherent entity in the realm of the mind. Seeking to define the genre of high fantasy, C. W. Sullivan III argues that J. R. R. Tolkien's work models the generic form and revitalizes the medieval Romantic structure. Tolkien articulated the concept of the "Secondary World" and "stressed the importance of its cohesiveness":

> [The story-maker] makes a Secondary World which your mind can enter. Inside it, what he relates is "true": it accords with the laws of that world. You therefore believe it, while you are, as it were, inside. The moment disbelief arises, the spell is broken; the magic, or rather art, has failed. You are then out in the Primary World again, looking at that little abortive Secondary World from outside. (Qtd. in Sullivan 304)

The girls stress the internal logic of the Secondary World as the crucial point for fantasy pleasure. Mastering the elaborate structure of the Secondary World is part and parcel of the reader's quest to experience a text such as *Harry Potter*, although the central hero would identify the text as masculine. Nine-year-old Jesse's assertion that "even though Harry Potter is a boy, it's like you're in the story. The words make you feel like you're in the story and you're there," cannot be understood without an awareness of her sense that the text meets, constructs, and revises generic standards: "*Harry Potter*'s like a mystery and funny and like it's lots of combinations in one story and stuff" (nine-year-old Jesse). Like Ruth, above, who views a text's difference in terms of its unique generic combinations, Jesse distinguishes the generic traditions that, she believes, inform the "one" object, producing the "one" aesthetic object from its generic contexts. The "inside" quality granted the reader about whom the text presumes formal knowledge creates the feeling among the girls that they are inside, or privileged participants in, fantasy worlds. Girls who read fantasy use a distinct language of immersion to describe their engagements with the texts. The reader must construct the coherence of a Secondary World not only through careful reading and filling in of the world's coherence, but also through recognizing and anticipating the effects of the text's generic "combinations," using her experience with form.

Recital of plot almost always is of secondary importance to the girls' explanations of the fantasy world's cohesion. Jesse enthusiastically describes the logic of the magic and groups created within *Harry Potter*:

> It's about wizards and stuff, and his parents are really good wizards. They went to this school called Hogwarts, which is like a wizard school. And they were really good wizards. There's groups like Ravenclaw, Gryffindor, and Slytherin, and that's like the classes, the classes that you're in, and I thought Harry Potter was going to be in Gryffindor and he was.

She anticipates the logic of the "sorting hat" (the sorting hat sorts the initiates into the school's groups) based on her understanding of the convention that the hero is destined for the best class. Harry's triumph is her triumph, but hers stems from the pleasure of decoding the author's use of convention and Secondary World construction.

The girls understand a symbiotic relationship between hero and villain in terms of the dialectical conflict between good and evil, understanding that the Secondary World can class its characters according to its archetypal logic and that the hero is important not as a character but as a construct within a formal system. The Secondary World delineates its structure by intertextuality, making visible its generic intertexts:

When [Harry] was really young, this bad guy came and all that was left of that family was his aunt and his uncle, which were Muggles, which in the book were people who weren't wizards. But his aunt had a sister who was a wizard. And they knew that [Harry] was a wizard and said his parents died in a car crash, but they really were killed by some bad guy because the dad put up a fight for the mother and baby and the mother was probably really easy to kill. And the bad guy which is called Voldemort, which was a really really really really really good wizard turned bad, sort of like *Star Wars*, like Darth Vader used to be Luke Skywalker's dad which was good and turned bad. And the fighting, Voldemort tried to kill Harry Potter but his mother's and father's love for him was so strong that when he touched him, when bad people would touch him it would feel like he was a porcupine poking them, but it was really just regular skin. And he got a zigzag scar on his forehead and he became famous after. He didn't even know he was famous and after that Voldemort lost his powers and nobody knew where he was. (Nine-year-old Jesse)

Jesse finds the classification of characters vital to the Secondary World's cohesive structure. Her understanding of the text depends upon both her familiarity and the text's intertextuality with literary forms, seen in her allusion to *Star Wars* as a generic reference. A film such as *Star Wars*, stemming from a fantasy tradition similar to that which engendered *Harry Potter*, marks a generic intertext in her mind, demonstrating the fact that she connects action adventure with fantasy on the grounds of character typology and the symbolic functioning of good and evil as two sides of the same coin. The hero and villain are intrinsically connected; the villain marks the hero through the reader's conventional understanding that the enemy is the mirror "other" of all that the hero embodies. She understands that this plot is an Oedipal one and that the villain marks the hero in a familial and seductive way, through her sense that fantasy is intertextual.

Eleven-year-old Vanessa identifies the logic of magic and the division of the "classes" and "groups" at Hogwarts as the central principles of *Harry Potter*. She contrasts her interest in the fictional world's coherence and classificatory system with plot ("just this boy" who does certain things) and content ("It's just this school"):

It's just this boy and all these other magical boys. It's called Hogwarts Express or something like that. And it's just this school for magic people and it's like karate, how they have red belts, or black belt, or white belts or something. It's like that but there's like different dorms and the beginners would be in this dorm and then the ones graduating

pretty soon are going to be in this dorm and stuff, and they all learn
magic stuff, and as the new ones grow up they learn more magic and
they're not supposed to use their magic. But [Harry] gets in trouble—
not like trouble—he throws a lamp against the wall. He has this cousin
that's really mean and he's a spoiled brat and he does magic on him
and his friend's dad has this flying car and they save him out of the
woods, and just they have a lot of magic. It's just this boy, he has a
lightning scar on his head because I forgot his name, but this guy was
like the king of magic. He tried to steal Henry, I mean Harry, and his
dad died from trying to save him, and then his mom died, and Harry
still lived. So his mom stood up for her son and died for Harry.

*Q: What's the plot of the story? What's he trying to do? Or is there
some . . . ?*

He's just like learning magic and everybody knows him because he's
the hero of all these stories about him and this scar on his head,
and they go, "oh that's Harry Potter" and stuff.

When I ask Vanessa to tell me the plot, her response reveals that the actual
plot is of little interest. In themselves, the characters are of little interest as
well, but as a system of formal relations with one another, the characters
gain interest. Characteristic of fantasy's conventions are its archetypal clas-
sifications (hero against evil; Oedipal structures) and arbitrary rules, such as
the rule of not using magic in the Muggle world. Also characteristic are symbols that call attention to their status as literary constructs and as symbols
from ancient traditions (tools of magic, flying, enchanted woods, scars that
preordain heroes and allow others to recognize him). Structural devices thus
frame Vanessa's understanding of the text as belonging to a certain genre,
one that places formal elements in sets of relations. The whole idea of a plot
belies the power of the text.

More important to Vanessa's reading is her "intertextual" analogy for
understanding how Hogwarts classes embody a system of formal elements.
Her analogy of karate belts provides her with a framework for understanding how people can be classified by a scheme that subordinates individuals
to social categories. Although the text is about "all these magical boys"—
thus power is male—*Harry Potter* does not invite girls to identify with the
hero. Both readers note the masculinity of the hero, but the fact that the
central hero is male and that the form itself stems from a masculine literary
tradition does not mean that girls identify with a male perspective to experience the text. Yet the ideology of the form suggests worlds organized by
male power, realized in character types.

APPRECIATING FANTASY BEYOND HERO

In discussing the form of high Romance, Frye implies that the form is essentially male:

> The perennially childlike quality of romance is marked by its extraordinarily persistent nostalgia, its search for some kind of imaginative golden age in time or space. . . . The essential element of plot in romance is adventure. . . . We may call this major adventure, the element that gives literary form to the romance, the quest. . . . The central form of romance is dialectical: everything is focussed on a conflict between the hero and his enemy, and all the reader's values are bound up with the hero. (186–87)

The girls note the essential elements of adventure, quest, and dialectical conflict when they discuss fantasy literature. But these elements become more important in their discussions than the hero's particular value system, suggesting that the search for an imaginative space thematizes the act of reading they desire. This search is thematized by but not identical to the hero, although girls expect the device of one hero to introduce them to the Secondary World. The hero of fantasy texts is seldom from the Secondary World and more likely initiated into its wonders through the sequence of adventure. Jessica says that girls and women want adventure, equating adventure with freedom, yet she does not equate the reader's adventure with the hero, instead equating reading itself with the act of adventure. The adventure derives from embarking into off-world aesthetic space. Thus the reader's "values" are bound to ideals of readership and storytelling forms.

Girls find the enchanted landscape of the hero's adventure more important than the hero himself. The land of fantasy contains a nostalgic "childlike" quality by virtue of its simultaneous dependence on an ancient past and a nonexistent referentiality. The land never existed but is, paradoxically, steeped in ancient symbolism. A psychoanalytic critic might see in the quest for this ancient but nonexistent land a vision of male sexuality, the perpetually nostalgic quality a mirror for the way the male is always searching for his first maternal love object and a lost time when he was whole. The masculine pronoun Frye uses to describe the hero, who comes into knowledge of his true self-potential—his real quest—through mastery of the land and the mysterious, is undeniable. Yet while the girls expect there to be a male hero, they rather enjoy the objectification of imagination as a "place" and identify with that place as a mental landscape. Ironically, the form itself empowers the girls to attend to conventions because it tends to exclude feminine values and reduce female characters to mere signs of the hero's progress, enablers, or even symbols for the (virginal) land itself. Paradoxically, the exclusion of girls and women from many high-fantasy worlds empowers the girls' readerly (even writerly) perceptions of the Secondary Worlds. Since they "can't really be a man in the Mafia" (or can't be a knight, or a Redwall warrior, or Harry Potter), they remain outside identification and, in the most cerebral manner possible, identify the means by which a fantasy text realizes the unreal and creates enchanted landscapes with certain logic, classification systems, symbols, conventions, and atmospheric effects.

THE MULTIPLE CLIMAXES AND QUESTS OF FANTASY

Important to this system of formal elements, in the girls' views, is the idea of affective balance between the two poles that define dialectical conflict—in terms of suspense and resolution, life and death, good and evil. Although Tolkien is reified by critics of high fantasy, the girls who read Tolkien feel he lacks balance and sides with the darker side of dialectical conflict. For example, Jessica describes Tolkien's fantasies as solely concerned with "guys and war" and eight-year-old Wendy describes *The Lord of the Rings* as "too scary," although she enjoys *The Hobbit*. The girls emphasize balance between emotional arousal and resolution as a construction of form:

> The next chapter [of *Redwall*] makes me kind of feel like to go on, it gives me a boost to read the next chapter. And I keep getting boosted to read more and more of it, like the names of the chapters do a boost too. And so it gives a boost so there isn't too much of a climax, well I mean there is a climax, but it kind of seems like there's more like a couple of climaxes, otherwise the story's like you're just working for the climax, you're not working to just read that chapter. And the *Martin the Warrior* ones, they're very exciting, and what happens is some books like the happy-ever ending, and nobody really gets hurt. But sometimes there's sad in them. Like in the books that I showed you that I really like, the *Martin* books, the *Redwall* books, they have like at least one animal dies in there and it's kind of sad but you know it doesn't have a happy-ever ending [pleased tone]. So you're like, "Is he going to get killed or something?" So you're not always so sure "this is gonna be the happy-ever-after ending." But you still know that this isn't too sad. There's probably going to be this hero and stuff, so there isn't too much sadness or too much happiness, but it's in the middle, and then it has the climax right that I like and it's adventure, and I actually kind of like having things about mice. And then in the stories I'm always expecting one person, like a hero base, like Martin or Martin's son, or Martin of Redwall or whatever, those kind of places-people, and then there's always like

these two little funny guys. They always run off with all this armor on, or like take these little wooden swords and they run off. They're pretty silly. So there's a lot of different things, so there's variety to it and you don't have too much adventure or too much nonadventure so it's just like right in the middle or everything you really want in a book. (Eight-year-old Wendy)

Wendy is looking for formal balance in the text's affects. She wants the text to arouse her yet control her arousal. Heightened emotions of uncertainty, suspense, sadness, and desire for more are complemented by her understanding of the way the text builds excitement with the chapter structure; denotes a "solid base" of hero; creates comic foils to the hero; and plays upon the convention of the happy ending with "sadness," meaning death of an important but secondary figure. Wendy knows what to expect and constantly measures the text at hand against an abstract generic standard that stands for the purity of balanced affect.

If the highest level of literary response includes emotional, intellectual, and critical significance, then eight-year-old Wendy's response achieves the highest level of aesthetic response through identification with form. In general, I found that developmental models of reading, in which critics specify stages of growth in reading sophistication, were inapplicable to my respondents. Paradoxically, Wendy's mastery of form gives her a vehicle for both expressing desire and mitigating it through affective balance. As reader, Wendy quests for multiple climaxes through the way the text constructs its chapters and sequences, but her physical pleasure is simultaneously an intellectual one, because she always remains conscious of the way form determines her response. The foils balance the hero, the comic balances the dangerous violence, the moments of joy balance the sad, the hero as device balances uncertainty in the Secondary World, and the small climaxes balance the length and time of sustained fantasy.

Girls find quest adventure thematizes the very structure of desire. For them, the specific object of a quest is not as significant as the structure of quest, which the impersonal reader can personalize. The girls define the central quest of a text differently from one another, translating the terms of the quest to mirror their own central desires. As literary critics, we might see Harry Potter's central quest as his desire to reach the sorcerer's stone, prevent Voldemort from achieving power, and thus save the land. But the girls find the quest structure formal and thus flexible, defining for themselves what Harry Potter lacks and quests for. According to Vanessa, the central mystery of *Harry Potter* is why Harry survives the death of his family. The text's major revelation occurs when the reader discovers that Harry's mother's love protected him and that she died to save him. Jessica is more enchanted by the processes of evil, and Vanessa, with security being given a tumultuous familial life. If each had identified with the hero they would have defined the quest by content—the title even announces the significance of the sorcerer's stone—but instead, they define the quest as a formal element, the content of which can be individualized.

THE HISTORY OF GENDER AND FORM IN
THE AMERICAN ROMANCE AND NOVEL

Because the girls enjoy the craft of story by attending to narrator and genre, along with the ability of those two elements to construct their vision of an alternative world, it is important to understand the connection between gender and genre as it developed in literary and critical history. This is particularly crucial if we are to take the girls' responses seriously and move beyond the idea that literature offers girls role models or lessons in identity politics—lessons that they seem to glean elsewhere. While many would agree that girls enjoy the very action of telling stories and that they employ narrative in a variety of settings to retroactively shape experiences, and while female characters in fantasy literature are a welcome innovation in the field of children's literature (e.g., in the work of Gail Carson Levine, Karen Cushman, Francesca Lia Block, and Tamora Pierce), the logic of the genre and constructed world hold more influence over the girls than the presence or absence of women in the textual world. The girls' appreciation of genre suggests that gender lies in the inner working systems of a literary world, of which characters are only a part, as recognized by Ursula Le Guin's departure from masculine form and world in *Tehanu*, her fourth Earthsea novel, for example.

An understanding of the history of gender and the novel, including novels for children, in both American and British literary history sheds light on the contemporary scene and the girls' responses. It is telling that girls turn to two British authors, J. K. Rowling and Brian Jacques, to explore fantasy and all its possibilities. In American culture, there has historically existed a certain negative bias toward fantasy literature, even for children, a bias inherited from a puritanical culture that doubted the usefulness of fantasy in educating a pragmatic subject. Gillian Avery argues this point in her history of American children's literature (pre-Baum). The "education" model of literature for children has been more predominant in America. Eighteenth- and nineteenth-century American literature sought to educate a gendered subject through model characters, as revealed by Avery's divisions between "Homes and Heroines" and "Frank and Manly: Ideals of Boyhood." However guarded against fantasy for children, however, nineteenth-century American culture produced an astounding array of high-Romance works, written for adults, by male authors whose novels depicted possibilities for young White men. The genre of high Romance in nineteenth-century America was used to explore possibilities for a masculine political subject and nation. The girls in my study turn to Europe for sustained fantasy works, but they *use* the form to imagine possibilities for alternative worlds of their own. I thus argue that they read high Romance (ancestor to fantasy) in a uniquely American fashion, developing their readings into desire for—and ways of thinking about—utopia.

BRITISH FANTASY FOR CHILDREN VERSUS AMERICAN ROMANCE

The high-Romance tradition has had very different meanings in British and American culture, meanings constructed by nineteenth-century literary history. Both national literary traditions stem from movements inspired by the Romantics, who elevated the value of imagination and the purity of the child's connection to imaginative ideals. Hence the "childlike quality" that fantasy worlds have come to embody over time. The sense of an enclosed fantasy space denoting a nostalgic view of childhood and past finds its fullest expressions in British fantasy for children. Conversely, in the American literary tradition, fantasy takes more the form of high Romance, denoting a perpetual openness to the quester in a new land. This openness of the quest in an enchanted landscape was not enclosed in the past but had to do with future political possibilities, consonant with the fact that the lone questers in the new land were male and adult, seeking a concept of self-made identity in a young nation.

When the girls insist upon literature as a Secondary World and use their participation in that world to fragment themselves from the limits of their "real" social roles, they claim the possibilities that high Romance represented among male writers of the American Renaissance. In Britain fantasy lands remained the domain of the child, and in America fantasy lands became national possibilities, placing ideals of American identity in the energies, if not bodies, of lone youths. In Britain, enchanted worlds were used to define the *child's* quest for self-possibilities, in works written by golden age children's writers Lewis Carroll, Charles Kingsley, George MacDonald, Robert Louis Stevenson, Rudyard Kipling, J. M. Barrie, Kenneth Grahame, and later A. A. Milne, C. S. Lewis and J. R. R. Tolkien. Their works were marked by longings for pastoral arcadias found in the ideal of a child at the center of their texts, most eloquently allegorized in Grahame's chapter titled "The Piper at the Gates of Dawn," from *The Wind in the Willows*. That chapter, interpreted by Carol Christ in her lectures on *The Wind in the Willows*, features a search for a lost child and, in that search, a glimpse of a forgotten wholeness in being one with nature, the sound of the wind in the willows, and the Pan figure that inspires poetic spirituality. In golden age texts, fantasy space is separated from "real" society, reflecting an idea that childhood is an entirely different land from that of adulthood, childhood being a lost period of time in which the possibilities of fantasy and imagination were open. Ultimately, the child who masters the enchanted world has to come home. Yet the fantasy space is always lingering in the past; "a bear and a boy will always be playing" in the 100 Aker Wood, and Peter will always be hovering outside Wendy's window, even though she is too old to adventure anymore. The utopia worlds are always threatened by the child's growth; Alice grows out of Wonderland, Mowgli is too much man so must return to the man-village at last, Christopher Robin has to go to school, and Wendy has betrayed the fantasy by growing up and reproducing. Even within Neverland, the crocodile's ticking clock symbolizes the march of time that will disrupt the ability to imagine and constitute in space a Secondary World. Fantasy separates the sociological and the formal worlds in the same way that my respondents do, but the girls refuse to close the boundaries between the two and use fantasy structure as a metaphor for that which the mind can materialize and imagine to be possible.

By reading British fantasy with an ideal of American transcendence of self through the imagination, the girls claim access to the ideology of fantasy as freedom, constructed by writers of American Romantic quests that structured the fantasy of self-making in a still-juvenile country. While writers of British adult novels of the same period were concerned with social realism, exploring the individual's relationship to society, American writers James Fennimore Cooper, Herman Melville, Edgar Allen Poe, Nathaniel Hawthorne, and Mark Twain expressed the possibilities for the American subject in the Romantic quest structure. The American Romance idealized the innocent youth featured in British fantasy, and turned him into a young man who discovers self-possibilities in a Secondary landscape, a metaphor for national land, Peter Hunt discerns in his descriptions of British and American fantasy:

> Not only do the complex layers of history embedded (as it were) in the landscape enrich the texture of stories, but the meanings of the landscapes themselves provide a subtext for the journeys: places mean. The American tradition of fantasy journey seems to be—at least to an Englishman like myself—one reaching outwards and westwards; it is a linear matter. Because there is little to dig down into, American fantasy tends to be set in secondary worlds. . . . The English, in contrast, are re-treading ancestral ground. Their reference points are more concrete, deep-rooted cultural symbols which seem to lie, sometimes literally, underfoot. (Qtd. in Smith 298)

In America, fantastic impulses reached outward into the American landscape itself: in the frontier of the American wilderness, haunted by Indians and witchcraft, in the uncharted seas where lurked an elusive white whale (Melville) and Arthur Gorden Pym's (Poe) utopian white land, and on the Mississippi River, a vision of escape and a quest for freedom, for White and Black (Twain). Even with the first successful quest fairy tale written specifically for children, L. Frank Baum's *The Wonderful Wizard of Oz,* the Secondary World is a thinly veiled allegory for America. Likewise, in Washington Irving's classic tale "Rip Van Winkle," still widely read by children, America itself is the fairy tale, the enchanted landscape for the European quester. Typically in the nineteenth century, this quest was a male experience. For the White man, then, America was the enchanted land denoting the openness of self-possibility, a place where one could really quest for more.

GENDER AND FORM IN NINETEENTH-CENTURY AMERICA

The girls' articulation of reading literature as a quest for adventure and symbolic landscape radicalizes the gendered divisions that both American literary history and critics have established between fantasy as male and social realism as female. High Romance defined the dream of the White man becoming anything he wanted in America, mapped onto juvenile energy, most evident in the way Huck Finn can take on any identity he wants to. As communities threaten to fix his identity, he simply lights out for the territories, so the quest for self-making is never closed. By contrast, the construction of the American feminine subject has largely been represented through social realism. American women writers of the nineteenth century stood against the tradition of high Romance, grounding sentimental and domestic novels in the home sphere and controlling the production of literature for children, for whom they followed Maria Edgeworth's ideology of rationality (Avery). Writers such as Louisa May Alcott, Susan Warner, and Lydia Maria Child wrote realistic coming-of-age stories in which girls learned to accommodate their characters to "real" social expectations, a different vision of citizenship from what the male writers had in mind. This was a conscious division; Hawthorne objected to those "damn scribbling women" writers and defined his vision of Romance against the novel:

> When a writer calls his work a Romance, it need hardly be observed that he wishes to claim a certain latitude, both as to its fashion and material, which he would not have felt himself entitled to assume had he professed to be writing a Novel. The latter form of composition is presumed to aim at a very minute fidelity, not merely to the possible, but to the probable and ordinary course of

man's experience. The former—while, as a work of art, it must rigidly subject itself to laws, and while it sins unpardonably so far as it may swerve aside from the truth of the human heart—has fairly a right to present that truth under circumstances, to a great extent, of the writer's own choosing or creation. If he think fit, also, he may so manage his atmospherical medium as to bring out or mellow the lights and deepen and enrich the shadows of the picture. (vii)

Writing this in his preface to *The House of the Seven Gables*, he connects the form to his pictorial intent:

The point of view in which this tale comes under the Romantic definition lies in the attempt to connect a bygone time with the very present that is flitting away from us . . . bringing along with it some of its legendary mist. (vii)

In the American Romance, legend, symbolism, and present purpose have everything to do with truths of the heart.

Only one girl, a very proficient reader, used the term *Romance* in the literary sense, citing the form's achievement of depth through its ability to create a symbolic, even enchanted, landscape of characters and actions. The subordination of character and "the probable and ordinary" to atmosphere and shadow is precisely what these girls appreciate and perceive as allowing transcendence of mundane life:

The book *Phantom* goes deeper into it than the *Phantom of the Opera*, the musical, does. I like that because the musical doesn't really explain it all that well but the book really gets into like the whole story, like the whole, how everything happened. And I like that book. I like the Romance part of it. I think that's just cool reading about that. It's about you know, the deformed genius and the chorus girl. I just think that's so wild reading about that you know. I just like how it goes deeper into the story than the musical does. You get a better feel for it. [It's] yeah, more of a Romance. I like the whole idea of the whole Romance thing. [It's] everything really. Like loving life you know, loving people and losing people that you love. That's where it all fits into. (Fifteen-year-old Ruth)

The "deformed genius" and "chorus girl" serve as meaningful categories only *within* the textual world; they are vehicles for both a "wild" read and a larger philosophical point. The text is "about" loving and losing people because it is *not* "about" the specific characters who love and lose; they are not of interest as men or women outside the book and it would not make sense to think of them in that way. This sensual kind of quest in the land of imagination was not in the scope of possibility for nineteenth-century women writers of social realism, who developed a didactic form to create "little women" and who, I believe, inform the perceptions of some critics who think that girls most need to read stories that teach them what girls and women can achieve in real life.

GENDER AND GENRE CONTINUE IN AMERICAN BOOKSTORES AND BLOCKBUSTERS

Although realism among male writers came into its own after the Civil War, the gender of American genre proliferated. Realism and the bildungsroman, Barbara White argues, remained in the twentieth century the dominant mode of expression for women writers reflecting on childhood and coming of age. This tradition of the American feminine subject coming into being through social realism, and the American masculine subject coming into self through fantasy, is sustained by popular fiction and film, even though contemporary fantasy literature is ripe with complex female characters and a whole genre of "role-playing" (world-playing) novels has come into its own.

Girls are highly aware of the fact that the category of heterosexual romance is marketed toward girls and women (the pinker section in the bookstore), while fantasy and science fiction targets boys and men (the darker section of the bookstore). Girls often mention their negative response to teen/heterosexual romance when I ask about their general experience of stories—anticipating the cultural expectation that they enjoy heterosexual romance novels, when I had not asked if they like heterosexual romance novels. For example, when I ask sixteen-year-old Amy to tell me about stories that matter to her, she immediately responds with, "Well, it's really weird; it's just that I'm not much of a romance movie person." Not only are the girls conscious of cultural rhetoric representing them as "a population in crisis" and "at risk" for loss of self; they also understand femininity as a genred construction and rebel against the terms. They know that films exploring the nuances of social relationships are called "tearjerkers" and that *tearjerker* means *feminine*.

The girls understand that modern action adventure films are fantasy worlds that utilize literary conventions in similar ways, which is why *Harry Potter* and *Star Wars* appear in the same response. Adventure films look remarkably similar to Romantic American classics in that they both imagine that a heroic quest to save the land united the White man and a racial other. Some examples of such films include *Lethal Weapon, Independence Day, Die Hard, The Negotiator, Indiana Jones, Karate Kid, Star Wars, Star Trek, Iron Eagle, An Officer and a Gentleman, The Wild, Wild West, Men in Black, A*

Time to Kill, and *Dances with Wolves*. Even *Robin Hood—Prince of Thieves* features a Moorish friend of Robin of Locksley.

That there exists an ongoing link between male fantasy and political subjecthood can be seen in the heroes' links to patriotic institutions such as the police, government, FBI, CIA, and secret service. Political power thus continues to be framed by collective fantasy about the potency of the White American male, often with racial others as enablers. Of course he needs a frontier, and so space functions as "the final frontier." The frontier, an enchanted landscape of utopian possibilities, calls upon the Romance of exploration and empire-building through voyaging to sea or into the wilderness or forest. The conventions behind these mythic narratives become the main point of interest for the girls, who use them to invent utopias for themselves, an example of which follows. The visibility of the form, learned through intense repetition, holds their interest largely because in the stories themselves, there are few roles for girls and women, other than to distract the hero from his mission or be given to him as reward. But that does not mean they do not forge their own points of departure from everyday life to enjoy collective American fantasy.

AN EXAMPLE OF UTOPIAN VISION

Many of the girls had utopian visions in their imaginations, either of alternative lands they could live in or alternative worlds that our own world could become. I present only one as an example because a discussion of all of them would fill another book:

> I'm a vegetarian and I really like animals, you know, and animalPower. And I really like deer. Deer's like my one animal. So I like to write a lot of stories about deer animals and how they get back at hunters. I change all the laws. Deer I worship. Most of my stories are about deer. They would overpopulate but that would be good and you know, natural predators are OK, so they would be brought back and it would be better ecosystem-wise and also like the humans, they're not the top creatures. They don't have to go and kill all animals and stuff, especially not deer. They're very cool, so graceful and wild. I've imagined I was a deer. Running free. If somebody kills a deer than they have to donate their lives to working for deer without pay. And all the land goes to deer reservations. And then there's going to be gardens and forests and security cameras. And it's better laws. Sometimes I make horror stories about deer, you know, like stories where people kill deer but the deer come back, you know, relatives and all

and they take out revenge. They're like innocence and all but it's a thrill. (Thirteen-year-old Ann)

Girls such as Ann articulate an environmental utopia by utilizing the conventions of fantasy, action adventure, and (in this case) horror, all of which stem from the high-Romance tradition, such as Arthurian legend. (Animal fantasy will be addressed in Chapter 7.) First, Ann identifies the land as in trouble, as threatened by dialectical conflict—by those who abuse the environment. She defines the land as a potential golden age with a past wholeness (graceful, wild, running free, gardens and forests), recognizing that the land has deeper knowledges than is apparent at first glance—knowledges of connectivity and ecosystem embedded within its mysterious, magical, enchanted inner workings. This threatened land is a past Eden but also a future, following the rules of science fiction (tight laws and security cameras) and even dystopia. The past yet potential Arcadia requires action adventure to be saved, and she recognizes that the use of these conventions is a means to power. Her utopia, shared by many girls who wish to save the animals and the environment, involves completely restructuring society.

Ann's story is a particularly interesting American theme in that Ann creates the dominant Secondary World figures as innocent but then makes slave-holding laws (for those who kill deer) and writes revenge stories in which the innocent kill. Ironically, girls aestheticize their reading and, by implication, disconnect literature from social issues, but they ultimately do so for a better understanding of how power operates in narrative space and social structures. Fantasy literature is never disconnected from social issues; fantasy worlds are used to critique or comment upon the real world, and questions of whether the form has a specifically liberating or conservative quality are ultimately unanswerable. However, the experience of the form is liberating for the girls because they use the form to imagine alternative universes of their own.

An interesting debate about science fiction opened at a panel on science and technology in literature (MLA, Chicago, 1999). One panelist asserted that science fiction "teaches" children that things are always changing, and another asserted that it "teaches" the thesis that no matter how much things change, they stay the same. The latter used the example of his disillusionment with *Star Trek*, its opening up of voyage and discovery within a militaristic venue. But setting does not define genre; as Nick Lacey points out, the writer of *Star Trek* meant it to be a Western in space, and actually, science fiction novels and films have very different strategies and forms, which we would do well to study along with the young. While it is impossible to say what the form of fantasy literature for children "does" as a whole, it is possible to assert that the fantasy form inherently contains an ideology of opening up Secondary Worlds or symbolic landscapes beyond "things as they are," just as the act of reading allows girls to imagine a secondary, nonsocial space for themselves in which they are beyond "who they currently are." The actual fantasy texts can often close these worlds or reinvent and reestablish patriarchal control, but because these girls are American optimists, they pay more attention to the notion of possibility embedded in the form.

The Genre of Identity:
Suspense, Action, Quest, and Gothic Form

They [mystery novels] go all the way to the spot and then they stop and
they go into another chapter and they start with a whole different subject
and then at the end of the book you finally find out what you wanted to
find out in chapter 7.

—Twelve-year-old Tae

WHY DO GIRLS enjoy mystery? How can they repeatedly experience suspense in genres they know so well?

The girls link a text's construction of their desire for action to its manipulation of suspense. When eight-year-old Wendy discusses her preference
for multiple climaxes in a plot, she reveals her emphasis on the constructive
rather than closing structure of the text. Just as the girls might select a text's
theme and believe that theme to embody a vision of the "whole," the girls
select aspects of form and believe those aspects to characterize the whole
genre. Even though both *Harry Potter* and *Redwall* restore status quo at the
end of the texts, as do most European fantasy and many American works of
science fiction, the girls insist that their knowledge of the form's impending
resolution is not important. They claim not to enjoy suspense because a resolution follows, which would define the text as a safe adventure. Rather, they
insist that the important component of the form is its prolonged, perpetually building suspense—its ques*ting*.

In this chapter I discuss the girls' attention to the way in which form
builds and gives shape to emotion, especially through texts that build suspense and those that prolong quest, the former making the reader or viewers
"want to want," and the latter promising purpose to the experience of "wanting." These structures are particularly evident in mystery plots, which require the readers to have active knowledge of form. Proficient with mystery,
the girls emphasize both emotional and intellectual desires to quest and re-
construct story from plot. The girls' understanding of structure and symbol

in mystery and horror bespeaks their investment in Gothic forms and tropes, which aestheticize emotion, particularly fear. Unlike other forms of fantasy, Gothic fantasy has historically been appropriated by women writers to express female concerns in both British and American culture. The girls approach Gothic fiction with an aesthetic stance to identify with an omniscient point of view on the story rather than with the female victim, subject to various "horrors" in stories and in life.

SUSPENSE

Suspense is theoretically complex because it bespeaks a kind of paradox involved in emotional response (Ryan 144–46). Readers of suspenseful mystery plots and viewers of suspenseful action films react to danger and intrigue as if the stories were real, the reader being completely immersed in the narrative situation, and yet suspense usually derives from a perspective of omniscience, dependent on the reader/viewer's knowledge of form, or the experience would not be pleasurable. However, since the reader/viewer knows the conventions, and thus knows that the suspense will be resolved and contained, how can she/he still experience tremendous arousal—again and again? The girls fluidly cite their understanding of form and their pleasure in feeling suspense, demonstrating fluid movement between seeing character viewpoint and form:

> Like I read *The Count of Monte Cristo* last year and I liked that. It's by Alexander Dumas. This guy, the count, he was just getting married and then some guy kind of backstabbed him and had him arrested and put in jail because he wanted to marry the girl he was marrying. And he educates himself when he was in this prison with this old man and he finds his fortune; this old man gives him this paper and it has nothing on it. He's like, "What is this?" and then one day the lights went out and he went to light it on fire and he realized that this was heat-sensitive ink and it would only come out when it was really hot. And so he reads this whole thing and finds this treasure and he goes back and he gets back at the people that have done stuff to him and even to the woman he loved because she married this other guy, he wanted to get back at her. It was kind of like, "Oh my god, I could never do that!"
>
> He has to overcome things in order to—this kid who he was very fond of, who always stood by him, wanted to marry this girl and he didn't like the girl or something, then he didn't want them together and then he realized that they want to be happy, this is all they want,

just so they're happy, that they want in life, and so he overcomes that and he gets them together. And that's the end of the story pretty much and he lives happily ever after. I liked it! It was very suspenseful. It was like a 450-page book. I read it in a little bit over a week. (Sixteen-year-old Amy)

Amy being particularly well versed in action adventure film, her preferred film genre, her pleasure derives from her engagement with genres she has previously understood as suspense-building. Amy easily switches from plot to a description of form, both what the protagonist must overcome and how suspense can be felt despite knowledge of the "happy ever after" that she knows will come. Amy attends to the count as a character, even comparing his actions to hers—"I could never do that"—because he embodies the literary universe of which he is a part (we do not meet counts these days) and because he is subordinate to form. He is part of the symbolic framework within which suspense operates.

In the following, Amy sees as the source of her pleasure in a book such as *Monte Cristo* her zest for action adventure. Paradoxically, the very predictability of conventions allows the girls to imagine emotion in external form, so emotion is experienced as a kind of bounded action. Amy contrasts her pleasure in action adventure with her avoidance of (heterosexual) romance (which we would call comedy). She appreciates the ability of action adventure to manipulate her solid understanding of conventions and surprise her:

Well it's really weird, it's just like I'm not much of a really romance-like movie person. Even though I have a boyfriend and all I do is like you know, we have good times together, we have our own little romance, like romantic thing going on, like *Runaway Bride*, I've never seen it. I'm more action. Anything that you're on the edge of your seat, you know? Anything with a thrill in it, something risky. I really like *The Blair Witch Project*. One of my movies that I really like is *The Rock*. Because it has Nicholas Cage and Sean O'Connor. Something with action in it, I'm more into that then. [Tells story of *The Rock*] You know, like, the guys won. They're [action adventure] all the same. They're always like that. It's kind of like suspense. That's what I mean when something where you're not, like *Blair Witch*, I thought it was really good because you didn't know what was going to happen. You couldn't predict and also *The Sixth Sense*, like at the end. [Explains major twist] It's kind of like this twist at the end of the movie. [Suspense] keeps you impressed.

I like not to know. When it's kind of obvious what's going to happen it's just like, a love story of course, you know from the beginning what's going to happen and sometimes I like where there's twists at the end. I like things that aren't going to just, otherwise I feel like the whole time you're like, "Oh I know what's going to happen." I don't really [imagine myself in it] because I know it wouldn't happen but kind of [what if] when I don't know what I'd do [if I saw dead people] so I don't know how to describe it, I don't know. I can't control what's happening in the movie. Like this is happening, like that's it. you know? In my usual life I have like the love story. [With stories] I guess it's that I'm watching from the outside and the [stories] that are good are good. I'll get into it if it's good. I mean I feel almost relaxed, like wow. I'm really fickle with my emotions and like with movies I do open up a lot with them. I cried at *The Lion King*. I felt bad for the little lion.

Amy's discussion features the paradox that she wants to not know what will happen in a film—"I like not to know"—yet the films she enjoys are "all the same." This posture of "not knowing" becomes, then, "not know-ing" how the unique text will use and perhaps twist generic conventions. The pretense of "not knowing" is bound to the feeling of losing control ("I can't control what's happening") and opening the self up to the experience of the text. She loses control to genre, conflating people and genre: "I'm not much of a romance person," "I'm more action." She makes a direct identification between viewer and form, as if there are generic forms of people walking around, and as if genres are solely defined by emotional response.

Because heterosexual romance and action films are both formulaic genres, we have to understand Amy's openness to one set of conventions over an-other through the fact that in adventure, she sees a symbol for her aesthetic desires, desiring to both "not know" and "know," a split and paradoxical viewing self that both understands the rules of genre and yet enjoys the pre-tense of "getting into it" and being expert viewer/pretender. The "twist" is the perfect metaphor to describe the way in which the girls view the text's status in tradition and their role when viewing the text, knowing and yet not knowing themselves, inside and outside both social identity and accrued story experience. The girls' awareness of structure becomes most useful to the girls when they can detect the twist; this parallels what Jameson argues is useful about formalist approaches to literature. When a significant change from conventional form can be detected, the artist or reader derives meaning from form. Yet even when they expect the twist, girls could imagine that they "don't know what is going to happen." The form that suspense and adventure take, then, symbolizes the process whereby the viewer becomes a vehicle for the action adventure of the text.

Storytelling conventions thus give to emotion itself shape and material existence in time and space. Suspense involves the process of the reading self opening up to the plot in a slowly building process:

> [Hope explains the plot of *Rigoletto*.] You *want* to make the other person figure out that it's not really them [who did the wrongdoing] and you just *want to know* what's going to happen but I like [that feeling]. I *know* what's going to happen but the other person doesn't so you *want* to hurry up and make the story get to the end so you'll know what really happens.
>
> *Q: So part of the suspense is the feeling like you want to get it resolved?*
>
> Yeah. Yeah.
>
> *Q: So is it good to know that it will be resolved? Do you know it will be resolved?*
>
> Yeah (shakily)
>
> *Q: So when does a story like that get good? When things are all complicated and you're in suspense or at the end when everything's resolved?*
>
> When I'm in suspense.
>
> *Q: Why is that good?*
>
> I don't know. I just *want* it to happen. (Fourteen-year-old Hope)

A state of "wanting knowledge" defines suspense for Hope, yet her awareness of form reveals that she *already knows*. How can the viewer both want to know and already know? The wanting takes on a life of its own, independent of the fact that the reader always already "knows" what will happen. The reader wants to *want*; this wanting is not dependent upon the text's revelation of knowledge. Rather, the girl's tension involves suspense as a response to certain "known" conventions of drama. The reader's want does not stem from pretending to "not know" or "wonder" what will happen next, but from the pleasure of witnessing how the particular text at hand uses, reveals, or twists conventions. Suspense derives from a combination of the text's engagement with conventions and the reader's experience of generic traditions, emerging from the viewer's unspoken question: "How is this particular text going to manipulate narrative time with its generic conventions such that I experience delay of gratification, continual delay of the knowledge I already know?"

Hope specifies the fact that pleasure lies in the "when and how" rather than in the "what," displaying an intuitive consciousness of the theory of suspense as defined by Alfred Hitchcock. The knowledge of resolution is only important insofar as that knowledge provides the boundaries for imaginative space as material form. This knowledge provides an end point at which the girl could imagine arriving if she could manipulate narrative time and accelerate the process. Suspense, however, is engendered by the text's control of narrative time such that resolution seems delayed and the constructive process elongated. The reader can sense the possibility of accelerating narrative time only because the text injects her into its framework for time and constitutes the reader as a construct-in-motion, being built and paced. The knowledge of resolution is thus only a necessary fiction in that it constitutes imaginative space as existing in time with "an end," the constitution of which (as a shape, a form) allows the girl to watch the text make unique the conventions she already knows. Thus it is the ability of form to constitute fiction as a real "space" and a structured object in tension with motion (plot development) that grants the illusion that suspense has its own building "shape."

"THE WHOLE WORLD-ENDING THING"

Suspense plots, particularly action adventure films, combine the quest of a hero with an epic structure. Journey through apocalypse to restoration of the land is the essential structure that many girls cite in their discussions of many texts, happy to summarize the texts in terms of form. They even gesture beyond fiction, showing how plots of news stories, for example, appropriate storytelling conventions. In the following, fifteen-year-old Ruth connects the apocalyptic structure with contemporary representations of the AIDS epidemic, but engages most powerfully with Stephen King's use of the structure in *The Stand*. Rather than lessening or cheapening the experience of literature, skillful use of conventional structure sharpens and enhances a text's power:

> [*The Stand*], it's not scary as much as it is gory and I don't really like gory a lot but this book is pretty much about the world ending and like 99.4% of the population dying and that part kind of made you wonder about all the outbreaks of disease, you know the AIDS, the

HIV, all that weird stuff. It just kind of makes you think what if that stuff ever became airborne, then we'd all be wiped out in days, and it was kind of interesting to be like, wow. That book I liked everything. It was you know, everything in the book. It touched everything. Apocalypse and love, life, and loss. Not as much but a little bit, just enough to make you think. Something about the book. It was different. I think that's why I like it so much. It's very very different from everything I've read before. It's just the whole, you know the end of the world, you know what would that be like and it's the whole good-versus-evil thing, and that kind of thing. It would be like an asteroid hitting the earth; that's influenced by Hollywood.

I do like happy endings a lot. When I'm reading a book and it's like very depressing at the end, because you think about that and it's like, why did that have to happen? You know, why couldn't they have like a nice happy ending? And it was a pretty happy ending. Yeah, it's the whole good overcomes evil and I like that. [But] it's just kind of like a curiosity, what would that be like?

A text "very very different from everything I've read before" can still be distilled as "the whole good-versus-evil thing," or "the whole good overcomes evil." It was clear to Ruth that the structure of the apocalypse repeats in books, films, and even news-magazine formats, the whole issue of "epidemic" depicted in similar structural terms. Many girls actually contrast stories with the news, showing a preoccupation with how stories are told on the news (I had not asked about the news, just about stories that mattered to them); twelve-year-old Tae objects to the lack of an aesthetic in the news, claiming that the news "throws people's pain away." The girls prefer to witness pain in the aesthetic realm, where it gains thematic meaning. But "the whole good-versus-evil thing," "good overcoming evil," undergirds the way a particular text might be "different," might use those conventions in "interesting" ways. If genre and structure become the means by which text and audience meet, then no stories are free of formula. Literary critics working in postmedieval fields tend to value unique rather than formulaic texts, equating popular fiction with the formulaic. But girls do not view formula and uniqueness as antitheses, suggesting that a text's uniqueness *rests upon* its selections and combinations of various formulas.

By becoming a formal participant of the text, the girls could regard two texts as structurally "the same," yet not the same in terms of the skill and content by which the texts work out their relationship to tradition:

My favorite movie is *Armageddon*. *Armageddon* was the better one. It was the other one, *Deep Impact*, that was not so good. It was the same thing. A comet asteroid. Well, comet was *Deep Impact, Armageddon* was asteroid but it doesn't matter. I wouldn't call it a horror story. Sort of like fiction. I mean world ending, but not horror. [She tells the story.] The world was saved and they got married. I like to be like on the asteroid you know, saving the earth and stuff. (Thirteen-year-old Ann)

Ann notes in her description of *Armageddon* that the female character stays on the ground while the important men in the character's life save the earth. However, Ann can still be on the asteroid just as Jesse is "there, battling" at Redwall, because Ann's perspective on the text is formal, emphasized by her intertextual allusion to generic "world-ending" fiction in which the world is saved and a marriage takes place. Ann identifies the central structural and archetypal good-versus-evil story, although she cannot think of the word for the genre, and equates the structure of "Armageddon" and its generic intertext with its sister film *Deep Impact*. Although the two stories are "the same" and share intertextual traditions, one uses conventions with more skill, in her eyes. In the end their specific content "does not matter," she says. It is the structure itself that transports her to its world: "I like to be on the asteroid."

I had expected the girls, in discussing form, to talk about happy endings, but I was surprised to find that their discussion of happy endings also includes a more significant understanding of how certain generic traditions emphasize response to happy endings and others do not. The girls thus have a sophisticated view upon forms of all kinds:

[I like horror films] to turn out OK. That's what I like. You know, everybody wishes for a happy ending, except it doesn't really happen all that much. But I don't really go to horror movies for the ending, but you do want it to work out. I could go to comedy movies and know that those will end up all right. Or romantic movies, and that's not what you go to when you want to go to a horror movie. (Thirteen-year-old Ann)

Although different genres can be structurally similar in terms of generic roots, certain genres emphasize different aspects of the same narrative structure. When nine-year-old Jesse defines *Harry Potter* as a combination of humor, mystery, and adventure, she, like Ann, evinces the sense that storytelling traditions are separate and that genres emphasize different aspects of narrative structure. One chooses to read or view different genres for different purposes and appreciation of different effects.

"THE HORROR, THE HORROR!": GOTHIC MYSTERY

Although action, fantasy, and high Romance are historically masculine forms, Gothic fantasy fiction in books and films is generally understood to be a powerful expression of female issues, among both writers and audiences (Kristeva, Masse, Berenstein). My respondents cite the Gothic form as steeped in conventions that are designed to produce responses of suspense and fear, continual deferral of gratification, horror of the mysterious and unexplained, lack or desire, and both emotional and intellectual need to quest. At first I thought that the girls enjoy Gothic fiction because such texts address fear but contain horror with conservative endings, allowing them a catharsis. Since the subject of brutality against girls and women would often arise in the interviews when I asked girls to tell me stories "about girls or women," I assumed at first that Gothic structures would ensure a happy ending to the scary story. But as thirteen-year-old Ann explains above, girls do not seek literary horror for its conservative ending; she could see a comic or romantic film if she wanted assurance that all's well that ends well. Rather, girls emphasize that the Gothic opens up the pleasure of fantasy and through appropriating conventions for materializing fantasy in their own minds, the girls author their own masterplots of horror and keep their fears of an unsafe world under control by identifying with omniscience rather than victim.

FORM OVER VICTIM, MIND OVER MATTER

Both mystery novels and horror films depend upon the reader's familiarity with Gothic conventions for emotional and even visceral response. The girls in my study are so familiar with Gothic conventions that they identify those conventions as "rules":

> Now, there's like, you know, there's certain rules that you have to have in horror stories, like whenever you turn around there's always somebody there, it always has to be nighttime in a thunderstorm, and something scary happens. All bad guys have to have bad aim with a gun, you know those kind of things. And then like regular laws of gravity and stuff. But it's always dark and all the killer people are always insane because something bad happened.
>
> I like horror movies, but not like the really bloody ones, like disgusting. I hated *Sixth Sense*. It was all gore. It was just really realistic and awful. Yeah, it has to be clean. It's like, this is nothing

like real life, so you know. [If we went to the planet of horror films] no one has any blood in their body. It's all just water, and there are no knives or weapons, well that sort of ruins it. All right, there's a rule. No one can hurt each other badly. No one can disfigure each other. There's no chopping off heads and arms and stuff, and nobody throws each other in fire. (Thirteen-year-old Ann)

Ann identifies certain "rules" "always" present in horror stories, rules engendering certain reader responses and absolutely crucial to the experience. There "have to be" certain effects produced by setting and action, close calls, mysteries in tension with motivations, and unveiling explanations for evil. Random evil cannot just stand alone, but nor can evil be "embodied" in the sense of graphic bodily violence. The horror is always a disembodied horror, differentiated by Ann from scenes of bodily mutilation. The horror, in Ann's view, should be embodied by formal convention rather than human character. Girls identify with Gothic form because Gothic horror provides a solid structure for fantasy. Even though almost all the girls identify with victims of real-life horrors depicted on the news (the Columbine shooting had recently occurred when I conducted interviews), they separate the Gothic aesthetic from life and, by doing so, imagine a disembodied horror—less gory and more dependent on literary devices—to affect the reader/viewer's mood and emotional response.

Ann's description of horror and her insistence that the form be differentiated from real bodies, especially female bodies that in real life *are* subject to various horrors, reveals girls' desire to embody the form rather than victim, usually female, of horror or violence. Later in the interview Ann explicitly links her understanding of Gothic conventions as bloodless spectacles to the fact that she is becoming a woman and has to bleed, expanding upon her visceral distaste for the real blood that womanhood engenders. The desire to separate Gothic as an aesthetic from real "Gothicized" plots is most apparent in eleven-year-old Nellie's differentiation of her experience of reading mystery novels from watching the news. When I ask her to recall stories about girls, she immediately mentions two news stories, one in which a four-year-old girl was drowned in a swimming pool and the other the story of Christina Williams, a young girl who was abducted. Nellie's experience with those stories makes her "imagine, like, what if I was that person, that got, that had something done to them. Like why would someone do that and what if I was that person out there?" To take control of her fear, engendered by identification with a person, she discusses the incident with her mother, and together, she says, they imagine "who did it" and "why someone would do that." They thus imagine a detective plot, imagining that they can solve the mystery and reenacting the narrative process that refocuses the plot from the victim to the slow revelation of evil and motivation.

Form becomes a way to deny identification with female character, offering the reader a generic rather than specific role in the text. Although she imagines herself as the victim when experiencing the "real" story on the news, Nellie denies identification with the young female detectives of the Mary Kate and Ashley mystery series (Olsen), even when I point out the contradiction. She suggests that mysteries are fun because she is an intellectual agent mastering form:

> I like mysteries [because] it's like something happens to a person and then they try to find who did it and why they do it and it's fun to read them because they're going all around wondering who did it and the clues, and it's interesting to me to see what they're doing and how they do it, until they find out who does it and why they did it.

> *Q: It is a good story if you're in the middle of it, is it good then? Or is it good when you find out who did it?*

> I guess you could say it's good both. Because it's good to try to get in the story and guess who it is, and then when you find out, sometimes you're right and sometimes you're wrong and it feels good when you're right. So you're pretty good at doing it and you guess. And then on the news, you don't know if they're going to get solved. You don't know what's going to happen.

Nellie sees no contradiction between the idea that she imagines herself as the victim of the news story and her denial of identification with Mary Kate and Ashley, characters empowered to solve such crimes. Nellie's mastery of form stands for an aesthetic identification and empowers her as a literary expert on form; she thinks of herself as "pretty good at doing it." Even if she is wrong about who perpetuated the crime, her aesthetic distance from the text allows her to expand her understanding of the form rather than worry about being wrong. She learns, by reading more from the series, that the form is constantly alluding to itself, setting up the convention of the "surprise." That a girl gets "good" at a form bespeaks Jill P. May's central point in *Children's Literature and Critical Theory*. May argues that exposure to literature involves children in a process of accumulating literary conventions, a sustained and always growing body of knowledge more complicated and substantial than that of any other field of cumulative understanding. The girls demonstrate that pleasure in form compensates for the uncertainties of narrative paths in life.

GETTING GOOD AT FORM

Older girls explain the importance of mystery plots in developing their mastery of readership. Thirteen-year-old Jessica, a fairly proficient reader, discusses how mystery novels helped develop her ability to make predictions based on her reading experience. Like many girls, she, when younger, would argue with a book's use of conventions and appropriate conventions to revise or reauthor stories in her mind:

> I used to read mysteries and stuff. Sometimes if they had a really silly ending, when they always skip over this obvious fact you know, like it jumps out at the reader, and I just like want to go in there and say, "Hey look at this," you know? "Go down this path" instead of going down the dark evil one, stuff like that. [Mysteries] they're just like, got your brain working more, so you're thinking harder or something like that. Trying to figure it out ahead of the book, or ahead of the reading.

In the girls' experience with reading the mystery novel, emotional and intellectual response combine in an acute understanding of form that can then be applied to all story forms, with more or less success depending upon how well the girls are educated in different genres.

The girls are so proficient with mystery that they sometimes misapply the form, showing how the way in which a girl perceives genre determines whether the text succeeds or fails for her. For example, fourteen-year-old Kristen thinks *The Scarlet Letter* announces its genre as mystery, by emphasizing Gothic elements and a mystery "who dunnit?" plot, framing the narrative with the introduction of bodily evidence (Hester and her infant) that demands explanation, in the course of which social intrigues emerge. By emphasizing Gothic elements, then, the text "should" have had other Gothic devices such as multiple plots, complications to the mystery, doubles, emphasis on spaces rather than psychological complexities, and little emphasis on social relations. The book does not fulfill Kristen's expectations:

> *The Scarlet Letter*, I watched both movies too; I read the book and then watched both movies because the book's hard to read. I thought that it wasn't a horrible book, like the worst book I ever read, but I mean I didn't like it that much because from the beginning, they tell you who the father is, they tell you that she's pregnant and that she has all this stuff happening and it's just one story. Some stories have other things going on in the stories, like especially soap operas and stuff, they have a million stories going on and this has one story. It's

simple. It's just about her and her baby and how people make fun of her and you can tell it in like a nutshell. It's like there.

Her dramatic Gothic frame causes the story to fail. She is disappointed that no real mystery emerges and that no complications to the mystery develop, viewing the text as one "simple" plot. She then views the text as "there" without her, as refusing her cocreative participation "inside." For her, the text is transformed from Gothic to character-in-relation-to-society, which then confuses her because (in her view) societal relations never become the text's predominant focus. Kristen has little framework for understanding the American manifestation of high Romance. Similarly, ten-year-old Elaine emphasizes the film *Now And Then* as a mystery. By emphasizing the mystery genre, she forecloses attention to the text's storytelling frame, which would imply the importance of the bildungsroman and the lasting community of women with roots in girlhood. The rules of form can foreclose other ways of appreciating a text if the girls do not see that different formal traditions are being combined in new ways.

SERIALIZATION: MYSTERY SAGA THAT NEVER ENDS

Although the girls expect that all will be explained by the conclusion of the mystery novel—not on page 2 with the look on Dimmesdale's face!—they also expect that the ending will be unequal to the possibilities opened up by the text as fantasy. Understanding the conventions, they simply reject or revise the endings they do not like, and thus appropriate the conventions as tools of authorship. Serialization allows them to appropriate authorship of Gothic conventions for themselves and imagine their own possibilities for a sequel. Because the Gothic text opens fantasy worlds and then closes them with unsatisfying explanations of mystery and magic, the girls would regard the text as one interpretation of the mystery, which could be reworked:

> I just got done reading an X-Files book. It's called *Empathy* [Steiber]. It's about a girl and she's in high school and she was really pretty and she went to sleep one night and some mysterious man came into her house and he kidnapped her and he stuck her in the basement of an unknown building, unknown to anybody, unknown to cops, unknown to parents, unknown to everybody. [Finishes story]
> Sometimes I get upset how they end the book, like this person never comes back again. Sometimes I get mad and I start screaming at the book! Why did you end it this way? I would have ended it *that* [other] way. I would have had the person like run away from the cops,

break out of jail and run away from the cops and hide in a different country and then come back with a sequel and he does something in New Mexico and then he runs away and goes back to Canada or something and does it again and then he finally gets caught and there's no way for him to get back out. I get so into the book I don't even want it to end. I want it to end and go to a sequel and then go to another one and go to another one and I want to find out like if the person goes to jail, if they die in jail or they get bullied by their cellmates or I want to know what happens. (Twelve-year-old Tae)

Tae's continuation of the story demonstrates the important tension the Gothic reader experiences between "wanting to know" and actually authoring the story. So familiar with and even embodied by Gothic form, this African American reader uses Gothic devices in her storytelling, controlling the revelation and repeating the word *unknown* to engage me with the mystery story. Tae begins to disagree with the text's construction, to argue with the text as an author, addressing the text as the imaginal agent: "Why did you end it that way?," "I start screaming at the book!" It becomes clear in her telling that any ending to the fantasy world would be angering, for it breaks the spell of the imaginary world's objective existence ("I don't want it to end"), yet the girls' desire to know or "find out" compels them forward, a problem answered by serialization, which renders endings temporary inconveniences in the life of the imaginary world.

The way the Gothic convention constantly alludes to and revises itself, however, can give the ending a different meaning. The convention of the twist begins to be expected and eventually becomes part of the tradition of the Gothic novel, in the girls' view, particularly if serialized. The serialization of detective fiction changes the shape of the particular text at hand to open up endings, Gothicizing rather than closing the story's possibilities. R. L. Stine's *Goosebumps* books, in fourteen-year-old Kristen's perspective, feature a different convention in that their endings "leave you hanging." Thus the end opens new possibilities of mystery and is instrumental to the process of unveiling knowledge. Kristen identifies the endings of the *Goosebumps* books as an important part of the thrill *because* those open endings allude to more conventional textual endings that contain mystery. She links *Goosebumps* endings with her engagement as imaginal agent "in" the text, a reader with the imagination to image from words:

I read a lot of scary books when I was little, like I read *Goosebumps* books. I must have about twenty of them downstairs that I used to collect. The mysteries, they're appealing. It gets you thinking. It's more creative. I read a mystery book and you don't know who it is. And you're thinking about it and you can create the person that you're thinking of in your mind.

If you read about a monster I can picture something so totally horrible, and then when you see it, you're like, "That's it?" Like some of the *Goosebumps* books they give you a picture on the front and you're like, "That's what the monster's supposed to look like?" And I create something more scary and it's just a lot more fun that way. Because it's like, "oooh." In my head I can picture it but just roughly. Not really every detail but I can pretty much picture what they look like and everything. [It's more scary] because you can't really actually see [in your mind]. It's like the picture of it. [And] it's kind of the thrill that [the text] doesn't turn out OK. Because most of the books, at the end they leave you hanging and stuff, and it's like, "Oh! I have to get to the end so I know what's happening." Like some of the other books that I read, that I think are going to be pretty interesting, I always cut myself short, I read the back first and then it's like, "No! Now I know what's going to happen. I've just ruined the whole book."

Although Gothic texts have stable conventions, the girls identify their presence as readers with "creativity," "imagination," and thought. The conventions invite their participation, knowledge, and experience with literary form. Kristen cites the dependence of the form on vague description as a site of reader entry, for the reader can create a "picture" of horror because horror depends on vague imaging, disembodied presences imprecisely evoked by one's imaging the words. The monster is scary because it is "the picture of" a monster, a presence foregrounding the idea of picturing rather than the picture itself. Kristen discusses the thrilling endings of the *Goosebumps* books in relation to the function of endings in other kinds of books; the endings "ruin" her experience of narrative time if she feels compelled to read the end first. She maintains a critical sense that knowing the endings of a text "ruins" the experience of stories, a sense that all the girls share even though they often expect the ending to be a cliffhanger.

GOTHIC LANDSCAPE

The girls imagine Gothic texts to be distinct from other imaginative landscapes. While the Gothic world is also a place to go, an object existing in space and time, the girls conceptualize this "place" as one of twists and turns, a site of multiple plots that "exist" simultaneously in the storytelling world. The mystery form's serialization adds new plots to the story place: thus when girls "go" to Gothic fiction they journey to a place with, on the one hand, very tight structure (quest sequence), and on the other hand, multiple twists and turns—even holes that suggest layers of places:

> I like mysteries a lot. In *Nancy Drew* [Keane] files and stuff, they make you want to keep reading it and reading it and reading it until you find out who did the crime and what happened, like why did this person jump from the window. Why did this person kill two people and then run away and kill himself. It makes you want to keep reading until the end and find out what happens. You don't know what's going to come and then when you find out it's like, "I never expected that to happen." Or they write a sequel to the book and it's better than it was before. I actually like when mysteries do that. They go all the way to the spot and then they stop and they go into another chapter and they start with a whole different subject and then at the end of the book you finally find out what you wanted to find out in chapter 7. (Twelve-year-old Tae)

Multiple plots disrupt and interfere with the central quest, the central "why" that needs answering. The structure motivates the reader to embark upon the central quest from the outside, an invitation the girls accept by giving the text the power to constitute the reader in its quest—"it makes you want to keep reading"—and the constitution of the reader as an intellectual agent who wants to research the "why," expects the "why" to be explained, and also expects to be surprised. To expect to be surprised is a rather paradoxical posture to take with a text. Girls train themselves to expect the unexpected, always conceptualizing an ending in advance of the reader's "arrival."

The mystery is a journey to "a spot," says Tae, a structure borrowing its power from quest fantasy/high Romance, but its constant deferrals of pathways define the world of the text as less "one" place to travel through and more the haunted house itself, in which different rooms and passages can all coexist simultaneously and advance their own plots. The form's propensity to switch between plots and delay the knowledge quested for (until "chapter 7," Tae says), creates the symbol of the Gothic world as a multistoried house rather than an enchanted land. For example, fourteen-year-old Carolyn engages with the conventions of the Gothic by imagining aspects of its form in her apartment. After seeing the film *The Haunting*, adapted from Shirley Jackson's *The Haunting of Hill House*, Carolyn imagines that one room in her apartment contains an evil spirit. She thus becomes author of a Gothic in her mind and evinces the sense that the Gothic is "a place" of many spaces, enclosures, and rooms:

> If I see a scary movie, that probably stays in my mind. Like the villain [of *The Haunting*] Hugh Crane. [I would imagine] something's in [that room.] And I think it's a spirit. It's a villain spirit. But I don't know whose it is. The haunted house stuff, that's cool.

The Gothic is thus a very spatialized form, defining its integrity as an artistic object separate from life, but complicating the aesthetic space of fantasy fiction by its multiple layers. Carolyn brings the conventions of the text into her own world rather than merely escaping social space through the fantasy text. The text changes the meaning of social space and makes its mark there through Carolyn's appropriation of narrative conventions. Carolyn authors and experiences the Gothic at the same time. Although she creates a villain in her mind, she does not "know" who it is (she does not even say "he"), enjoying not the "who" but the "how," the means by which she scares herself in her own textual "place." She hovers between omniscient narrator and unknowing reader by taking the structure of Gothic form and identifying that structure with the haunted house, a typical setting for the Gothic story but not simply a setting she draws out from the text. Rather, girls denote the haunted house as a symbol for the Gothic's multiple imaginative spaces, which co-occur to produce an aesthetic object.

HOW THE GOTHIC DOUBLES

Girls expect the Gothic form to feature multiples or doubles of spaces, characters, and plots, which threaten the integrity of "one" unique hero, story, villain, or discursive story place. The element of the double they link with other narrative forms, such as the convention of the twin on television (*Sister, Sister*; *Full House*'s Mary Kate and Ashley, also stars of the written mystery series), the idea of which they really like. When discussing twins on television, they demonstrate the fact that they identify with characters on television shows, discerning TV twins as representing the ability to have a piece of self and yet a friend, perfectly bridging their real-life needs for both individuality and connectedness. Yet they define doubling within the Gothic as ultimately a doubling of the text's world by their own imaginations of fear, as produced by Gothic conventions. That is, they could take a Gothic device and author that device in a new context, expanding upon the device to shape their own fantasy. The girls would imagine and pretend Gothic forms to scare themselves and their friends, and ultimately materialize their own imaginations through Gothic story. It is, then, the text's Gothic form itself that ultimately doubles, reproduced *in* and *by* the girls' imaginations:

> I used to be real scared of movies and stuff. Like stupid stuff, like dolls that come alive. I used to always turn my dolls around in my room because I was so scared of them. And I know it's make-believe. Like Chucky (*Child's Play*), or something like that, I would always be afraid, because I had a lot of dolls in my room and I would always ask my mom, once or twice a night I couldn't sleep, I'd be like something's under my bed, an I can't sleep, my doll's looking at me, I swear to God it just moved.
>
> I hear stuff in the house. I know it's like the refrigerator [but] I'll get real warm. My face will get real hot. I'll be real hot under my covers. And I'll pull my face under the covers and just lay there real still and I won't move for like fifteen, twenty minutes and then when it goes away I'll just go to sleep. So I'm like all panicking and everything and I'm just like, "I'm not leaving my room. I don't care how bad I have to go to the bathroom." I'll just sit there and look around and wait until it goes away. (Fourteen-year-old Kristen)

Kristen's discussion features many versions of the device of doubling. The doll stands as a double for, or the underside of, "the human" and also "the child." It gains most of its uncanniness, however, from its doubling of femininity; Kristen's own dolls are external symbols for a female childhood steeped in certain feminine ideologies. The Gothic project could be described as doubling domesticity to explore the dark underside of domestic ideology. However, the most important double of Kristen's description is her own imaginal agency as a double of literary form. She knows that pretend fear is structured by literary conventions and "make-believe," but in her mind she externalizes fear and gives it material form, which takes on its own agency. Imagining that evil lurks in her own house, she waits until "it" goes away, as if her imagination—given Gothic form—could then wander around at will. She links this production of a Gothic object ("it") to desire, arousal, and a sexualized image of herself "real hot under my covers." This sexual embodiment of the reader through response and identification with form, however, stems from an immersion in the devices that constitute the aesthetic rather than a specific story, despite her example of *Child's Play*.

The girls become extremely animated storytellers when they use Gothic conventions and tell stories of creepy occurrences. They would tell me stories with Gothic form and they claim expertise in telling such tales to their girlfriends. Even the youngest girls in my sample articulate the importance of the form in objectifying or materializing imagination, connecting literary form to their ability to appropriate conventions for their own purposes:

Scary stories are fun to watch and fun to listen to.

Q: Do most scary stories turn out to be a blanket in the closet [alluding to her telling of Terry Harshman's Porcupine's Pajama Party] *or not?*

No.

Q: Do you like it better when it's just a blanket in the closet or do you like just the scary story—doesn't matter whether it's true or not true?

I like just a blanket, or anything just in the closet. Because that's what these books usually just turn out to be.

Q: Do you know when you read a book like this that it's going to turn out to be just a blanket or something like that?

Yeah.

Q: Is that a good part of reading a book like that or not?

It's a good part.

Q: Why?

Because if you read them a lot of times you know what's going to happen and because so it won't be that scary to you. [She explains all the fears that haunt her in her life.]

Q: Do you think grownups know that there's that scary stuff in your mind [referring to her fears of dreams, things she's found in her yard, "bad grownups," etc.] that you're worried about? Or not?

No. I don't think they do. No. But I think they knew when they were kids.

Q: Do you think they need to know that?

Yeah. I think they do need to know that.

Q: Do you think they need to do something about it or just know?

They don't need to do anything about it, because some scary things just help you get nicer things in your mind. Because if you think about scary things you say, "Calm down, calm down, start thinking about good things." And then you start thinking about some good things, better than you would if you just start thinking about good things. If you do that it's real fun.

Q: Is that anything like turning into an animal to fight the bad things? [referring to the way she told me she imagines she could fight bad grownups]

Yeah. Because it's part of your imagination. (Eight-year-old Angela)

Eight-year-old Angela, with less developed literacy skills, uses Gothic form to work through fear. Scary stories provide forms by means of which she externalizes and objectifies imagination *as* fear. By learning the conventions that make Gothic worlds possible, understanding that the monsters at the end of stories usually turn out to be just blankets in the closet, she also learns how imaginative space can be constituted with storytelling forms that separate the story from real life. Gothic forms define and delimit fear such that the reader can give form to her fears, objectify them, and send them away, because the materialized imagination is experienced as an inherently powerful action. The literary form thus not only enables expression of her reality, but also gives her an imaginative way to transform that reality.

GOTHICIZING THE FEMALE

Unlike the high Romance or fantasy form, the Gothic has been equally utilized by both male and female writers. It has had particular value for female authors who wish to express fears of being persecuted in domestic, often patriarchal, spaces (Ann Radcliffe, Charlotte Perkins Gilman, Harriet Jacobs) and of becoming the dark double of the feminine—the monster or the madwoman (Mary Shelley, Emily Brontë, Gilman). The Gothic novel, introduced by Horace Walpole in his seminal work *The Castle of Otranto* (1765), flourished and achieved its fullest expression in British literature after the French Revolution led to a reign of terror. Works such as Edmunde Burke's *Reflections on the Revolution in France* and Mary Shelley's *Frankenstein* represent revolutionary energy as a monstrous force unleashed upon the genteel sensibility. The Gothic, in some sense, seeks to privatize or domesticate political horrors and thus symbolically contain and explain them by deflecting attention from political reality. But since domestic space *was* the political scene for White middle-class women, the Gothic form quickly became a way for women writers to express feminine captivity in houses, patriarchal villains in the disguise of fathers and husbands, and femininity thinly veiling monstrosity in processes of birthing. Masse has recently explored the ongoing meaning of Gothic films for female spectators and readers in *In the Name of Love*. Berenstein argues that female viewers of classic horror films identify with the monster as well as with the female victim. The reproductive grotesque continues to be a central theme of modern horror films, suggesting that anxieties about the female subject and body find expression in Gothic tradition, parallel to the expression of male political possibilities being found in the continuing film tradition of action adventure fantasy.

Just as the girls expect standard formal elements of fantasy such as a male hero, villain, and even foil, the girls implicitly expect Gothic horror to unsettle cultural boundaries and formally express the position of girls and women in culture, at risk for becoming victims or monstrous bodies, while striving to be participants and producers of culture. To deny identification with the former, girls prefer the posture of omniscient reader/viewer: the spectator. When thirteen-year-old Ann emphasizes the idea that the generic "rules" of the horror film require bloodless fantasy, she symbolically emphasizes the way in which the aesthetics of horror allow her to imagine herself outside a social identity rooted in the female body. In speaking of her body, Ann Gothicizes her own menstruation, even bestializing her own menstrual blood. She says she reacts to her menstrual blood as she would to the smell of a dog, with disgust. The blood's refusal of boundaries bothers her, and thus she seeks in the Gothic an alternative existence to her embodied identity as a girl-becoming-woman. Julia Kristeva asserts that the true horror within Western culture is the female body itself. Female body fluids, in her view, fall into the category of the abject: "It is thus not lack of cleanliness or health that causes abjection but what disturbs identity, system, order. What does not respect borders, positions, rules. The in-between, the ambiguous, the composite" (4).

The horror of the Gothic is "the uncanny" (Freud), the most familiar (self, femaleness) become most unfamiliar (bloody, beaten, monstrous, reproductive). Ann cannot even describe the scene in *The Sixth Sense* that terrifies her the most. She only refers to the scene as the one that occurs directly after the child character uses the bathroom in the middle of the night. I had to see the film myself to interpret her terror. The scene entails the child's confrontation with a woman (a ghost) whom he thinks is his mother when he sees her from behind. He follows this woman into the kitchen and says, "Mama?" When this figure turns, we (and he) see that this figure is actually a dead person whose body shows signs of domestic abuse. This dead woman turns to the child and yells at him as if he were her husband, screaming that his dinner is not ready and calling him foul names. The "horror," then, is that the maternal figure anchoring the home and the child's life is, underneath, this horrific figure of domestic incarceration and abuse, a monster terrorizing the female viewer (Ann) who is quickly growing into a woman. If fantasy form expresses political and environmental utopia and dystopia in American culture, Gothic forms formalize cultural fears of and disgust toward the female body, and express a female condition of subservience to and fears of patriarchy—both in the external culture and internalized or marked on the self.

Similarly, fourteen-year-old Carolyn Gothicizes the story of her great-grandmother, a significant figure in her life although they have never met. She is taken with stories of her great-grandmother, who "made bad choices" in life and married an abusive man; in order to protect her children from this husband her great-grandmother had to send her children to a home and never see them again. This sacrifice of her great-grandmother moves Carolyn, who sees this woman as a brave protector, yet victimized and destroyed. We could view Carolyn's fascination with *The Haunting*, based on Shirley Jackson's novel, in this light. The film certainly takes as its issue the transformation of domesticity into horror, its heroine on the one hand "punished" for not liking children and, on the other, terrified of becoming the dead villain's wife. The heroine even sees herself pregnant in the haunted house's carnivalesque room of mirrors and recoils with horror. The character's redemption from the film's initial scene, in which she obviously detests her nephew, however, comes with her great sacrifice to set free the spirits of all the children trapped by the house.

Rather than emphasize the quest through enchanted lands made possible by fantasy elements, the Gothic emphasizes the mysterious and horrific aspects that enchanted spaces and quests obtain in domestic space. Aestheticizing fear through Gothic form allows the girls in this study to visualize the conventional means by which aesthetics control fear and empower both storytellers and listeners. Because they see a structure of thought in place in the literary and cinema text, they identify their reading/viewing imagination with this structure of thought, preferring the position of omniscient (godlike) power to female character as point of entry into the fictional world. Perceiving the literary structure of the imagination is power.

Cherchez la Femme:
The Problem of Verisimilitude

Actually, I haven't read too many stories about girls. I like traveling
through magical places. . . . I actually like it when I'm going to another
place, another place.

　　　　　　　　　　　　　　　　　　　　　—Eight-year-old Wendy

WHY WOULD READING about girls not be magical? Why would it be like
staying home?

The girls' aestheticization of texts reveals their desire to experience
alterity and fantasy through the stories they seek. To experience alterity in
literature, the girls tend to prefer fiction that depicts action-oriented male
social worlds. However, by doing so, they do not support Fetterley's thesis
that male experience itself is viewed as universal. Rather, texts representing
male experience stand for alterity from the female reader and thus more
readily conform to the girls' aesthetic philosophies. This alterity initiates a
chain of responses. In defining male depictions as alterity, girls evince the
awareness that no experience is universal, but that literature voices alterity
and that alterity provides a means to visualize the universal aspects of texts,
namely form and theme. Male-female binary codes inform their appreciation of literature because they seek to define the text as fantasy *for them*. To
appreciate the text representing female characters and social worlds as fantasy and alterity, girls could construct the text's difference from their own
lives, denying any connection between their own social worlds and the characters in, for example, *Little Women*. The pains they take to separate stories
about girls and women from a sense that they, too, are girls-becoming-women
demonstrates that they can appreciate female social worlds in fiction if they
take an aesthetic stance.

The respondents' equation of difference with action- and fantasy-
oriented male literature asks us to consider the relationship between readers
and realism. A text's realism lies in the eye of the beholder. The film *Clueless*,

based on the story of Jane Austen's *Emma,* looks like an exercise in hyperbolic, comedic stereotype to me, but not to my respondents, who live the comedy and are quite conscious of the comedy "inherent" in their everyday social interactions. The issue of literature and film as representational arts involves the implicit assumption that readers/viewers perceive verisimilitude. When the girls read or view a fictional text that they perceive as more mimetic than a Secondary World (see the discussion of fantasy in Chapter 3), they either resist immersion, map traditional genres onto the narrative, or analyze narrative structure, strategies, and plot. They often impose generic tradition upon the mimetic text to create a site of identification with form, showing, in my view, *both* a sophisticated refusal to be duped by realism's illusion of independence from storytelling conventions, and the need for guidance in decoding the narrative strategies of mimetic texts.

ALIENATION FROM FEMALE CHARACTERS IN WRITTEN FICTION

The girls often voice a rhetoric of alienation from female characters and social worlds in written fiction. This is partly the result of the lack of imagination in the books to which they are exposed and partly the result of their reading stance. For example, ten-year-old Becky reads *Amelia's Notebooks* (Moss), a series written in diary style by a female character of approximately Becky's age, but she could neither tell me any particular story nor regard the text as imaginative space: "*Amelia's Notebooks.* I have a couple books in there. I have almost all of them because I read them the day that I get them. This is a girl about my age. [Q: When you're reading this, are you imagining that you are her or that you're like her?] No. I just usually just read it" (ten-year-old Becky). The *Notebooks* are not of further interest to her—she has nothing else to say of them—and a character of her age and gender has no more relationship with her than does any other character.

The girls simply have more trouble defining as aesthetic objects texts with complex female characters. Realistic female characters could serve as casual acquaintances rather than powerful ways to experience a narrative situation. For example, twelve-year-old Margaret notes some overlapping characteristics between her and *Little Women*'s Jo. Although she did not spontaneously mention *Little Women,* I asked about it when I saw the book in her bedroom. But neither the overlap between herself and Jo nor the narrative situation of the character is particularly meaningful to her. (She had both read the book and seen the 1994 movie.) Although she regards Jo as an attractive character, she describes the text as "sort of but not really" important to her:

If I'm like in a real imaginative mood I'll be like that's me. Jo. I like
Jo. Because I love writing and I write all these stories on the com-
puter. Like about my life and about growing up and everything, but I
change the names. I like how [Jo] gets along with guys and how she's
more of a tomboy and how she's adventurous. I just think that's cool.
It's sort of [an important story to me] but not really.

Margaret has a moment of recognition in Jo as a stable character, but the
character is merely a coincidental example of a person who happens to like
to do certain things. In fact, Margaret begins the interview by telling me that
tomboyism is a self-attribute; tomboyism and authorship bridge her and Jo's
"lives," but the bridge forecloses the possibility of attending to the *story*—
the literary frame—and instead, Margaret treats Jo like a real person in a
more naive and less engaged response.

   Oftentimes the girls who mention a relationship with a literary character bring the character into their world and ignore or forget the actual narrative, citing irrelevant coincidences between reader and character. For example,
fourteen-year-old Kristen, after telling me the themes and story of *That Was
Then, This Was Now*, by S. E. Hinton, meditates on how she and the text's
peripheral female characters may be connected. She mentions extraneous
information by switching gears from the text's "issues" to the issue of female
character/identification (because I asked):

   Well there is a girl in that book this one kid goes out with. He's not
   the druggy kid, the other kid's the druggy, his friend slash brother.
   And that was a really good book too because it had racial issues and
   peer pressure and drugs and everything that you can imagine was in
   that book. And I could sort of imagine; there were a couple girls in
   that book but the main one I sort of thought that she was like me in
   some ways. Not really though. Because she was a good student, she
   played soccer I think. I'm pretty sure she played some sport. In that
   way, but not because of the stuff she did. She used to be a nurse and I
   don't see myself being a nurse because I don't like to be around blood
   and all that other stuff. So I really couldn't see myself in that way.
   But I guess around like school and stuff like that.

The question of relating to character deflects focus from the "issues" the text
presents and the quality of the book. Kristen maintains appreciation of
the text's contemporary focus on difficult issues but offers a relatively odd
comparison between herself and the female character, completely irrelevant
to the issues of the text. The character comparison ("like me") results in a
shift to the everyday extratextual self, career choice, and mundane behavior

("around school"), deflecting attention from the issues that Kristen identifies as the text's main issues—"racial issues and peer pressure and drugs and everything that you can imagine."

Both the bibliographic model for reading and the teen problem novel of literature would suggest that the experience of the character would be meaningful to the reader in (or about to be in) a similar narrative situation. However, the girls consider reading "about girls" to be mundane, appreciated for information rather than for identification, theme, or meaning:

> [I read this book] about this girl that went to Washington with her class, and it was really exactly like what I did and stuff. And it's just like this girl that went to Washington with her class but she got lost and she got to meet the president and all this stuff. He helped her find her class and stuff like that. When I read it though it was actually informing me about what I was going to see in Washington, like the Washington Monument and stuff. Most of the books I read have nothing to do with my life and that's the reason that I read them. It's kind of like something new. If it already happened to me and stuff, I don't get as excited about it, like the girl who went to Washington. It's kind of not a big deal to me. (Twelve-year-old Angie)

Angie does not regard a character "like her"—sharing identity category or enacting her specific situation—as "a big deal" in literature. If she had seen the character as vicarious self-experience, then she too could fantasize about meeting the president. Unimpressed, she reads for information about the setting. Similarly, nine-year-old Jesse tells me that she once read a biography of "an Australian girl" who found a cure for polio. Jesse's own aspirations include becoming a veterinarian so she can "help" those she loves—animals. When I ask her if she is "like the girl" in the story, she denies it, but adds that she wants to visit Australia.

Even to a fourteen-year-old, who immediately tells me that she feels the world to be increasingly dangerous, the story of Anne Frank has no significance. She just "could not relate" and, in fact, cannot relate to "books about girls." Many of the older girls recall reading series books about girls when they were younger, but could not remember any particular plots. They claim to have read them because they were easy (quantity requirements for school): "They were real-life kind of put in characters in a book. Didn't really think anything of it though" (fifteen-year-old Ellie). Girls of all ages think that when they were younger, they liked books (such as Julie Edwards's *Mandy*) with female characters whom they could pretend to be. But it was hard to interpret this response, because the girls also think, in *theory*, that "the gender thing" is a ruling principle of whether readers will relate to particular

characters. One girl, for example, thinks that her brother emotionally responded to John Knowles's *A Separate Peace* because he identified with Finny,
"a guy."

HOW THE GENDER OF FANTASY BECOMES BOUND
TO THEIR APPRECIATION OF LITERATURE

Because the girls understand themselves as female teens, male universes and
principal characters more readily stand for alterity in fiction. The girls equate
"maleness" with the construction of imaginative space, with the realm of
pretend and adventure. When nine-year-old Jesse discusses the gender of
pretend play, she associates her tomboy tendency with her desire to play
pretend: "Girls who are all fancy or something wouldn't want to get dirty
and wouldn't really dress up in clothes, like pretending they were other people
or something" (nine-year-old Jesse). In her view *girl* is antithesis to *pretend*;
tomboyism denotes the structure of pretend itself—her ability to unhinge
imagination from experience. She associates being a girl with "being" one
specific identity, thus with the question of "being" as social role. She next
explains the game she likes to play with her male neighbor, Spying on the
Grown-Ups. To her, the activity of spying stands for the power of vision.
She contrasts this feeling of "being invisible" and "spying" with the time she
feels most like a girl—on picture day. She explains that on picture day, she
has to dress nicely and "just stand there hugging a tree or something." Female identity becomes intertwined with "specific" identity and social objectification, the antithesis of all the values advanced when girls discuss their
motivations for engaging with fiction.

The "meaning" of literary experience and the "meaning" of female gender intersect and become a binary code; the male-female binary often gets
mixed up with this primary binary, and could easily be mistaken for it. Literary experience stands for vision, presence, creation, transformation, action,
liberation, philosophy, and transcendence, while female gender—in the girls'
minds—stands for "fixed" role, objectification, responsibility, growing up,
social identity, relationships, limitations, and "real life." Girls repeatedly tell
me that with girlfriends they pretend real-life "female" situations, like house,
mother, "living on your own," and dress-up. Thus they construct a meaning
for being female, defined as being socially identified and as "in process" of
growing up, rehearsing for specific roles—and thus not so much about
"present" identities as about social roles of the future. Literary experience
per se is genderless, but the choice of texts with male characters associates
male with *other* and with reconstitution as reader into a more imaginative,
radical, liberating, pretend-oriented space. Eleven-year-old Vanessa likes to

imagine she could be a boy for a week, not for what a boy could do, not for liberating identity, but for a radical experience of "difference," "a different" point of view. This "different" point of view epitomizes the function of literature in their lives.

The meanings the girls accord to the male ↔ female binary code, mapped onto the literary experience ↔ social identity binary, mirror critical discourses that suggest that girls and women are relational. Toward the end of each interview, I asked each girl to imagine an all-girl planet and tell me what the planet is like, a technique I learned from researcher Cindy Clark. The girls produced remarkably similar images, summed up by the image of social experience among girls who seek social activities together (shopping, beach parties, pool parties, pizza parties, movies, etc.). One fifteen-year-old described the all-girl planet as "*Clueless* gone crazy!" Girls see the planet as a relaxing and comfortable environment in which makeup and accoutrements of femininity could be shed without penalty, but for all my respondents this environment would grow boring. The stereotype motivating this vision is the idea that girls and women are entirely relational beings, grounded in social realism, while boys and men are the figures that shake up those "realities." Girls are relationship-grounded "talkers" and boys the figures who can transcend the limits of social relations. For example, twelve-year-old Margaret voices the need for "guys" in these terms, typical of the girls' responses:

> The all-girl planet wouldn't be boring because girls mostly you can talk to and everything. But sometimes you need some adventure sometimes; you need someone who'd yell at you, someone who'd teach you discipline and mostly guys are like that. Girls don't really make fun of everyone, but guys are usually the troublemakers, but sometimes you need a troublemaker or two. Life is boring if you don't have troublemakers. It'd be incomplete. [You need] adventure.

Within the very concept of *male* there exists an enemy and protagonist, an adventure and quest, the possibility for change and transformation. Within the concept of *female* there exists perpetual novelistic realism, perpetual social exploration, perpetual talking in the vein of verisimilitude. Mirroring the gendered aspects of genre in American culture and literary history, the girls feel *male* to be a means for an inherently dramatic and intriguing plot.

This equation of male with fantasy led me to reflect upon the feminist theorists who have previously had an impact on my thinking, and on how our culture might create an environment in which girls learn that *female* is a code for social and *male* for adventure, which literary forms certainly help sustain. Whether female "relationality" is viewed as the result of identification with maternal presence (Chodorow, *Reproduction*), moral theory

(Gilligan), or sociological realities of female labor (Dinnerstein, Ortner), theorists imply that men "imagine" and "create" complex aspects of culture more than do women. In fact, when women do create and produce something anew in the form of a child, we call it "reproduction." Even French feminists, who are less interested in the social conditions of culture and more in the unconscious and physic conceptualizations of the body, are explicit on this argument; in Hélène Cixous's "The Laugh of the Medusa," imagination itself is *male*. The girls in this project show that they claim a right to fantasy and imagination.

AMERICAN GIRLS AND THE FREEDOM TO FLY

Partly, this alienation from literature "about girls" represents the respondents' tendency to equate "books about girls" with mundane life and historical fiction, which is quite different from thinking of fantasy that happens to have a historical setting. When I ask eight-year-old Wendy if she can recall a book about a girl or girls, she distinguishes *The American Girls* from "magical places":

> [*The American Girl* books] are the kind of books where I just read them. I don't exactly feel like I'm seeing it or am in it. [In reading Janet Shaw's *Kirsten*] I'm like, "OK, well the bear, OK the dog got hurt," or like, "Oh I feel kind of happy, she's happy," or like the honey, they sell the honey she got. Or I feel kind of happy. But I don't exactly feel like I'm seeing it or am in it, but I feel just like happy and I'm going, it's just like happening. I feel like it's happening or something. It's happening in front of me. It's like, "OK they get some fish," and then, "The dog gets stung." It's hard to explain but it's like they are going through the pages.
>
> Actually I haven't read too many books about girls. I like traveling through magical places. It just brings me. *Anne of Green Gables* [Montgomery] and *A Little Princess* [Burnett], those are really nice. I don't exactly travel to another place but I get a little feeling. I still feel kind of a little firm because it could happen. I actually like it when I'm going to another place, another place.

The partial identification of "Oh she's happy, I'm kind of happy" is offset by Wendy's separation of herself from books about girls—"they're just happening"—through passive voice and complacent emotions; they give "a little feeling"; they're "nice books"; they leave her "firm" and unchanged, not diffused or transformed. Paradoxically, the very discourses that address and

reflect her subject position (female experience) preclude her "inside" participation and vision. She speaks of *The American Girl* books "happening" as
if the stories are real. When Wendy discusses adventure with male heroes,
she feels that she actually travels through imaginative space, immersing herself in the text for a vision: "In reading the *Redwall* books you kind of feel
like you're just right there seeing it. You're a thing watching, and you're
watching everything going on." Presence is the result of voyaging "into" the
book, a process undercut by the more feminine "nice feelings" of the "books
about girls," books that more gently "happen" in front of her. Although many
of the middle- and upper-class respondents had *American Girls* dolls and
books, they told me that they "arrange" the dolls "to look pretty" and had
no interest in the books. Typically the dolls and books were purchased by
adults. For example, on the way into my interview with nine-year-old Jesse,
Jesse's mother enthusiastically showed me *Kirsten*, which she purchased for
her daughter because Jesse and Kirsten are both second-generation Swedish
American. Jesse had no interest in my questions about the book, preferring
to discuss *Harry Potter* and *The Last Unicorn*.

Thirteen-year-old Jessica describes girls' quest for alterity through aes-
theticism as flying, which, to me, means defying the boundaries of the self in
social life. At the end of the interview I always had the girls sort images to
match "the mood of girlhood and womanhood." During this task, Jesse chooses
the image of an airplane to describe the mood of both, an airplane poised pre-
cariously on a cliff: "It looks like they're learning to fly because girls want to
fly, and women, some of them are pilots, or like on a boat and they want to go
off and do adventures and stuff like that." When I ask what it means to want
to fly, she elaborates, "Like being free." An image of flying suggests that when
texts conform to the reader's philosophy of what good literature should be,
they lift the reader from grounded social worlds such that reading itself is an
adventure. Yet content in which the reader sees everyday girlhood becomes
too real and loses aesthetic appeal. The reader crashes, so to speak.

CONSTRUCTING FEMALE STORIES AS FANTASIES

I found one instance in which a girl, fifteen-year-old Nicole, immediately
said that she loved to read about girls. Intrigued, we discussed her reading.
I found that she was reading books about girls because it was summer and
she was experiencing a lack of female community, which a textual world
could invoke:

> My best friend, I haven't seen her in a while because she's been on
> vacation and stuff and so I'm reading all these books on girl rela-

tionships. It helps me a lot if she does something, if she goes off with her boyfriend.

Nicole consciously constructs the text as a fantasy, fulfilling her longing to be reenveloped in female community. To overdetermine this wish she says she is also reading *Tryin' to Sleep in the Bed You Made* (DeBerry and Grant), a story of female friendship. In her mind, she anticipates a scene to reenact when her friend returns, one that would perform the pain of forced separation from the relationship that, in many ways, defines her as Nicole.

Even when the text is "about girls" and the girl enjoys it, appreciation stems from the girl's constitution of the text as alterity from self and life:

> I usually read V. C. Andrews. *Flowers in the Attic*, I've read that one. That's the one that got me into them. It was kinda weird but it was interesting, different. It's about these girls, different girls' lives and all this weird stuff that happens to them. It's kinda like their whole life you know, each book is a different part of their life and the stuff that happens to them. It's not really like life because nobody has lives like them. It's just interesting. It's not like I want to be like them. I'm watching it. It would never happen. I wouldn't really change that because that's what makes it interesting. It's more fun to read a book that couldn't happen, you know books are kind of different [from movies]. When you read them yourself you want to read different kinds of stuff I guess. In books it's good because you can imagine what they look like, how they would be saying it; it's not really spelled out in black and white like on TV I guess. While I'm reading a book I imagine what they're doing and where they are and stuff. I'm not really in it with them I'm just like watching it, kinda like I'm watching a movie only it's in your mind. You're making up the setting and stuff because you can make it up however you want.

Although *Flowers in the Attic* is "about girls," Lily denies the characters and narrative as a social allegory representing domestic abuse, despite the irony that the topic of abuse against girls and children would spontaneously arise in almost every interview. Lily views *Flowers in the Attic* as completely separate from life. She creates this separation by citing the text's visible Gothic conventions and the medium of words, which look nothing like what they represent, completely dependent on the imaging of the reader (Esrock). This is a common assertion that I analyze in Chapter 6.

The girls who find literary female social worlds meaningful do so because they construct the text as an aesthetic and a fantasy, from which they draw a thematic vision. For example, twelve-year-old Randi repeatedly views the recent film of *Little Women* and, in her recent past, enjoyed the novel. Her discussion of the text details aspects of female relationship, from which she draws a meaningful, moral theme that transforms her sense of self, but she achieves her understanding of the text by separating her contemporary life and self from the world of the March sisters:

> [*Little Women's*] about these four sisters who grew up together. Like a long time ago, it was in the 1800s or 1700s or something like that. They come together. Like one time a sister Beth, one of them, gets very very sick. That's during Thanksgiving going into Christmas, and the family pitched in and one of the girls sold their hair. She had long beautiful hair, but she got it cut up to here and sold it, just so they could have the money and take her to a hospital. And I think that's amazing. If my brothers ever did that I would love them to death. But they don't have any hair.
>
> She survives through Christmas and New Year's but eventually she gives up on life and that's a very hard time for a family, to lose one of your sisters that you loved very much. And then the mother gets pretty sick and in the meantime one of the sisters got married and had two kids and they're very sick. And Amy is the youngest one; she meets a guy that she loves very much. And Jo's the oldest one who sold her hair and she goes to I think it's London and meets this guy, I think he's a reporter. And she didn't know that she loved him until the end. And I think that's like four sisters mining together. Some families like brothers and sisters they just grow apart and they never talk to each other and I think that one, even if one of them gets married and has children, one of them falls in love with another guy and one of them is dead, and one of them is still trying to find love, they still stick together in whatever they do. I like that they're four sisters trying to get through life together.

Randi expands the text's female community as "the theme," reifying community to the extent that she revises the plot and recalls the sacrifice of Jo as a sacrifice for a sister, and she maps sickness onto several characters in an effort to hyperbolize the mechanisms by which the theme of female community emerges. Yet in regard to her engagement with *Little Women* in relation to other contexts in which Randi imagines scenarios—including playing dolls, imagining her stuffed animals, and dreaming about "what she'll be when she grows up"—Randi insists that her experience of *Little Women* is profoundly different. She does not imagine being the female heroine, using her brother rather than herself to visualize identification with Jo. She cannot imagine being in that story, because she frames the story as "long ago"—

thus in fantasy, nonexistent space—and she maintains that gender is not a defining connection to the text: "I don't have sisters and I don't really know what they're going through. Their family's so different I can't even imagine that. It's so different":

Q: Why is it good for you to have a movie like that? About that?

Because it reminds me that you can get through anything. I rented it right after my grandfather died. He died pretty suddenly and it just got me through it. I was thinking about how to get through it, how they did. And how they survived it and how they survived their sister dying. And I was trying to put it a way of, like switching it around and putting it in like what position I'm in with my grandfather and that's what I was thinking about.

Randi interprets a theme that moves beyond a narrative situation, and she can then apply the theme to her own life. She brings the world of the text into social space to transform her understanding of social complexities, after constructing the text's alterity. By denying identification with the text's principle heroine(s), Randi develops an expansive perception of the text and backgrounds the issue of Jo's struggle against patriarchy and female community. Jo's ambivalence toward her family is backgrounded to such an extent that in her version, Jo sacrifices her hair for her sister. Randi thus even exaggerates the minimalization of men that is effected by the text, an interpretation enabled by the film's many scenes in which the men literally dissolve into the background.

The theme of imagination and discovery in a literary text can become a mode of identification with a female character. The theme of creativity is, in general, appreciated in literature—for example, "making things from nothing" in Johann Wyss's *The Swiss Family Robinson*. When ten-year-old Kelly narrates the story of *The Lion, the Witch and the Wardrobe* (Lewis), she reveals that she experiences a partial identification with Lucy because she views Lucy as thematizing the creative role of the reader, embarking upon a textual adventure to describe a world in the wardrobe. She expands Lucy's role as empowerment:

This professor had a house with a wardrobe in it and Lucy this one girl she went in the wardrobe and she noticed that it was sort of like branches but she thought they were coats and it was sort of cold in there, so she grabbed a jacket and she put it on and she was feeling around and she felt some bushes so she went as far as she could even though she didn't feel the back wall. She kept on going and going and she ended up at a big pole. And so everyone didn't believe her and so she said well please believe me, please! And so Peter, this other boy or Edmund, this other boy, they played hide-and-go-seek again and they went in the wardrobe because he sort of thought Lucy was telling the truth. [Continues story]

Lucy, she had the dagger and stuff, and she was the one that was helping out Aslan really well. She was just really helping him out, and all the brothers and sisters were doing it too and so they had all of their armor and stuff on, and shields, and Lucy had the shields, it was a shield and the dagger and the knife, to help Aslan.

Kelly's rendition of *The Lion, the Witch and the Wardrobe* stresses the role of the female character in thematizing adventure in and discovery of a Secondary World. Kelly's rendition of the text thematizes the authentication of the female voice in the processes of discovery, travel, and adventure. In her storytelling, she enacts the process of response as desire to discover, travel, and use the text to open up the self to another world. The story of Lucy's discovery gains more importance than what actually occurs in the land of Narnia. We can also see that the problem Lucy confronts, in Kelly's version, is the conflict between "female" as inherently "social," needing community validation, and desire for a transformational experience. To Lucy it matters that others believe her discovery and authenticate her role as adventurer. To Kelly, this matters because Lucy stands for Kelly's desire to discover a world behind the wardrobe.

In Kelly's story of the text, the emphasis on the long process of Lucy's wondrous discovery within the domestic leads directly to Lucy's role in the battle, Kelly's central revision. Kelly voices the refrain that Lucy helps with "the shield, the dagger, and the knife," ultimately rivaling the triadic structure of the text's title. For me, C. S. Lewis's text is as pure an example of patriarchal values as I can imagine. However, there are many different ways to focus on and interpret a piece of literature, which is its beauty. One can select pieces for interpretation and forget the rest. As an adult, I was astonished to find that Colin takes over Mary's story in *The Secret Garden*; as a child, I simply focused my imagination on Mary's secret world and forgot the rest.

STRUCTURING TEXTS PERCEIVED AS VERISIMILAR

The problem with many texts that have complex female characters and experiences in fiction appears to be a more general resistance to realism. When a fictional text is assigned as informational or historical reading, the girls regard the text's verisimilitude as its defining quality. They then resist the text's presumption that the reader should draw a relationship between themselves and the characters of the text's social world:

> Social studies books I don't like. English books are way better than social studies. [A good book] has to be action packed, mystery. Like in *Killing Mr. Griffin* [Duncan], it was a good book. It wasn't really action packed. It wasn't really mystery. It was just really good because I couldn't imagine somebody doing that. [Recaps story] At the end they finally get caught. I forget how but they do. They get caught somehow. I think the wife finds out about it. And the one kid who's like, who started the whole thing, he snaps. He's like a psycho; at the end he turns weird. He starts to set this one kid's grandmother's house on fire and then turns into a weirdo. It was just really good. It was captivating. You couldn't put it down. I read four chapters a day. (Fourteen-year-old Kristen)

The power of *Killing Mr. Griffin,* for Kristen, stems from its allusions to generic traditions that build the action before turning attention to characters and social intrigues within the alternative world. The narrative world provides the context for, and the appeal of, the characters. The "action/mystery" structure that Kristen perceives in *Killing Mr. Griffin* defines the character's category as "psycho" and "weirdo," a product of *that* world rather than a mundane category from her world.

The girls do not understand the formal qualities of realistic literature, other than "it was/it was not really action, mystery." Realist texts turn literary conventions into matters of human psychology (Jameson); what Kristen traces in *Killing Mr. Griffin* is the transfer from formal traditions, necessary to her pleasure, to individual psychology and the veiling of power and social structure. It is the switch itself that "captivates" her and defines the text's difference from generic action and mystery, although she has no precise means by which to describe the effects of the shift from conventional action form to exploration of human psychology.

By foregrounding psychology, memory, character, emotion, and bildunsgroman, the realist text has the surprising effect of being less an artistic object—less "out there," the girls say, and less distinct from sociological context—of both the artistic production and the reader. Paradoxically, then, the text with more visible literary conventions engages these girls as a participant in its structure (in Amy's description below, suspense) while the *realist text* is experienced as predictable and mundane! Below, realism is linked to "female" and "social," and thus as status quo, "normal," and consequently lackluster reading:

Things that are out there I find interesting. Right now I'm reading a
book *My Ántonia* [Cather]. I'm not finding it very interesting. It's
about some girl and pretty much this guy remembers about this girl
that he knew and how she changed. It seems pretty normal to me. It's
not like anything thrilling. Like I read *The Count of Monte Cristo*
last year and I liked that. (Sixteen-year-old Amy)

The overtly Romantic structure engenders suspense while the realist text,
which should be less predictable, does not. Suspense and interest thus do not
derive from the girls' engagement with the plot, but from their engagement
with genres. In *My Ántonia*, characters are not constructs but "normality."
In my view, these readers are so American—which means to believe that "the
psychological self" is just a natural view of personhood—that bildungsroman
or first-person reflective, engaging, or dissonant narrations are not perceived
as forms but as "just pretty normal." The girls cannot "see" form and theme
in literature they perceive as realistic because, I believe, no one has ever
problematized realism for them and made them understand that the twentieth-
century interest in representing consciousness and psychology was not
always of interest to storytellers and is not always of primary interest to
non-American writers, which is why I begin each children's literature class
with the antibildunsgroman picaresque *Pinocchio* (Collodi).

STRUCTURING PSYCHOLOGY

When confronted with the realist text, girls work through the texts by trying
out different formal approaches. A realist text could then become most interesting if it were both uncommon and "a true story," gaining a value that
was separate from the mimesis of the textual world yet dependent on recog-
nizable storytelling conventions:

My favorite book of all time is *Sibyl* [Schreiber]. It's a classic. It's
about the girl with multiple personalities and how she recovered and
stuff. It's just how she recovered. It's a really good book because she
developed her personalities from, like she was awfully abused as a
child and then she overcame that and at the end of the book she
finally became one with her personalities and stuff. I think it's a
really interesting book because it's all true they say, and somebody
could be like that way, and have just fifteen personalities and stuff.
There's sometimes, like in school and somebody's, I think maybe I
could have two [personalities] but they're not like horror and peace-
ful. My favorite name is Ann and when I'm with my friends I'm Ann

and I feel really good and I'm at peace and so I'm hanging out and having a good time but when I'm alone I'm just staying out and I'm not as good as Ann. I'm sort of alienated and stuff. I don't have connections to the world or something.

I like the part [of *Sybil*] that she gets over it and even though she has this awful mental disease she still has a lot of friends that stand by her. And she lives sort of happily ever after and stuff at the end. You know, she's all one. (Thirteen-year-old Ann)

Sybil is a clear bildungsroman approach to character as a developing psychology. The character herself, however, has multiple personalities such that she becomes a social world, a storytelling world of characters, the form of which can serve as a working structure for Ann so that Ann can understand herself. She likes thinking about herself as having more than one personality, one social and connected to the larger society just like Sybil's most likeable personality. Although identification with the character is the end result, Ann only achieves this identification by distinguishing the text's narrative structure—the slow road to being "all one." Sybil lives "happily ever after" and, in effect, works through the abuse that initiates the plot (but not the narrative) and the "social world" that Sybil embodies. Ann finds the book "interesting" not because of its verisimilitude, although the text's verisimilitude makes her work on its structure, but because of information external to the text—that the text *is* a representation of a real life. Thus the text thematizes the issue of representing identity. In *Sybil* Ann identifies a quest for identity but identifies less with the quest and more with the storytelling world within Sybil and the structure of personality integration. She identifies less with the narrative situation than with the structure of the narrative situation, identifying not with Sybil's problems but with her internalization of literary form—the novel of social manners and Gothic within the mind.

Sybil is organized by means of a detective plot, narrated by Sybil's psychologist, who serves as the seeker of truth. Ann does not identify with the female sleuth, who is empowered to solve the mystery, but with the structure of Sybil as a text, a mystery interpreted or "read" by the narrator. Sybil's split self gains interest through the slow revelation of knowledge that undergirds the psychoanalytic model for the self, positing the self and the mind as topographies, as layers of "people" (characters) simultaneously coexisting in different "spaces" (like a haunted house). Discussing the text in terms of a quest and multiple personalities that the character *"created"* (authored), Ann engages with the text on the level of a structured storytelling world, which she could then appropriate to describe her own life. By deciding that the character authors a social world and quests for integration, Ann authors her own self as a social world and makes the text come "true" in her own self-understanding, just as she understands part of the text's value as its reference beyond the text—its reality as well as its truth.

As a text that gives literary form to the individual psyche, *Sybil* perfectly exemplifies the way in which character derives meaning from formal traditions when they are used to represent psychology. While romantic types such as "deformed genius" and "chorus girl" serve as dialectical elements within a formal structure, the psychology of character holds interest if it expresses a literary structure of meaning. This is the central insight of psychoanalytic criticism, which asserts that narrative texts are manifestations of psychic processes (Brooks) and that even dreams are like densely structured pieces of literature (Freud, "Interpretation"). Texts that display the literary and linguistic structure of the mind invite the girls to identify with characters not through an inherent connection between reader and character but through the reader's engagement with the forms by which the literary character is constructed. The detective plot that structures the revelation of Sybil's unconscious is meaningful to Ann because it conforms to the quest of the mystery novel, the structure that Peter Brooks describes as laying bare the interworkings of narrative. In *Reading for the Plot*, Brooks defines the detective plot as the sine qua non of narrative desire, revealing the interworkings of narrative structure through which the reader is constructed as a desiring subject and that drives the reader forward as he/she "reads for the plot."

STRUCTURING EMOTION

Just as they define as suspense their response to structures that delay gratification, girls discuss the ways in which the narrative structure of the realist text controls the reader's emotional response. They often voice preference for stories that begin by invoking sadness and then end happily. They ask that verisimilar texts give emotional response shape and closure, attending to the experience of narrative rather than to genre when the text represents "life": "I like stories that are sad but have a triumphant ending. But like sad stories, like *Message in a Bottle* is another sad story [besides *Little Women*] but it doesn't have a pretty triumphant ending. I cried for a long time after that movie and that movie, I mean I liked it, but the end was too sad for me to handle" (twelve-year-old Randi). Girls expect a text to give them a concentrated emotional experience and resolve the emotion with narrative closure. They value the resolution of the verisimilar text more highly than they do the resolution of fantasy and Gothic texts.

Girls feel that most realist texts operate upon a principle of tragedy. By invoking the form of tragedy to describe the verisimilar text, they make the subject matter conform to an aesthetic shape. Roberta Trites (*Disturbing*) asserts that meditation upon loss is a common concern of the adolescent novel. More than the symbols they are in children's literature, death and sex are the two biological imperatives with which the teen in the teen novel must come to terms. Doing so gives boundaries to an individual life, constructing a life as a bildungsroman. The girls discuss the literary theme of loss as narrative principle:

> I think sad stories are better than happy endings and stuff. It's more tragic. You want to read on to see what's going on but, we had to read this short story. It's about this boy who leaves his little brother who was only three and he had something with him and he couldn't walk and the kid teaches him how to walk and everything and we're like, "Oh this is a really nice story" and then at the end, the little boy gets on his nerves so much that they're running through the field one day and the little boy eventually learns how to run but the boy runs so far ahead of him, because he didn't really care if he caught up or not, and he just collapsed and the boy didn't know about it and he found him a week later, not a week, but a couple of hours later and there was blood all over and he was dead. It was just sad. I mean that was sad. Everybody was like [gives a look of horror] and it was just sad.
>   That's the kind of stories you should read because something could happen like that. It's something real. That could happen if you had a little brother who had a [dis]ability. I can relate to that, because my grandmother just died and I was real close to her for a very very long time, I mean for all my life I knew her and I grew up with her and she was like my second mom. She was one of my best friends and I love her so much. She just died in January. Reading that makes me like, yeah something bad could happen like that because I know with that something bad can happen like that. (Fourteen-year-old Kristen)

The realist text invites identification with character through a circuitous route, positing a structure for meditating upon significant themes of life, the preciousness and uncertainty of life itself. Death is, and is expected to be, a powerful narrative action, proliferating narrative possibilities. Death serves as the lack or desire that initiates and motivates the need for story. From a very short story, Kristen analyzes narrative structure (triumph only to startle and set up horrific sadness), and uses that structure to reflect upon herself. In doing so she constructs the text's reality as an emotional one. The relationship between reader and character emerges from thoughtful decisions about a text's structure and its revelations of "real" horrors—murder, abuse, death, and pain.

Film and "Reelism"

We might talk about books, but I don't know. We talk more about stuff
that's really happening. When you [quote a movie line] to your friends,
you all laugh because you remember back when you saw the movie. [In
books] you're not really watching [the story] together. And in books, I
don't know, sometimes you interpret things differently.
—Fifteen-year-old Lily

Movies can't take you to other places that books can.
—Eight-year-old Wendy

WHY ARE MOVIES not "other places" but also "stuff that's really happening?" How is the experience of a world in written fiction different from the
experience of a world in film?

For the girls, literature requires engagement with a world entirely of the
imagination; to identify the theme and then apply it to the reader's situation
or understanding of social life requires the reader to author an adaptation
and do a tremendous amount of "eye-opening" work. However, films more
readily provide girls with a model of adaptation and performance of text;
thus visual media allow them a greater experience of identification with female characters. They are explicit about preferring stories "about girls" in
film to those in literature. The medium of film symbolizes an industry organized around the story*form* of role-playing performance. The girls' perceptions of film as a medium involve a paradox and register their confusion about
growing up as a genred experience. Although they emphasize the impersonal
readership and viewership of both literature and film, when discussing the
actual experiences of participating in the story's unfolding narrative, the girls
feel that film somehow has a more direct dependence on the real world of
referents than do the stories in books. They define this reality in various ways,
some girls attending to the way in which the popularity of certain films organize their social worlds and can be used as social currency, some attending to the performances of particular actresses, and some attending to the

reality of the film industry. Ultimately, they mirror critical endeavors to define characteristics that distinguish literature from film by contradicting themselves, for while believing in the verisimilitude of films, they continually cite instances of film's effects, design, and illusions.

Because film has a greater influence on popular culture and invites more attention to female character, and perhaps because it displays wonder at emergent technologies, the girls read less and see more movies as they grow older. I argue that the girls' conflation of the imaging of film with mimesis and "real" cultural worlds reveals an unspoken belief that growing up "should" be accompanied by more appreciation of verisimilar fiction, a belief advanced by the stories we tell about literary history (Romance to realism), and children's versus adolescent literature. These narratives of maturation are mirrored by the perception that twentieth-century literature "grew up" with the emergence of film technologies and with the social uses of the movie theater as the theater of adolescence.

EMPOWERMENT OF FEMALE CHARACTERS

When fifteen-year-old Nicole, the one girl who liked to "read about girls" because she missed her "summer sister," speaks of identifying with the heroine of the film *She's All That*, she demonstrates interpretive and moral confusions. She twists the story and characters to conform to her recognition of a relationship between herself and the female (Galatea) character:

> A lot of movies have come out where they're about teenage girls growing up. [In *She's All That*] this girl's a senior and she's the biggest nerd in the entire school. She's always to herself, hangs out with the people, other people would be geeks, and computer nerds and artists, people where they just paint and do nothing else, and get straight A's and stuff like that. And then these two guys make a bet to see if they could turn her into the prom queen and they did it and she transformed pretty much with the help of her best friend.
>
> He liked her for who she was, not for what she looked like because before she changed and did all her hair and everything she was kind of odd looking. [Elaborates] [The story] just shows people transforming I guess from girl to woman and people accepting you for who you are during that transformation. I like that one. No one liked her and no one bothered to get to know her. She's basically like what happened between my eighth- and ninth-grade years. They like portrayed that character to be like me, how did they do that? And so I sometimes I just think that someone has been following me and did

my life as a movie and that certain part, I thought that was really
neat, just that one movie I'm like, "Oh my gosh, that's me, from
eighth- to ninth-grade years."

Nicole's relationship with the heroine is twofold; she recognizes herself in
the character and in the situation. They share a similar story of metamorphosis. Because Nicole is inside the character, she cannot figure out what to
do with the dubious quality of the male bet. The character cannot resolve
this problem in the text, and thus Nicole has little perspective on the power
dynamics that inform the problem, which is typical of girls who have perceptive vision of power dynamics in fantasy or "guy" worlds but not in stories
with conventions they cannot "see." Nicole wants the story to be about female
metamorphosis. To some extent the film interprets the Pygmalion story in
this light, foregrounding the unique complexity of the heroine and portray-
ing the central hero sympathetically. However, film as a medium depends
upon "showing" metamorphosis, delving into issues of character appearance,
which produces Nicole's confusion. She does not know that female empowerment and Pygmalion cannot be reconciled, because she does not know the
myth.

Nevertheless Nicole wants the female heroine to be empowered with a
metamorphosis just as thirteen-year-old Ann wants Cinderella, in *Ever After*,
to "stick up for herself" and is angry when she does not: "I'm thinking [when
I'm watching] if I were her I would just have kicked that stepmother." The
actresses on the screen invoke ideas about female metamorphosis *and* narrative structure. When nine-year-old Rose speaks at great length about her
favorite film, *A League of Their Own*, she both identifies with the female
characters and unpacks narrative structure, ultimately grasping the theme
that "girls can do anything boys can." Rose explains that she and her friends
adapt the story in their pretend play, telling me that each of her friends plays
characters from the film. While this sounds like unmediated identification (I
thought it was at the time of the interview), in analyzing her incredibly detailed and interesting discussion of the text, I discovered that the means by
which she arrives at character identification derives from her fluid movement
between empathy with characters and appreciation of narrative structure:

> Girls doing what boys can do and they got to do it. They were
> playing softball and they ended up getting in the Hall of Fame. The
> baseball Hall of Fame. There was like this whole exhibit of them
> playing softball, softball and pictures, and then coming back when
> they're older knowing "this is what I did," that the boys didn't do it
> and we did it. No one else. It shows girls can do anything that boys
> can do.

[She vividly recalls the scene in which a military telegram arrives.]

Dotty didn't play for awhile and then she came back and played and then the other girl's name was Kit and they were sisters and when they got into the Hall of Fame, they both came with their children, their grandchildren and showed them what they did, and they kind of explained it to them and then when they saw each other they went up and said, "Hi," and gave each other hugs and stuff.

Pausing Rose's telling for a moment, I wish to point out that her narrative moves in a circle, beginning and returning to the narrative action. This circularity symbolizes an important aspect of the text—the fact that the text's frame focuses on Dotty and Kit's presently existing families (meaning they *did* in fact reproduce) and their role as audiences of Dotty and Kit's achievements. Those families, in Rose's following rendition, become roles for viewer response. Rose thus differentiates narrative structure from plot, and she further distinguishes plot from her construction of the text's "whole" message—that girls can do anything boys can. The text "shows" this by its framing, the opening of the Hall of Fame to these women, and by its tale—the operations of the female league. However, the scene Rose most vividly recalls has nothing to do with this theme. She recalls the development of the coach from a stereotypical gendered character to a sensitive team player. She recalls this by detailing the scene that posits the importance of the text's historical setting—the fact that war could make these women lose husbands (and their social roles as wives) any moment. When I return to this question later, however, Rose has no interest in the historical context of the war. She finds it important that the story takes place "long ago" (like Randi, in discussing *Little Women*), connecting this historical frame to the "fantasy" because, she asserts, the story could not happen in today's world. Later, she does not even remember that a war frames the story at all. The fact that the girls are able to play because the men cannot is completely forgotten structurally and thematically, although she recalls this emotional scene.

Specific textual details thus come and go in her discussion, but the overall structure that she creates unifies her vision of the text. She continues:

That was like a long-time-ago story that people played. It was kind of based on a true story, or it was kind of made up to look like it was way back then. Because there's time change and everything. Then you wouldn't have people who are crazy as they are today. Like a lot of people are crazy at baseball games and stuff.

[When I was watching the film] I was thinking that they do a very good job teaching them how to do things because if they could

get into the Hall of Fame then I think they would be a very good
teacher, and then one of the grandchildren was a girl and so I think
that if one of them taught her that she could grow up and do the
same thing, play softball, and be just like her grandmother.

[My friends and I played it together like this:] I would be up to
bat and I would be the fourth player and pretend I came to bat, I was
either got out the first three times or struck out, then at the last time
it was the end of the game, no one would ever, bases were loaded,
they were winning by three points, and I hit it and it went, had all of
the runs going and no one, everyone screwed it up because they knew
I wasn't a good hitter and so I hit it way back into the outfield and so
they weren't that far back. So all the runs went in and we ended up
winning the game. Because we were pulling ahead of them. We all
played it together. We didn't organize anything. All we organized
was the batting order and who plays what. We were all watching the
movie together and then when it was done we went, "Why don't we
imagine that we're in that movie?" Then we did that. [Then] twenty
years later they open an exhibit in the Baseball Hall of Fame and then
all the players, they're grandmothers now, so they bring their grandchildren with them and they show them what they did. And then a
few years later one of their grandchildren ends up playing and doing
kind of the same thing and they made a new exhibit of it. A new
team. I added that. To know that other girls achieve that. Did that
again. And not just once but twice.

Rose plays a scene from the film by appropriating the structure of the scene
and the similar structure of realistic drama itself. She does not name herself or
her girlfriends after characters, but they clearly inhabit character positions.
Rose appropriates the conventions by which dramatic scenes are set up and
enacted. Pressure accumulates and culminates in a last-minute triumph. One
failure, two failures, then last-minute triumph, after mounting pressure, also
describes Tae's identification of the dramatic structure of *Ghosts of Mississippi*. Tae keeps repeating the structure: first, a Caucasian jury convicted the
Black man, then a new Caucasian jury convicted the man, then a more representative jury relieved his guilt. Rose's pretend play reveals her identification
with and appropriation of narrative structure (a structure the baseball game
sets up as well with three strikes and you're out), such that the end result is an
embodiment of new characters on a team. She pretends the thematic ideals
that the characters represent, through the complicated process of sorting and
appropriating the conventions by which the film structures its story.

The storytelling world is for Rose more "enchanted" than a today world
because of the setting's "long ago" quality. While the girls resist a piece of

fiction as historically significant, historical setting can frame a story's "once upon a time." Rose's appropriation of the story's working structure, not its historical achievement, defines her ability to write a sequel for her social community to enact. She authors a continuation to the text to further explicate the theme she finds important, the theme of generational continuity, or role-modeling *within* the text. She reproduces the theme that "girls can do anything," making the text reproduce itself thematically and structurally. Ironically, then, to engage with the text, Rose works to produce the text's storytelling structure and translates the structure of adaptation into her social life. The ease with which the respondents move between formal awareness and seeing themselves in the film plot contrasts with their responses to literature.

THE ROLE FILM PLAYS IN SOCIAL LIFE

Girls more readily translate films into social possibilities because they experience cinema in the context of friendship communities. Girls often use films as social currency. In their social environments, girls quote lines from films to establish who is "in" and "out" of the group (who had and had not seen the film). In addition, films evoke a memory of social cohesion:

> [I like] movies I could talk about with my friends. When I see a movie, my friends automatically know what it's about because everybody in my class goes to movies most of the time—a lot. When I read a book, it depends on what kind of book, if it was a book we read in class I might talk about it with my friends, and if it's a book that I just read I'll still talk about it with them but it doesn't have the same impact. (Twelve-year-old Angie)

Another girl states that her friends might only discuss a book that they dislike. But films that the girls appreciate are thought of as fictions embedded within "real" social narratives and relationships in life, within the rhythms of "girl talk."

The girls often speak of seeing and renting movies with friends. A slumber party has to feature a film and food, embedding the medium of film within female community. Films are seen as inherently more connected than books to "real life," to a structure in which girls might more directly enact the form of the text's social world, because seeing movies is an inherently social experience:

> We might talk about books but I don't know, this just wouldn't come up [referring to a series books that many of her friends had read]. We talk more about stuff that's really happening. We'll quote lines from

[a movie] when something happens if it just pops in your head you know, quote a line from it, but it's not really like that's how life is, it's just funny. Like we'll be driving in the car because I have my permit and I'll be with my friends in the backseat and we're about to hit and we're like, "Oops, my bad" like when [the *Clueless* heroine] says that, or like, "Should I write them a note?" or like we'll just say little things like that. I have a friend who knows the whole movie *Clueless*; she can quote any line, just sit down and repeat the whole thing.

When you [quote a line] to your friends, you all laugh because you remember back when you saw the movie. Everybody knows what we're talking about and it's just funny. We'll have other things, besides movies, like inside jokes, like something that happened one night, we could just be like, "Oh remember blah blah blah" and like somebody else is like, "What?" (Fifteen-year-old Lily)

Lily illustrates the tension between regarding the film as an aesthetic form and seeing it as a social experience, an event in "life." She contrasts books with her communal discussions of "things that are really happening." Film quotations are woven into the social fabric of life by their taking on social currency and thus standing for the means by which the social group is "really happening" in social space. Yet the film is not "how life is"; rather, girls use allusions to film to display their contemporary sensibility. It is inherently impressive to the group that a member can display knowledge of the entire film of *Clueless*, and that display of knowledge constructs a vision of "how life is" for the girls in their extratextual social space. In considering how *Clueless* operates in their lives, Lily decides that the characters in the social world depicted in the film are "like us," thus establishing a social relationship with the text. The characters mirror her community in a comic manner, and thus the narrative context reveals the characterization of the form of her own social world.[9]

Girls actually claim to experience films in two distinct ways—one as a viewer of the story and one as a girl within her social scene. When she speaks of *The Craft*, fourteen-year-old Alevay contrasts the role-playing she enacts with friends to the experience of actually seeing the film:

I can relate to *The Craft* because I think a lot of girls think about being a witch because it'd be kind of fun to not necessarily use your powers for bad, but it could help you a lot to have magical powers because you wouldn't really have to worry about things. Maybe to get a guy to like you or get a good grade on a test when you're doing a test. You could get all the answers to come to you with no problems or if you get a good job or do whatever you want to be. If someone's being mean to you, you could just embarrass them or make them fall or something. [I don't picture myself as one of the witches in the movie but I picture] myself, like hanging out with them or something. Kinda like a secret-type thing. I think when you see the movie, you always like say with your friends, "Oh I'd be her" or something like that, but when you really stop and think about it you'd kind of just be yourself but doing like the type of things she does. If that makes sense.

The idea of performing the female role is useful in terms of social discourse ("you say with your friends, 'Oh I'd be her'") and female community, she suggests. When she considers her actual viewing experience of the film, she imagines that the female character and viewer are distinct; she does not picture herself as a witch, but she establishes her self-presence ("hanging out with [the characters]") in front of the screen. However, films are both stories and models for adaptation into social life. Alevay—and other girls, she thinks—imagine that they obtain the power of the witch to transform their everyday lives, and indeed her friendship community is transformed by the idea of the coven. In her social community, Alevay enacts a role-playing experience, acting out the scene in which *The Craft*'s female characters play "light as a feather, stiff as a board." Through adapting the text together, they perform the female roles represented in the film.

Alevay and Lily express a common belief among the girls and critics that interpretation of books is personal, completely in the working mind, while interpretation of films is both personal and social, reinterpreted by a social community. However, the girls demonstrate the importance of the visual component of film by paying attention to actresses more than interpreting the texts themselves as real. They tend to prefer a certain actress and stress the actress's role in discussing the particular character she portrays, showing that they feel not only that films mirror forms of social worlds, but also that the "real person" playing the character's role is part of their social group and the text's meaning.

ATTENDING TO ACTRESSES

Girls equate actresses with particular styles of representation, in the same way that they might identify a book series or an author with a particular genre of books (R. L. Stine, V. C. Andrews, Anne McCaffrey, Donald Goines, etc.). They establish a relationship with an actress's career and feel her presence to be inseparable from the character at hand. When thirteen-year-old

Ann discusses one of her favorite movies, *Ever After*, she calls the heroine Drew Barrymore rather than Cinderella, showing that no pure experience of character is possible in a culture of stars. She maintains that films have a much more direct connection to a viewing experience in which the girl becomes a character, because she can view a structure of performance:

> Books are sort of harder [to imagine yourself in]. What I do in movies, say like, "If I were that character I would do so much different and stuff." There's magic in the movies. That's why I want to make movies. I want to like leave people with inspiration, like my feeling.

She imagines a film to be a more direct rendering of a filmmaker's vision and emotion, the "magic" or "inspiration" of the movies as a medium. The magic is its invitation to *feel* its inspiring actors and actresses. The film embodies a double experience of impersonally experiencing text and personally relating to an attractive industry with magical roles for talented people.

The girls believe that films influence people's behavior. For example, fourteen-year-old Kristen agrees with the decision to adapt *Killing Mr. Griffin* (Duncan) as *Teaching Mrs. Tingle*: "She doesn't die in the end so but I think because *Killing Mr. Griffin* was a good book, but now I'm not so sure that you would want to give it to kids because of what happened about the bombing and Columbine." Similarly, thirteen-year-old Jessica objects to the way in which adults perceive teens negatively—as representative of "trouble"— yet are the ones influencing them by making movies. Many of the girls object to the representation of teen girls in films; sixteen-year-old Olive resents the practice of having older women play teens and "expect us to relate," while twelve-year-old Tae critiques the high school depicted in *The Faculty* as not like high school at all. Measuring films against their realities, none of the girls actually imagine the fiction of books to mirror reality or have this kind of influence.

A film's actual mimesis is entirely in the eye of the beholder, revealed by the fact that girls contradict themselves by constantly attending to the constructed nature of the films. Filmic illusions and effects have interest because of their emergent technologies and because the girls like to become expert viewers. They scrutinize actresses, costumes, settings, and inconsistencies. They appreciate their expertise as viewers when they detect moments that reveal the craft of the medium, visual "mistakes" and inconsistencies that they believe they have detected. They thus evince a sense of "intertextuality" by medium, looking at how each text not only responds to other texts and actresses's careers, but how it responds to the medium itself:

I watch a movie like three times. I pick out the little bloopers, like any movie I can tell you everything that's wrong in the movie. [About *Maverick*,] I liked all the fashion. The way that Jodie Foster, she's in the blue dress, I love that style and stuff. And it was bunch of train chases and gambling and it was a movie almost like a soap opera, the way they have the camera in their faces and that you're like part of the movie, like their lives and stuff. You're just made really into it. I looked at [the blue dress] as how the actors themselves adapted to their character and stuff, like if you put on a certain, in theater if you put on a certain outfit that you know, doesn't fit your character as you think the character would wear it, then you act totally different and you don't like it and you can't do your best. But if the dress was like, "Oh this is perfect," you go out there and it's like you're all into character and you do it like a million times better. And I compare that, let's say Jodie Foster in this movie, to another movie that she was in, with a different fashion, different era, and I'm like, "Oh she adapted so well," and she did. This came out in this movie and she had more of this in that movie.

By attending to various visual effects and the means by which they can be achieved, the girls often reify the film as carefully crafted design, design that *"makes* the reader into it." Their sense that film is a more verisimilar art than books is thus a product of their use of the text. They define the medium's verisimilar quality differently, by the film's role as social event, constitutive of reality, or visual realism. Yet all the qualities that make a film more "real" can be traced to the girls' practice of foregrounding film as "design." Thus they define the design of the film as the performance of verisimilitude, and the design of a book as a product of mental fantasy.

GROWING UP WITH FILM

By drawing a relationship between film and visual frames of reference for their own identity performances, the girls believe that the role of a film changes in their lives over time because their identities change, as described by an Asian American girl:

My favorite movie is *The Little Mermaid*. I loved it when I was really little, like she used to do all these little things, I liked the mermaid part. I always wanted to be a mermaid, so that was fun. Now I watch it because I knew every single word in the movie and all the songs. It's fun to watch with my friends because they'll laugh at me and

stuff. Only the friends that know the songs can come over and watch
it with me. I usually have like a sleepover with like one friend. She
brought the movie when we went camping and we watched it every
single night of the entire week. We'd copy some of the words that are
really important or stand out. All the songs we sing. I think [watching
it now] is the friends and I sharing this little moment that we have.
And it's more fun watching it with my friends who used to watch this
when we were little.

It's sort of different [now]. When I saw it with my friend we just
like noticed these little things in the movies that we didn't notice
when we were little, you know a lot of things change you know, it's
not like that anymore. You know the prince isn't going to come and
everything so stuff like that, just makes you wonder. Like there's no
mermaids. There are no mermaids. And because my father would
never do that. He'd never turn me into something else. [When I was
five] it was the princess thing. (Fourteen-year-old Alex)

The film's movement from fantasy to social form is shaped by a girl's consciousness of *her* changing realities—her growing appreciation for the difference between text and life, a reflection spoken with sadness. Alex's memory
of the text evokes her past and present realities, the former embedded in
fantasy and the latter in her social world. Her final summation of "the princess thing" sounds like "the whole world-ending thing" that another girl uses
to describe action adventure. "The princess thing" means that she once viewed
the female character in the context of the storyworld, a reading of genre that
she seems to think a much simpler reading. Because fairy tales are perceived
as a genre for only the youngest readers, unless they can be updated with
verisimilar qualities (*Ever After*), she reclaims the film for her social circle
and thus can still enjoy it. She revises her understanding of the text, from
fantasy to "unrealistic" fairy tale, theorizing that the film constituted a world
she thought possible at age five. At her current age, she "knows" the prince
will not come; she "knows" her father is not the king, who is willing to sacrifice his daughter so she can be happy; and she "knows" that the film is
pretend. Demonstrating her understanding that within ideologies of childhood she is "supposed" to reject fantasy and fairy tale, she also suggests that
she cannot let the text go. To keep it meaningful, she shifts the text from a
representation of a Secondary World to a reification of social space, such
that the text still holds its spell over the "real." Her whole idea of reality
shifts with re-viewing the text, and she begins to define the text's genre as
heterosexual romance rather than fantasy.

Having rejected *The Little Mermaid*'s idea of heterosexual romance as
not "like life," however, she reembeds the text into a female social commu-

nity and enjoys the community it creates around her, in life, by actually giving form to female community. When I ask what she likes about *The Little Mermaid* now, she says "the merfolk community," fantasizing that she would like to be part of a community under the sea. Because films are texts of social worlds *and* social events with friends, they construct communities:

> I'll see [*Austin Powers*] with my friends and then we'll repeat it and then we'll just have a really good time playing parts of the movie. We'll remember this part and we'll just laugh it off because it was really funny. *Stepmom*; there was this movie and my friend and I just completely cried so that brought me and my friend really close together. (Fourteen-year-old Alex)

The community "plays" the film's parts not because the girls are embracing possible social roles created by the film, but because they are embracing their "real" social roles as film consumers and communities organized around entertainment. They experience cultural identity through the film as event.

THE PARADOX OF FILM, MORE NOVEL THAN LITERATURE

> It's not like that anymore. You know the prince isn't going to come. Like there's no mermaids. (Fourteen-year-old Alex)

The girls' discussions of films feature the paradox that film is imagined to be a verisimilar art, yet the design of an industry. This paradox bespeaks an important conflict between their desire for fantasy and alterity in fiction and their awareness of a cultural ideology that defines growth as movement *away* from the genre of fantasy toward the genre of social realism. Just as they map the binary code of male ↔ female onto the code of fantasy (aesthetic appreciation) ↔ realism (social performance), they map a binary code of imagination ↔ mimesis onto fictional books ↔ fictional films. The girls' perception of their own viewing and reading practices demonstrates that they resist and yet also succumb to ideologies lurking behind the selection of literature for children: the American tradition of equating fantasy/fairy tale with children's literature and verisimilitude with adolescent literature. The girls do not feel entitled to continued immersion in fantasy novels as they grow older. This segmentation of fantasy into the children's genre is less prominent a concern in film, which distinguishes the age-appropriateness of different films by certain violent and sexual content but which does not maintain a strict division between child and adult by virtue of theme, genre, or the age of the hero or heroine. Even animation is a cross-audienced genre.

A predominant tradition of children's literature denotes fantasy as the proper mode of younger children with more and more doses of "reality," or "realistic literature," as the child grows up. Because Romance is an older form than realism, Frye asserts, critics construe the development of realism as a kind of evolution of sophistication—as growth itself. This idea of formal evolution has been mapped onto child development and recommendations for children's reading, although any trip to Barnes & Noble reveals that the literary scene is changing and we are seeing a new appreciation for (and marketing of) fantasy, science fiction, mystery, and "role-playing" (really world-playing) novels for all ages. Even critics are beginning to inquire into science fiction, and emergent technologies (in the digital age) are profoundly reshaping the aesthetic aspects of publications for children (Dresang). Although popular fantasy and science fiction have remained staples since the turn of the twentieth century, the complexity of modernism drew attention away from popular forms. Robert Latham has noted the relationship between the writing of Joseph Conrad and H. G. Wells, but the canonization of the former reveals the value that critics have placed upon psychological complexities and their relative downplaying of Secondary Worlds, and it also makes clear their favorable opinion of the modernists who rejected rather than revised the Romantic traditions of the nineteenth century (49). The academy's esteem for the novel character and for psychological complexity reveals an investment in ideologies of the individual liberal subject (Jameson) as superior to the social dynamics that an alternative world can make visible. Novel theorists have paid more attention to the literary achievements of nineteenth-century realist masters because realism undoes convention (seen also as the job of adolescence, you could say), and transfers focus to character and social scene.

The "building" of character has come to stand for a central cultural narrative about growing up. Narratives that denote child development as a genred development from Romance to realism, from form (formula) to character, from convention to uniqueness ("tradition" to "individual talent"), produce the reductive sense of the child and fantasy literature as "a simpler genre," as "not quite full-bodied characters"; as not quite "subjects" in their own right. Ursula Le Guin, speaking at the University of California, Berkeley, lamented the arbitrary canon-making decisions that equate literature with realism. The narrative that maps a higher sophistication onto literary realism has to do with critical valuation of character, the complexity of character being the defining feature that differentiates realism from high Romance, according to Leslie Fiedler's definition of the distinctions between novel and Romance, in *Love and Death in the American Novel*, which he draws from Hawthorne's distinction in Hawthorne's preface to *The House of Seven Gables*.

As the girls grow older and feel that they are supposed to know that "there are no mermaids," they experience more and more films, fewer and fewer books. Underneath their confusing and contradictory discussions of films lies a belief that they should follow the path defined by our stories of literary history and by the course of children's literature versus the adolescent novel—that they should give up immersion in Secondary Worlds and come to terms with "what's really happening." Because the mode of the adolescent novel largely conflicts with their appreciation of more Romantic forms, the girls turn away from literature entirely and feel that they move "into the real world" by experiencing more films, another narrative of story evolution mapped onto twentieth-century media.

In an amazing manner, films have replaced the popular, communal novel of the nineteenth century; they are better immersive novels than, well, novels. Teen girls have seen a synergy between coming-of-age and film, deciding that film is a better symbol for the relationship between life and story, both because film invokes adaptation of text to performance and because the movie theater—that precious space that is both public and private, communal and individual—has come to symbolize the theater of adolescence, that transitional "space" (Winnicott) between self and culture, parents and friends, personal and shared experience, childhood and adulthood. Movie theaters are perhaps the most widely used forums for imaginal experience. And where else can you find coming-of-age as affirmed as it is in the rite of passage that is defined in the move from G to PG-13, to PG, and—oh! finally—to R: the Real/Reel sign that you've come of age.

Beauty in the Beast:
The Power of Metamorphosis

[Pretending to be an animal] really makes you reach inside and pull out explanations that you never thought you'd think of. It's a different way of expressing how you feel and who you are and stuff.
—Fifteen-year-old Ellie

Is READING like playing Let's Pretend? Or not?

Glimpsing the girls' self-reports of pretend play is quite intriguing because many teachers of literature view children's capacity to imagine literary worlds as an extension of the children's capacity to pretend. In stories they "write" for themselves to pretend, the girls identify with the narrative form of performing another person and imagine that they embody female characters, shifting focus from story theme and omniscient point of view to a self-directed role-playing drama. I found adaptation of literary stories rare except in the instance of the animal character, which the girls choose to identify with in *both* literary and nonliterary forms. When reading, seeing, or pretending stories of animal narratives, the girls fantasize complete embodiment of character, emphasizing the body, movement, and narrative possibilities of being an animal. Their narrations of animal-pretend lend themselves to a reading of role-playing as an expression of identity and serve to exemplify the kinds of responses to human female characters of fiction that I thought I would analyze when I first began this project.

ACTING IN PLAY: A DIFFERENT TRANSCENDENCE OF SELF

Although the subject of pretend play frequently arose during the interviews, most of the girls insist that they do not pretend stories they have encountered only in books. However, they do pretend scenes from books if the books have been adapted into film. Adaptation involves important shifts in meaning. Eight-year-old Wendy, familiar with both Barrie's book and Disney's adaptation, demonstrates that she reads *Peter Pan* in a different manner from how she pretends the story:

> I'm not the kind of person who likes exactly pretending that you're exactly in the story. There's only one story that I pretend that I'm in, and that's *Peter Pan* and all those places. I like being Wendy. I like *Peter Pan*. There's one kind of sad part in it, and when, like, Peter Pan and there's no time. This is like the real story, the original, not the Disney or kind of changed kind of *Peter Pan*—this was pretty much the original story. And so it was Peter Pan had lost the time and he wanted to come and see Wendy and he didn't want Wendy to leave but Wendy needed to go back. So Peter Pan, so Wendy's mother met Peter Pan, let Wendy come over about three [months] or maybe a month, do housecleaning and do things with Peter Pan, and so then Peter Pan returned for like a month every year but Peter Pan started splitting into like five years and then he ended up never coming back. And then he came back when Wendy was all grown up! And Wendy had a child and I felt kind of sad because Peter Pan started crying because Wendy was all grown up. And when you're all grown up you can't really come back. And then Peter started liking Wendy's little girl so that was kind of happy. But I still feel a little sad about that.

When I ask how she pretends Wendy, she claims, "I'd do like exactly what Wendy does. I like to be what Wendy does, and I like what happens to Wendy in the story. That's the only story I pretend I'm in." In the context of pretend play she pretends the female role, the "nice motherly kind of person," scripting a feminine part for herself. In describing her reading of *Peter Pan*, by contrast, she focuses on its major theme—the sadness and permanence of the fact of growing up. When she adapts *Peter Pan* to her performance, Wendy loses her reflection on growth as "sad" or tinged with nostalgia, happily playing the "motherly," grown-up role.

Identifying with the conventions of performance in film, girls adapt the texts to those conventions and direct themselves into the female role of the performance: "One of my favorite characters is from the movie. It's Robin Hood actually. One of my wishes is Robin Hood were real. Because I'm sort of in love with him. He's so cool and things. He seems to rescue people and stuff" (eight-year-old Honey). Honey extends the story of *Robin Hood* as a narrator or author, but by bringing the text into a form of performed drama, she prefers to embrace the female role of love interest rather than pretend to be Robin himself, a "trousers role" that I would have expected girls to enjoy before I began this project. The girls differentiate their dramatic self-direction in role-playing pretend from their impersonal role "in" the literary text when they read. Ten-year-old Becky explains that she enjoys imagining roles she might achieve in life, as demonstrated by a "lifeline" she has on her bedroom wall, featuring roles like Miss America and president. However, she explains that reading makes her feel not presence as a social role, but "like you're on the rooftop," which is why she reads. Girls who act in school plays speak of role-playing experience as the possibility of self-transcendence by one's actually becoming someone else: "[In acting the part of Yum Yum] I got to feel what she would feel and everything. You can feel what's happening to them or their problems and different feelings that they have" (fourteen-year-old Hope). She claims to experience *empathy* with the character she both constructs and acts.

Although the interpretive action is different, identifying with the conventions of pretend performance also engenders a feeling of self-transcendence and a quest for alterity. In the following, fifteen-year-old Ellie describes dramatic role-playing in terms of her desire for alterity, in a way similar to the way in which Olive desires a vision of a different social world in *The Godfather*, "far off" from "who I am":

> We step out of [our lives, when we act]. We can't worry about [what's bothering us] and we don't have to worry about that because that's not us at the moment. You go to theater and you become someone else. It doesn't even enter your mind what's going on in your regular life. It's just a total escape from reality. I love that. If in the show you're playing a fifteen-year-old girl, it kind of lifts off because you can create the own problems for your character but the farther stretch away the character is from your actual person, like if I have to play a forty-year-old attorney or something like that, it's a really far stretch from who I am now, so the farther it is the farther you get from reality.

Like reading, acting enables the girls to imagine that they escape their everyday selves and "reality," suggesting that motivations for, if not experiences of, reading and acting are similar. For example, fifteen-year-old Ruth discusses reading as escape: "[Experiencing stories] it's like escaping what's actually happening and going to what hasn't happened, you know? What didn't happen? It's just all from someone's imagination and I like that better." The distinction between the two experiences, however, lies in the form with which the girl identifies and by which she interprets meaning. When acting a story, the girls become someone else, and when reading, they become "someone's imagination."

Like eleven-year-old Vanessa, ten-year-old Becky pretends to be one of the performers singing and dancing with the Spice Girls in their video. Like many of the girls in this study, she enacts scenes that she has seen and plays dress-up, a process involving embodying role and authoring detailed scenario, as adapted from scenes she has viewed:

> I have at least two boxes of dress-up. There's like Japanese person, Japanese clothes in here, rabbit ears, Voorhees stuff. But sometimes we pretend we're from another country or something. [She pretends modeling for me and explains how she and her friend would set up.] We'd have socks for where the lights usually are when you come down the big, um, when you come down the big walkway thing, you know, going [pretends modeling walk, exaggerating hip movements] we walk like this! And then we'd change real quickly and we'd do another one. "And now a word from our sponsor" or something. (Ten-year-old Becky)

When Becky explains how to role-play a model, she makes me see it. She enacts the movement of the "character," and sets the scene with words and props, both directing and acting her imagined story. When critics discuss music videos and media images as relentlessly presenting images of girls and women for the viewer to identify with, they well predict how girls experience the form of performance in such texts. Music videos are pure sound, movement, voice, and montage; while they have point of view, their editing style deemphasizes narrative form and highlights artistry as a role-playing activity. Many of the girls differentiate role-playing with props and dolls from reading, one girl even noting that she likes to play *American Girl* dolls because she can create the conversation, whereas in reading the *American Girl* books, "someone else" makes up the conversation.

THE APPEAL OF SPECIES METAMORPHOSIS

Older girls who recall pretending to be characters in films, however, would often shift during their discussions to a re-creation of the text's alternative fantasy world. In the following, fourteen-year-old Alex identifies with the communal world within the text and the different "species" living there:

> When I was little I used to pretend that I was in the same situation. But a little more like I think that'd be really cool to have fins and just swim around and do other things. [She admits that she is the opposite

of the mermaid Ariel, from the film *The Little Mermaid*, who wants
to be human.] I always wondered what it was like to be in the ocean
because it took me awhile to learn how to swim and I always liked
the ocean and the fish and being able to swim instead of walk and
things like that. It's sort of different. I'd swim around in the coral and
humans they'll be like, "Wow. I saw a mermaid!" That'd be fun.
Dolphins—I love dolphins too so I'd swim with them. I always
looked for mermaids when I was at the ocean or something. But I
never found any. I'd have to have a friend. I'd be very lonely without
a friend. I like a [mermaid] community.

As she speaks about pretending a narrative situation, the fantasy takes on
a life of its own apart from Ariel's narrative situation, which is her initial
point for discussion. Alex reenacts the way in which a fantasy world actually allows the viewer to move beyond the feelings and desires of a particular character to identify with a larger social structure, "I like a [mermaid]
community"—the form of creating a social community in the alternative
world. Part of the appeal of mermaids seems to be their status as an alternative species in an underwater world—the power of fantasy that a non-
human society materializes.

One particular kind of literary fantasy appeals to many of the girls:
animal fantasy. While girls deny direct identification with the human characters of social worlds in fictional literature and embrace role-playing possibilities in narratives they define as "real-life," they *do* imagine themselves as
the animal character when reading, viewing, *or* pretending stories of animal
societies. They thus complement their postmodern sense of the self's spectator role "in" literature with a material longing to inhabit the animal form,
stressing the bodily power, movement, and revenge plot they enjoy when they
imagine themselves to be animals. When thirteen-year-old Ann writes horror stories about deer who take revenge on hunters, she appropriates the
conventions of animal fantasy, utopia literature, American fantasy, and science fiction to write plots that self-consciously allow her to imagine she is a
deer and can run wild and free, if only the hunters can be rigidly controlled
and punished. The girls' animal role-play enables them to identify with a less
powerful species, but the animal plot enables them to quest to become something more. Animal stories interrogate the borders between species, or "nature," and environment, or culture. The quintessential questions of the animal
hero are, What do I have to accept as natural? What can be changed? What
is merely cultural? Are Wilbur and Babe to be meat or can they become more?
Animal fantasy gives the girls a way to imagine enacting themes of freedom
and social change. I believe that their embrace of animal pretend is enabled
by the success of environmental rhetoric. The girls appropriate "save the

animals" themes and imagine themselves as the vulnerable animals that require future utopia.

EMBODYING THE ANIMAL NARRATIVE

Twelve-year-old Shelley remembers enjoying the story of *Babe* (King-Smith) for its interrogation of these "nature or culture" questions. Similarly, eight-year-old Honey defines the central drama of *Charlotte's Web* (E. B. White) as whether or not "Wilbur will be the farmer's Thanksgiving dinner." For her, the power of the text lies in how Charlotte tricks the farmer. She remembers the very words spelled out in Charlotte's web, emphasizing the theme that animal characters have alternative ways of speaking, tricky and subtle ways of establishing voice and challenging the social organization of power: "[Charlotte] used her web [to save Wilbur's life] and she wrote words in her web, such as *terrific, radiant,* actually I remember one of the things she wrote is *some pig.* And *terrific.* And she tricked the man and then [Wilbur] turned out to be a prize pig" (eight-year-old Honey). Honey's identification with the tricky animal allows her to imagine that she too could "play a trick," in her case, on the Rat of *The Nutcracker* film, a character that scares her. Authorship puts him in his place.

Girls link their engagements with animal stories to their general love of animals, demonstrating the fact that their definitions of the animal story conjoin aesthetic and nonaesthetic appreciation. Animals and animal characters readily stand for alternative selves and gain multiple meanings. In the following discussion, nine-year-old Jesse asserts her general love for animals, including the common assertion among girls that they would like to be veterinarians or somehow work with animals in the future, and then details her imaginative play of the female unicorn in the film *The Last Unicorn*:

> I like to read about dogs because they're my favorite animals. And at the library they have a section on dogs and a section on pets and stuff, and I've read almost all the dog books in that section. At school they have papers, what you want to be when you grow up and every single time it says on it, it says a vet! Because I love animals. One of my favorite movies was called *The Last Unicorn* and I watched it about 10 million billion times and I memorized the whole story, the whole movie. I did [imagine I was the unicorn] because it was this girl [who] can turn into a unicorn and she was the last unicorn because this bad guy, he had this bull which was like made out of fire and the bull went out into the world and chased all the unicorns into the sea. And she met the bull when she was a unicorn and got away from him

and turned into a person again. When she was a person she was
practically white sort of because unicorns are white, and she was
really white and her eyes were blue—really shiny blue and stuff.

Books with animals attract Jesse because of their depicted subject. Although
the unicorn of *The Last Unicorn* is also a girl/woman, Jesse pretends to be
the unicorn part of her, embodying the female character because she is an
animal and a symbol for animal metamorphosis. Indeed, Jesse identifies with
the very metamorphosis of the character from animal to girl to animal, the
character role-modeling how Jesse can transform herself into the animal. The
unicorn is a unique character because she is the "last" and "only" unicorn,
a heroine whom everyone in the story wants to entrap, but whose power rests
upon the fact that she can change her shape. Jesse continues her narration
by telling me that she imagines fighting the bull and uses shiny plastic to
represent the sea; for her, the defeat of the bull is the climax of the story. She
remembers neither the unicorn community nor the love interest, showing that
the character's power derives from her ability to allegorize the fantasy of
becoming an animal, rather than romance or quest.

Jesse self-consciously understands her enactment of the unicorn as a
symbolic expression of her identity, telling me that *The Last Unicorn* is one
story that would be produced on "the all-girl planet," which we travel to in
our imagination at the end of the interview: "I don't think boys would really
want to watch, you know, a movie like that." Many girls, when I ask them
how their lives would be different if they were boys, theorize that they would
not like animals as much, nor would they keep so many stuffed animals.
Pretending to embody animals and enjoying images of animals are, for the
girls, expressions of gender.

The idea of metamorphosis thematizes response to the animal story,
through which girls could enjoy the idea of changing shape, tricking or de-
feating those in power in ways only animal characters can, and leaving behind
the limits of being a young girl—in their eyes, a vulnerable position. Eight-
year-old Angela imagines that she has the metamorphic powers to transform
herself from child to animal in order to travel between the kid planet, animal
planet, and grown-up planet—this is her fantasy of how animals, children,
and grown-ups inhabit different lands and entirely different natures and
cultures. In her vision of becoming an animal hero, the girl needs to become
a beast to protect these sacred divisions:

> A bad grown-up would let you in their house and put you into a boiler
> or something. [I'd turn into] a crocodile, then I would try to get them
> and bite them; but if that doesn't work I'll turn into a monkey, then I'll
> swing on them and poke them in the eye. (Eight-year-old Angela)

This heroism demonstrates that girls not only imagine that they protect themselves, but also use animal fantasy to express rage at being the site of adult victimization. A fear of being eaten, one that animal stories evoke, becomes Angela's own oral greed. She uses the conventions of fairy tales, adventure fantasy, and mythological metamorphosis (even science fiction) to defeat evil. In Angela's mind, bad grown-ups would refuse to approach the kid planet once they knew that "kids can turn into anything." The very knowledge that children are metamorphic creatures would, in her mind, deconstruct ideals of childhood/girlhood as vulnerable and keep the bad grown-ups forever suspended in space, with no land to inhabit. Angela's narrative animal identification performs a symbolic deconstruction of adult-child power dynamics, seeking in narrative an imagination of social change, just as do Ann's imagined stories about deer.

THE BRAID OF ANIMAL LITERATURE AND IMAGINATIVE LIFE

Many young children's books feature animals, and indeed a cultural association between children and animal stories has denoted certain animal books as "for children" in the oddest ways. For example, *Black Beauty* (Sewell) does not announce itself as written for children, nor does *Animal Farm* (Orwell) or *Aesop's Fables* (Aesop), but all have been put into children's curriculums. In Carol Christ's words, from a lecture on *Black Beauty*, "Animals as characters appear principally in children's books. . . . animals duplicate the feelings that adults have toward children. They are cute and attractive to pet" (31).

In classic children's literature and American fantasy literature, those who cross the borders between human and animal societies for a new sense of self are often male. The theme of *The Call of the Wild* (London) is similar to that of *The Wind in the Willows* (Grahame), *The Jungle Books* (Kipling) and countless manifestations of the theme of boys and men who "dance with wolves." Such stories allow plasticity between children (or an American Adam) and the animal kingdom. While animal literature suggests a Western tradition of thinking about national history, the packaging of animal stories for children suggests a duality: adults think of children as domestic presences, as protected pets and pasts, but they also think of children as a form of feral wildness, in need of civilization. Uncertainty about the feral wildness lurking within the child finds expression in horror fiction, fable, and fairy tale. Part of the continuing appeal of "Beauty and the Beast" and "Little Red Riding Hood" seems to be an uncertainty about the relationship between girls and beasts: does the girl desire the beast? Is she aroused or terrified by the panting wolf? asks Angela Carter in her different versions of Red Riding Hood (short stories of *The Bloody*

Chamber and screenplay for *The Company of Wolves*). Are girls cowering, like Laura of *Little House*, or fantasizing about being Spirit, the essence of the American frontier? In the wonderfully wild story *Carmen Dog*, by Carol Emshwiller, a woman who wants to be an opera singer is transformed into a dog; only then can she feel free to howl. Animal stories have always been used for allegorical purposes; in Orwell's *Animal Farm*, *Carmen Dog*, and Marie Darrieussecq's *Pig Tales*, the allegories have a political purpose.

The girls embrace the ideology of childhood that links children with animals—and lowers them on the food chain—for their own purposes, using animal fantasy to question cultural definitions of childhood as in need of adult protection. I quote the following young girl's elaborate imagination of *The Lion, the Witch and the Wardrobe* (Lewis) because like the girls who fluidly identify with both characters and narrative structure in films, eight-year-old Honey *owns* the metamorphic powers of both book and film because they depict a powerful animal kingdom:

> One of the things I have been dreaming about is that I would have magical wings and unicorn horses with wings and lions that are magical, and they can fly without wings. They only do what I tell them to do, like if I say for a lion to destroy something then he would do it. But if I say to the lion to ride him, then he would. [The lions and unicorns] are my pets and I also have pet deer because I adore cats, dogs, actually I pretty much adore all of the animals in the world. The unicorns are magical and the unicorns would be used, they could sort of cast something. And if I told them to do something, well if there was someone that was dangerous like a witch then I would tell them to put the unicorn near them, or if they just aim it, then they could shoot them and return that witch into a statue that couldn't harm anyone. They could shoot magic. Well, I could turn her into some good person, like you that comes riding along with me, or if I want, or if she's bad enough, and her heart could not be changed like that, I would turn her into a statue.

> Q: *Have you ever read a story like that?*

> Well, actually one of my favorite stories that gave me the idea is *The Lion, the Witch and the Wardrobe*. Unicorn magic can do many other things than save lives. They don't have to use their unicorn thing. I actually have a little bit of magic too, and the lions have more magic than the unicorns . . . [I have] millions [of lions]. Well, actually they don't always use their magic. They only use it if they can't use their fighting skills, although they never die. Because if I put a sword

into their side, it would be as if I was poking a needle into their skin. If I poke that in and then I took it out, and I did it several times, and I stuck arrows into their side, they could have their wounds healed a lot faster.

   I want to be as least older as I can. Actually I would want to be younger because when I was younger when I was scared my mom and dad used to comfort me. Well, actually I don't need to be comforted because I don't really need to be scared as long as those lions are around in my imagination in that life. As long as magic is around me because with so many magic I can't be harmed, and I can use my own magic to protect myself.

Honey's lion and unicorn fantasy stems from but far surpasses the story of Narnia. She only titles the text because I ask, and she views the fantasy as *hers*. The way Aslan transcends mortality and conquers evil fuels Honey's dreams of protecting herself in a world she fears (her very first assertion in the interview is that she is home-schooled because "fools with guns" lurk in public schools). Her belief in animal magic is associated in her mind with early childhood, both parents and transitional objects (Winnicott), which underscores the subversion of Honey's use of the animal to express her power, rage, and even violence.

   I call attention to the narrative imaginations of the youngest respondents because they demonstrate how imagination is a means to power and how fluid the lines are between certain types of metamorphosis literature and personal fantasy, as Shirley Brice Heath demonstrates in her study of her young children who are exposed to many works of fantasy. Young children approach animal fantasy and utopian literature and film with the same attention to structure and character issues with which the older girls approach female characters of film but not literature. The location of the animal fantasy in her mind, rather than in the text, enables Honey's articulation of self-empowerment, contrasting the rhetoric of textual power that many readers voice. Both protected self and agent of protection, she is simultaneously the animal's kingly spirit and strength, the commander of the magic forces in a hierarchy over imaginal experience, and a magical force with her own transformational abilities to change threatening forces. She protects and divides from herself the vulnerable, frightened part of herself. With animal fantasy Honey actually possesses "a little bit of magic," because she has authored "so many magic" around her.

   By narrating a part she can role-play, she both appropriates the narrative logic and challenges the construction of adult-protected childhood and girlhood, fantasizing about the impenetrable skin and phallic properties of lions and unicorns. In fantasy she is the piercer and the voice of command, the doubled power of the character and author. Literature gives children the conventions by which to author fantasies in the mind, argues Bruno Bettelheim in *The Uses of Enchantment*, which I always assign to my students because they are so reluctant to read "scary" or "disturbing" content to children and are trapped by their view that literature teaches values and ideas (such as violence) rather than forms that empower the young reader to narrate and thus control the fears and anxieties that all children have.

The girls use animal fantasy to appropriate a rhetoric of power to be found in the animal kingdom. By identifying with animals and animal stories, they engage with powerful questions about what it means to be a girl and experience body and desire. When the girls assert their love of animals, they often speak of animals as cute and cuddly rather than wild, and they identify their stuffed animals as symbols of their maternal feelings toward animals. But when girls actually spin narratives of animal characters, they emphasize the wilder side of animals, the ferocious rage that animals express. In stories animals often "get away" with ferocity because they are driven to violence by oppression, motivated by the need to protect their species—often their young. Fourteen-year-old Carolyn describes herself as a "fun" person who is also "brave and strong" when necessary, characteristics she derives from Baloo of *The Jungle Books* (Kipling): "He was fun to be around, he liked to have fun but he also scared people away, when he had to be, he had to like be strong and scare [the tiger]." The animal character is a conscious component of self-characterization.

While it might seem that girls lower themselves on the food chain to "become" animals, the girls themselves stress the ability of small animals to become mighty in stories, the theme that eight-year-old Wendy draws from *Redwall*, when she says that small animals become mighty and that as a reader, she is "a little animal" watching the whole. This process is thematized by many children's stories that are organized around "The Ugly Duckling" structure and theme, from *Rudolph the Red-Nosed Reindeer* (R. L. May) to *Dumbo*; the hero's lack of communal power derives from a "default," but the default becomes his strength and allows his rise to power.

It is the very process by which girls imagine they can escape their human form that defines their fantasy of power in animal role-play, and their ability to imagine themselves engaged in a social crusade to change the world. In the following, eleven-year-old Vanessa links her ability to pretend animals with transcendence of gender:

> I love, like I'm so in love with animals. It doesn't matter [what kind]. It could be a snake. It could be a tarantula, even though I'm afraid of them. I like them. I used to write a lot of stories. Like me and my sister, I'd pretend that I'd be a jaguar or a koala and my cousin, his name is Justin, he'd be an elephant or something. And we'd pretend

we're in the jungle fighting like these trees or something. [Another story I wrote] it's about, my cousin, my sister, and me, a long time ago, my old friend, her name is Francesca, it was like, all of us, and it was about like we were all animals.

I would try to be a veterinarian when I grow up. It's just like *Jumanji* or something, I'm running, trying to catch all these animals, but instead of kill them or something I'm going to help them. I've pretended to be a panda and [my cousin] was a horse and Francesca was a little eagle, and I turned into an eagle and then my cousin would turn into a bear or something. And we'd all have these powers and stuff, and people can be trying to catch like the forest on fire and we'd attack them and then that's how we'd live. By eating them. Actually I was a koala. I'd climb a drain and jump on them and then my cousin would come, because he's a bear, or he was a bull. A bull or a bear. He's like a bull and he'd ram into them and then my best friend would come, and like bite his ankles or something, like turn into an eagle and fly away and just put them in a ditch or something.

When I think of being a koala, I would think of a girl then I would think of a boy. I wouldn't think of how I look, I'd just be a character. I wouldn't have a name or anything. I'd just be it. I'd have the powers, like Sabrina [in *Sabrina the Teenage Witch*] to go back like—years ago and just like disappear, to change into somebody else, and change somebody's voice, or make a fire or something.

The animal is either androgyny or gender fluidity, but as the imaginal and pretending agent, Vanessa imagines herself outside identity discourses, associated with name and body. "I'd just be it," she says, as if animal pretend allows her to just *be* in a material and unperformative sense. Through the animal, Vanessa feels her ontological "being," because she needs the body to enact rage and see results. Vanessa expresses a common desire among the girls to avenge mother nature, indicating an ethic of care through the guise of environmental awareness. She revises the plot of *Jumanji* to save the animals rather than to assert the dominance of the human being. Within the ethic of ecology, the girls can express rage and desire, because they disappear from personhood and, by doing so, imagine that they transcend feminine codes of behavior. The koala, which others might see as cute, cuddly, or childlike in the domestic sense, is in her story roving female desire that becomes an elusive, unnameable "it" beyond gender, language, and human body: "I wouldn't think of how I look. I'd just be a character. I wouldn't have a name or anything. I'd just be it. I'd have the powers." Vanessa not only ascends on the food chain through the animal fantasy, but also dreams of devouring and punishing those who offend nature.

OUR BODIES, OUR ANIMALS

The older girls voice a rhetoric of animal identification as regression, displaying their belief that animals link them with early childhood and allow them to regress, even while they imagine animals in plots of power. In fact, when I walked into the bedrooms of the girls, I encountered hordes of stuffed animals surrounding even the oldest girls' beds. Sixteen-year-olds discuss the importance to them of Mickey Mouse, and twelve-year-olds discuss the importance of Tweetie. As though reading from a Winnicottian textbook, the girls explain how the important stuffed animals connect them to relatives and friends by symbolizing gifts and relationships, and mediating transitional space as girls differentiated themselves. Ann's gardens, forests, and frolicking deer bespeak the pastoral memory of early childhood, which fifteen-year-old Ruth describes as a time when the self was "authentic." Animals stand for the girls' desire to protect the authentic (early childhood) self, to "save" that self and thus link the authentic self with ecological politics:

> I've had this thing for awhile where I want to be a vet, because I love animals. I wanted to find a cure for rabies for the longest time. I mean I'm the person, I cry at animals movies and not people movies because I just love animals and I'm not like much of a people person so I love animals and I wanted to save an animal's life, but I didn't want to have one die during surgery or put them to sleep. I wouldn't be able to handle that. I often do volunteer work because I volunteered at a refuge one summer a couple years ago and that was so much fun. I loved it so much. And I think volunteer work, like just help the animals and without having to, you know, put them to sleep or cut them open. I just love them. I grew up on a farm so animals were my first friends and I've gotten used to them and I don't really care for people sometimes. You know, seeing how nasty and evil and stupid they can be. Animals I love because they just understand you, you can talk to them and they don't judge you. They love you for who you are. I love that about animals. (Fifteen-year-old Ruth)

Ruth's comments establish links between desire for a profession involving animals, a desire for the political agenda of saving the animals, and desire to protect the early childhood self that animals represent, thinly veiling the girls' desire to create a world in which girls are safe and free to be themselves, free from "nasty" and "evil" human beings. Animals stand for the girls' desire to just be—to just be a happy, material being without social accoutrements or "judgments," to be selves that society just understands and will not judge.

Love of animals substitutes for fantasizing about having children, yet falls into its rhetoric: the ethic of care and emotion. Fifteen-year-old Ginger wishes to be a puppy and romanticizes youth as "puppy playtime," describing animal fantasy as a quest for both regression and progression in a traditional feminine plot:

> I just remember all the good times, I just remember when I was three. We used to, when we got [the dog] we used to hold her and she felt all chubby. I remember that. Always [I have a calendar] with puppies. They're my favorite animal. They're cute. Maybe when I'm older and have kids, [I'll get another]. [I imagine] puppies playing with my kids. I'd like to be a puppy because all you do is lay down all day and play. You don't have to do any work or schoolwork or anything. [If I was a puppy] I'd play with little kids. [When I grow up] I want to be a doctor and I want to have an office in my house so I could watch [my kids] grow up and I don't want to work. I want to see them grow up. I don't want to work all the time, but I want to be a doctor too.

Animals and children become synonymous in the girls' rhetoric, and animals are often thought to protect children. Ginger imagines that animals and children can both play and "just be." Animals invoke a maternal pastoral at the same time as they invoke the girls' desires for their own youth, perceived as less complex. The girls use animals to double for children as "species," paralleling cultural ideologies, but want to mother animals to actually mother themselves, the child-self within them that feels vulnerable. Although sociological critics such as Nancy Chodorow understand girls as identifying with mothers and thus reproducing the roles of mothers (*Reproduction*), my respondents identify with the maternal aspects of animals and through doing so, reproduce the symbolic value of mothering through caring for animals.

Ironically, the fantasy that displaces maternal feeling onto animals involves a self-conscious denial of motherhood as a potential role of the future. Once the girl introduces the topic of animals, which often occurs quite early in the interview, the discussion inevitably leads to the issue of children and the future:

> I like animals. I want to be a vet when I grow up. I love animals. They're really cute and they've been here forever, you know. They sometimes seem real smart, like smarter than humans sometimes. Like cats, especially, and dogs. I just want to help them out because a lot of them are sick and endangered and stuff. I know I could actually do something for the animals, well you're trying to help

the animals and you're battling humans in a way, trying to keep
them off. One thing I do know when I grow up is I don't want to
have any kids. I want to be a vet and I probably want to live like on
a huge farm and like on another continent like in Europe some-
where, or maybe in Africa or something like that. [Kids] are really
annoying and this world's already overpopulated enough. They cost
a whole lot and if your husband leaves you you're stuck with this
huge responsibility. I don't want to have that. I don't really care to
have kids. [Animals] are a lot better. They don't cost as much
either. (Thirteen-year-old Jessica)

In Jessica's view, animals symbolize something deeper than human society—
some alternative knowledges and nobilities. Her vision of the animal as symbolizing a wise pastoral society—an "other land"—is linked with a reality
of contemporary female oppression, the understanding that the ethic of care,
in human society, occupies women's time and resources. This understanding
that material conditions create power imbalances and oppression, however,
translates into her creation of an "other land" in which she could battle the
powers that be and save those who suffer. Animals bear all the feelings girls
have toward "female" as *species*—what is unique about girls and women,
and what makes them vulnerable. But animals also bear the ways in which
girls evince a Romantic ideal of children. Pretending to be animals bridges
two important impulses: the desire to stay young and the desire to have power,
incompatible fantasies given dominant constructions of childhood. Like
Honey, nine-year-old Rose, for example, pretends to be her pets because "you
can't get hurt as easily. You have all that fur to protect you and you won't
get scraped." I have already noted that Ann identifies with deer to imagine
she can transcend a menstruating body, which she says disgusts her and makes
her feel "sick as a dog."

   Animals represent bodies that are less vulnerable than the bodies of
humans, a theme directly contradictory to the girls' impulse to want to save
the animals, which are viewed as "sick" or "endangered" and threatened by
humans. Thus the animals bridge yet embody contradictions in how the girls
feel about themselves as inhabitants of female bodies and desire to feel about
themselves—strong protectors.[10] This ideal of being protector rather than in
need of protection is linked to a feeling of ambivalence toward the role of
mother, a role of a person who protects children yet who occupies vulnerable status in culture. Rose, for example, connects her animal pretend to her
fantasies of babysitting when she gets older, choosing the image of babysitter
as an alternative to mother. Eight-year-old Honey tells me that all her stuffed
animals are girls, because she prohibits "breeding." Sixteen-year-old Shereen
voices the idea that with children she could just be herself, separating love of

children from the enterprise of mothering and thus equating love of children with self-essence:

> I have a lot of friends that try to change for different friends or boys. I've lost a couple friends because they were trying to change, and it bothers me. They're not being really who they are. I know who they are and it's not how they're being. I like children because they're so innocent. They're honest. You can always be honest with a little kid.

The ideology of childhood as innocent and without guile results in fantasies of being "with children" to truly be oneself and avoid heterosexual focus. Twelve-year-old Margaret feels that the image of a cat expresses the mood of being a girl, because "the cat's part of her"; fourteen-year-old Kristen answers my question, "What makes you *you*?" by saying, "My animals . . . I like animals, never be cruel to animals and stuff." Thus expression of kindness to animals is also an expression of resistance to growth.

Animal identification is a denial of womanhood but not maternity, a denial of childhood but not the authentic self the girls locate within childhood, and a denial of gender as a category but not the abstract interconnectedness of the ecological social movement, typically fraught with feminine metaphor. Pretending to be animals invites girls to play out violent narrative fantasies yet maintain a feminine, maternal sense of ultimate social good, of caring for animals as a kind of children—particularly the child-self within themselves. Animals fundamentally stand for an embrace of, and longing for, a presence "within" the material body, distinct from the ways girls do not express enthusiasm for their own bodies. They mostly define their bodies as a "pain" or inconvenience.

TRANSCENDENCE OF HUMAN FORM

Fifteen-year-old Ellie illustrates the fact that animal pretend represents an ideal of transcendence from the female body, speaking of her fascination with the movement of the actors in Broadway's *Cats*, adapted from T. S. Eliot's *Old Possom's Book of Practical Cats*:

> The cats of *Cats* didn't speak to get their emotions across, they moved to get their emotions across. And that shows, you know, there's different ways than just screaming and yelling about it or whatever. The dancing and the running just kind of free my mind of everything. I mean I dance; it's almost like there's nothing else in the world you'd rather be doing except for that. The actors in *Cats* move

like cats. Their reflexes and their actions and everything are so similar to something you'd see in an animal, that it's just kind of fascinating. [Pretending to be an animal] really makes you reach inside and pull out explanations that you never thought you'd think of.

And that's kind of what you do with the whole animal thing. In New York, the whole theater's turned into a junkyard. I turned around and there was just this big box because you're transformed down to the size of the cat and how the cat sees everything. And you're kind of brought into the show. [Pretending to be a cat is] kind of like expanding your limits, what you think you're able to do and this is kind of like pushing it a step further than you'd ever thought you'd go. The emotion [you'd express playing a cat] is kind of the same—in the acting like a human and acting like an animal. I don't know if it's necessarily a different kind of form of emotion that you get to express but it's still like the cats are acting almost like people. It's just how deep the emotion is, and how you have to express it, how it comes out.

[In usual life] I feel better when other people tell me their problems. I love to sit there and listen. I will sit there for hours on end and listen to people complain or cry or really share in detail how they're feeling. I can really think of some way to get them to be happy again or get them to forget it and that makes me feel better. But I don't like telling people my problems because I figure if they have problems they don't want to hear mine, [whereas if I'm pretending to be something else, like an animal,] it's a different way of talking to people, if you're in a character. It's a different way of expressing how you feel and who you are and stuff.

Ellie emphasizes complete embodiment of the animal—to move like cats do, shed the limits of the human body, pursue identification to its limits, and thereby creative narrative space to imagine a different point of view (scale, in *Cats*'s theatrical space), heighten emotional intensity of experience, and express through dance and movement what she cannot express in her real life. Many girls voice the value of receptive listening to others, defining themselves through social role. But in pretending to be an animal, as Ellie articulates, girls reach inside themselves and expand the limits of their social role by imagining qualities desired in another species. Ellie stresses voice rather than ear, and depth of emotion through embodiment, rather than transcendence of self through becoming the impersonal "watcher" of the text. Animal pretend is a "way of expressing who you are," reflecting a direct discourse of identity. This identity is not the same as the girl's human identity, but it is another way of exploring and expanding the self. Animal pretend thus shares the same impulse as appreciation for literary experience: expansion and recognition of everyday boundaries.

Coda: Tapping Girls' Responses to Reading

THE GIRLS in this study feel that the capacity to imagine is inherently empowering and that the aesthetic act of reading enables imagination throughout life. Attention to form provides them with a way to appreciate literature and a means by which to both connect reading fiction to experiencing film and separate their identity issues in life from their appreciation of fiction.

Adults are often trapped by the ways we see pieces of literature; from our vantage point, a literary text may be valuable to us in a very different way from how it becomes valuable to a child. A personal story demonstrates this. My own daughter recently suffered from fears of the dark, and I, literal grown-up that I am, decorated her bed with powerful female characters, including the level-headed Dora and the superhero PowerPuffs. She enjoys both television shows, so wouldn't these help? Not in the least. Her brilliant preschool teacher finally read to her *Franklin in the Dark* (Bourgeois), which became her companion each night. She preferred to externalize her issues into a turtle hero, who is as frightened of the world as she. I thought, "Of course!" And the moral of "Beauty in the Beast" may be not only that gender dynamics inform the tale, but also that the beast is the part of the female self that needs to be integrated by the narrative structure of metamorphosis.

Form is a site of both familiarity and challenge, with potential for a great variety of discussions in the classroom and beyond. I remember how challenging it was to read epistolary style in ninth grade, when I first read *Dracula* (Stoker). Reading *Dracula*, I was greatly assisted by a syllabus that was organized by a familiar theme, literary and mythic monsters that challenge their creators. Comparing forms and keeping themes constant make innovative form visible and meaningful. Further, I believe that we need to seriously consider these girls' interests in intensely dramatic fiction. We cannot shy away from literature with graphic, violent, and sensual elements (see also Power, Wilhelm, and Chandler for teaching Stephen King); they hold the intensity of narrative power and desire, which children first learn to appreciate in fairy tales, animation, and oral children's culture, this last a very violent form that also demonstrates young children's ability to appreciate and adapt form in rhyme, song, and chant. They then turn to film for its storytelling power.

Epic, quest, suspense, myth, mystery, legend, tragedy, and melodrama capture larger-than-life experiences that leave the mundane world far behind. Rather than insist that children appreciate realistic literature, we can assist them with making formal connections between verisimilar literature and the more dramatic forms they find pleasurable. The responses of these girls suggest that teachers who are committed to a feminist and multicultural canon could capture their interest by including on their reading lists women's and minority novels with fantastic elements, mythic worlds, and epic structures. In a recent interview with a thirteen-year-old girl on another project, I had barely begun asking questions when I was given an enthusiastic account of her reading *The Mists of Avalon* (Bradley) for her language arts class. On the whole, I have found it rare for children to gush about their English classes, even when they define themselves as readers. More commonly, I find that teen girls happen upon something they love, such as *The Red Tent*, and recommend the books to one another without expecting school to engage them or share their appreciation for experiencing alternative worlds. While the girl mentioned above relished books by Tamora Pierce as well as those by Marion Zimmer Bradley, most of the girls I interviewed were unfamiliar with popular female fantasy writings. The contemporary young adult literature scene beckons them with the work of Francesca Lia Block, Gail Carson Levine, Karen Cushman, Theresa Tomlinson, and Monica Furlong, authors that could be recommended to girls and invited into the classroom. However, there are also ample opportunities to link their appreciation of contemporary literature and film with classics.

Because these girls have altered my understanding of why literature matters to them, and because I teach undergraduates in teacher-preparation programs, I would like to reflect on ways to enhance the readings the girls already do and comment on how I have shifted my own teaching practices to focus on form and adaptation. I am continually making form visible to my students in the hopes that they will bring this lens into their language arts classrooms. I wholeheartedly agree with Jon Stott, Denise Nessel, Bette Bosma, and Anita McClain, who argue that the formal features and patterns of fairy tales, myths, fables, and legends give children a "grammar" of literary construction through which to appreciate literature and make comparisons between increasingly complex types of texts (Pugh). The applicability of this grammar to study of film makes it particularly relevant to contemporary literary study. However, this coda is particularly geared toward retaining the interest of teens in literature because teen girls are most likely to tell me that their English classes are composed of historical approaches and that they are not encouraged to make formal connections and thus expand their knowledge of literary grammar. Teen girls are far less engaged in their language arts curriculum than are younger girls.

COMPARING FORM ACROSS GENRES

Many of the girls strictly divide generic literature (fantasy, mystery, adventure, and "chick lit," they say) from "all the other" literature. For them, literature "that could happen" is the "serious" literature that occupies the bookstore section simply labeled "literature." They shy away from this category because its primary purpose is to "teach lessons" or "communicate a message." However, they feel that they are "supposed" to read "real literature" as they grow older. As I demonstrated in Chapter 5, they struggle to forge connections between realistic texts and the literary structures that inform them, such as adventure quest, mystery, myth, folktale and fairy tale, tragedy, elegy, and comedy. For example, Kristen's and Ann's application to literature of forms they understand, such as in *Killing Mr. Griffin* and *Sybil*, enables them to unpack the actions and plots, thus feeling in the presence of a structured and "captivating" universe. Actions and narrative situations are often related to traditional forms, while realist texts use particular narrative strategies to create and explore character motivations, social dialogue, and, often, the narration of consciousness and feeling. These strategies become more visible once different formal approaches are applied to verisimilar texts, which can allow meditation on profound human themes.

To get my own undergraduates to understand form and help them work with teens to make connections between literature and the action adventure genre they so appreciate, I have them study the roots of Romance and its permutation into Western, Gothic horror, fantasy, science fiction, and action adventure film. I ask them to encourage teens to draw connections between many different forms of fantasy, comparing the various storytelling forms that utilize fantastic elements or create enchanted shadows for particular effects. My students love to connect the high Romance form of American male authors with action adventure films, discussing the subordination of character to action and world, even democratic epic. This actually allows them to investigate how American folk roots depend upon racial and gender archetypes that then repeatedly appear in literature and film. One of my classes read *Huckleberry Finn* and presented the White-"racial other" fraternal relationships in *The Last of the Mohicans* (Cooper), *Moby-Dick* (Melville), *The Narrative of Arthur Gorden Pym* (Poe), and various action adventure films, including films that substitute a woman or cyborg for the "other." In a delightful twist, the alien and cyborg have become both American Adams and machines in the garden, as analyzed by Leo Marx, which helps them understand the theme of *The Iron Giant* and *Terminator* in the context of literary history. For example, the scene in which the child asserts authority over the cyborg-terminator in *Terminator 2—Judgment Day* parallels a scene in *Huck* but demonstrates a shift in the White man's frontier. Two of my students presented this Black-White structure in *Field of Dreams* and *The Legend of Bagger Vance*, both of which feature Black male characters who "enable" the White man's dreams and then, like the Native American in *The Last of the Mohicans*, conveniently disappear into the sunset. Formal comparisons allow amazing connections between Dante and a film such as *Terminator 2*, or *Oedipus Rex* (Sophocles), *Hamlet* (Shakespeare), and *The Lion King*, the deep structures that make literature matter to today's multimedia youth. I believe structural connections to be a highly sophisticated form of thinking among youth, one that could stimulate even greater appreciation for our cultural heritage of storytelling.

I recommend Nick Lacey's book *Narrative and Genre* as a source for learning about specific comparisons between narrative structures and genres of film and literature. He compares everything from romance to Westerns to science fiction to melodrama. He is also useful for teachers who wish to employ analysis of deep structure in the classroom. A teacher can use Tzvetan Todorov's theory of narrative structure, Vladimir Propp's analysis of the narrative functions of characters, or Claude Lévi-Strauss's analysis of binary opposites in myths, to apply to all kinds of texts (23–71). Sometimes a text seems to present a powerful female or minority character but it actually puts that character in the formal position of victim or enabler, according to the deep structure (53–54).

In discussion, teachers and discussion leaders can assist readers with understanding how writers and filmmakers themselves speak of their genres, along with the conservative nature of form in media that have more commercial interests. There are also many wonderful works that use magical elements in new ways, such as Laura Esquivel's *Like Water for Chocolate*, both novel and film, which features the theme of frustrated desire, endemic to adolescent and young adult novels. Magic realism allows "the real" and "the unreal" to coexist on the same plane. Many contemporary women writers develop new points of view on fantasy, legend, myth, Secondary Worlds, and longings for quest. There is a place in the classroom for feminist re-visions of everything from detective fiction to fantasy series. In-depth study of the corpus of a single author who employs a variety of forms helps readers investigate both genre and theme. For example, Margaret Atwood utilizes Gothic mystery, fairy tale, parable/fable, metamorphosis, fantasy, realism (various narrative strategies), and dystopia to refocus points of view and ask different questions about the female condition (*The Handmaid's Tale*, *Alias Grace*, *The Blind Assassin*, *Surfacing*, *Lady Oracle*, *The Edible Woman*, *Cat's Eye*, *Bluebeard's Egg*, *The Robber Bride*).

EXPLORING NARRATIVE STRATEGIES

Texts that people take to be a record of an event often rely upon older structures of meaning just as much as they do on forms that are perceived to be more formulaic. For example, when my students study racial archetypes that inform courtroom mystery drama, such as in the books *Puddn'head Wilson* (Twain), *To Kill a Mockingbird* (Lee), and *Their Eyes Were Watching God* (Hurston) and in films such as *A Time to Kill* and *Amistad*, the students collaborate to write a trial in which Black lawyers try White "criminals," investigating the intersection of form and race in inherently dramatic plots involving such acts as rape and murder. My students love to apply the narrative situations of "Little Red Riding Hood," "Cinderella," and the Perspephone myth to mother-daughter structures in coming-of-age literature. It allows them to perceive, for example, the vilification of mothers and look closely at how characters in realistic literature are given psychological complexity rather than simple motivation or "good/evil" status. It allows them to appreciate how form determines perspective in Jamaica Kincaid's *Annie John*: "When [my mother] laughed, her mouth opened to show off big, shiny, sharp white teeth. It was as if my mother had suddenly turned into a crocodile" (84). The deployment of this perspective on the mother epitomizes the metamorphosis of the adolescent girl, but it also demonstrates that fairy tales have mature themes even if they have simple forms. Their coming of age content makes them well worth revisiting in the teen years.

Study of something like the Pygmalion myth allows in-depth appreciation for the structure of metamorphosis informing Genesis, *Pinocchio* (Collodi), *The Velveteen Rabbit* (Williams), *The Sand Man* (Hoffmann), *Frankenstein* (Shelley), Hawthorne's short stories ("Drowne's Wooden Image," "The Birthmark," "Rappaccini's Daughter"), *Pygmalion* (Shaw), *My Fair Lady*, *The Taming of the Shrew* (Shakespeare), *Kiss Me, Kate*, and other films such as *Weird Science*, *The Rocky Horror Picture Show*, *Ten Things I Hate about You*, *Mannequin*, and *She's All That*. Different versions approach the desires of the characters and strategies of metamorphosis in different ways; the students can compare the strategies of magic with the ways in which various realistic texts build up the complexities and consequences of creating life. I asked my students to imagine women creating the perfect man and received many stories of female scientists and cooks who bring machines and soups to life, but it also made them think about modern films in which women realistically attempt to "change" a man and usually cannot (such as *Heartburn*).

In their writing, teens can take folktale, myth, and fairy tale structures and make them more verisimilar, learning the way in which dialogue, the narration of thoughts and emotions, and "showing" versus "telling" actions can be manipulated. The teen girls in this study appreciate *Ever After* for its versimilitude, but they could also read adult fiction in which women writers grapple with the lasting legacy of fairy tales. For instance, Angela Carter's *The Bloody Chamber* and *The Company of Wolves*, the poems in Anne Sexton's *Transformations*, and Joyce Carol Oates's *Black Water* can all be read as exploration of the consequences of the Cinderella story (the theme "If you await your prince, you'll be left drowning, with nothing but a shoe"). They could also read the ironic *Who Will Run the Frog Hospital?* by Lorrie Moore.

It should be obvious to my readers that I do not believe in a separation between adolescent and adult fiction. Just as electronic media cannot differentiate between child and adult audiences—and thus, Niel Postman asserts, the concept of childhood is disappearing before our eyes—I do not see merit in withholding certain subjects in literature. Why it is that children can see anything of horror on television or in film, but that educators and parents should wish to censor the same subjects in books, is quite beyond me. Literature allows sustained reflection on the forms and expressions of human experiences that is simply not possible in viewing a succession of three-second frames.

Readers in the classroom benefit from comparing narration strategies such as omniscient with limited point of view, and engaging with dissonant first-person and epistolary. In a recent group interview that I conducted, I found that once I asked the right questions, the group of sixteen- to eighteen-year-olds was able to analyze the different effects of presenting a story as a memory, as in *A Separate Peace* (Knowles); using dissonant narration in *To Kill a Mockingbird* (Lee); encountering engaging and immediate telling in both *The Bluest Eye* (Morrison) and two films (*Ferris Bueller's Day Off* and *High Fidelity*); hearing a character who is also the subject of irony in *Huck Finn*; and experiencing epistolary form in *Are You There God? It's Me, Margaret* (Blume) and *The Color Purple* (Walker). They had never studied first-person strategies and found it fun. The group thought that *The Red Tent* used an engaging narrator but featured some moments of dissonance and even epistolary-style immediacy of action and emotion, which they elaborated fairly well ("This feels like a close friend telling me a story," or "This feels like an old person remembering something that happened a long time ago," "This is like when my brother tries to be funny and make people laugh," etc.).

Literature uses first-person narration and the representation of consciousness more effectively than does film, but it is noteworthy how much the girls in this study prefer omniscient narration. Even Ann, a proficient reader, ignores the actual psychologist storyteller's point of view in *Sybil*. Equating omniscience with power and first-person consciousness with "just normalcy," these girls might develop more appreciation for the multiplicity of effects

achieved by first-person narration if they had some formal training. Literature with multiple narrators, such as Julia Alvarez's *How the Garcia Girls
Lost Their Accents* or *In the Time of the Butterflies* and Alice Childress's
Rainbow Jordan, can be discussed along with films that experiment with
multiple points of view, such as *Drowning Mona, Courage under Fire*, and
Basic, and both literary and film texts that experiment with representing
memory, such as *Beloved* (Morrison). Strategies of representing memory in
both literature and film could be connected. Exercises that call attention to
narrative strategy, such as rewriting passages in different verb tenses and from
different vantage points, or changing a scene to dialogue (adapting to a screenplay or play) help develop an understanding of the representation of subjectivity, so crucial to many twentieth-century novels and to humanist study.

INVESTIGATING POINTS OF VIEW

Fiction that has been adapted or retold in a variety of forms draws attention
to the different points of view that can be given to a story. People are drawn
to films, the girls say, because they want to compare their vision of a story
with "someone else's interpretation." They notice how adapted texts shift
focus:

> This one [the *Jekyll and Hyde* musical] isn't focused on Dr. Jekyll and
> Mr. Hyde. It focuses on him *and* people around him. Like the lives he
> affects. I like that. I like that version better than the original version,
> because the original version is really gory and all that stuff and I
> don't really care for that. There's also a lot about love and stuff and
> the fact that he dies in the end. I don't remember if it's at his wedding
> or not but that kind of makes you really think about, you know,
> almost how short life is, you know? It's just the whole. Something
> about it really clicks with me. (Fifteen-year-old Ruth)

The aesthetic stance allows appreciation for a great variety of stories and
forms. Just as Shereen imagines alternatives, rewritings, and authorial de-
signs in *Black Girl Lost*, girls can imagine and seek out two or more differ-
ent versions of a story. Some interesting pairings might be Margaret Mitchell's
Gone with the Wind and Alice Randall's *The Wind Done Gone*; Kenneth
Grahame's *The Wind in the Willows* and Jan Needle's *Wild Wood*; *Beowulf*
(Heaney) and John Champlin Gardner's *Grendel*; or Herman Melville's
Moby-Dick, or The Whale, and Sena Jeter Naslund's *Ahab's Wife; Or, The
Star-Gazer*. Anita Diamant's *The Red Tent* is a current favorite among
sixteen- to eighteen-year-olds whom I recently interviewed because it imagines

the story of Jacob from the perspective of his daughter Dinah, opening up a new vision on a familiar story. Beautifully written, complicated, feminist, and with multifaceted appeal, this particular book straddles the worlds of women and teen girl readers. As such, it exemplifies a profound engagement with form, theme, and subject.

CONCLUSION: ENCOURAGING THE AESTHETIC STANCE

These girls show a fascinating plasticity in moving between the forms of storytelling they appreciate and the ways they adapt form into their imaginations, using storytelling conventions to make connections across texts, create their own utopias, imagine themselves as powerful animals, and scare themselves as a way to aestheticize and send away fears. They experience intense pleasure and intellectual development at the very same time. I believe that an understanding of the aesthetic stance and how aesthetic actions bring creator and reader together could change the focus of discussion and enhance the appreciation of young readers for the powerful fantasies and timeless themes that inspire authors and, quite often, filmmakers.

The aesthetic stance allows appreciation of worlds that are not consonant with the personal values of the reader. This gap between who one is and what one can "see" demonstrates, for me, a kind of thinking that goes beyond things as they are. It is this kind of thinking that supports appreciation of difference itself. It is this kind of thinking that has the potential to develop respect for others and their points of view. Fictional literature is uniquely suited to bridge the issues of a *specific* community represented in a story and the forms and themes that literature gives to human experience. I emerge from this study fascinated by the possibility that we can present multicultural women's literature in a more aesthetic fashion, through which *all* readers can learn to appreciate alternative points of view and different worlds, both the literary world itself and the shifting points of view that texts encourage readers to take.

Interviews as Texts:
A Methodological Discussion

IN THIS APPENDIX, I place my methodology in the context of trends in qualitative research, demonstrating how my research design takes advantage of
the innovations that occurred in social science throughout the 1980s and
1990s and blends methodologies from the fields of anthropology, sociology,
psychology, and literary criticism.

THE CONVERGENCE OF LITERARY AND NONLITERARY TEXTS

Cynthia Lightfoot's chapter "The Interpretive Turn" in her book *The Culture of Adolescent Risk-Taking* best expresses the influence of literary concepts such as interpretation on current thought in social science:

> The thesis that our interpretations express and constitute who we are and what
> we know has been broadcast within philosophy, psychology, anthropology,
> sociology, political science—within virtually every discipline that concerns itself
> with the organization of human activity and social praxis. This multidisciplinary
> "interpretive turn" has been taken from the well-traveled road of *hermeneutics*,
> a paradigm associated historically with the exegesis of literary, especially reli-
> gious, documents. In allegiance to this tradition, human interaction and culture
> are construed as readable *text*. . . . This basic notion has been articulated to in-
> clude three basic assumptions: (1) that texts and their congeners—narrative,
> autobiography, voice—impose coherence on reality rather than correspond to it
> directly (they are inventive); (2) that writing a text is an inherently social, dia-
> logical, or semiotic affair; and (3) that texts are constructed and reconstructed
> in and over time, and carry their histories forward through time. This consti-
> tutes the triumvirate of modern interpretive theory. (38–39)

Many social scientists have turned their attention to how people represent themselves in language and narrative (Briggs; Mishler; Seidman; Kvale),
viewing language and stories as culturally situated and socially produced

texts, just as literary critics have increasingly done as a result of the influence of theorists such as Bakhtin, Jameson, Barthes, and Lacan, who have articulated models for viewing language and literature as social consciousness. Although social scientists study oral or unpublished texts and English scholars study published texts, both social science and humanities scholars agree that language shapes self-understanding and that language is cultural. Thus there is neither truth outside of language nor an objectifible, empirical reality beyond "the narratable," a philosophy that has profound implications for the status of interviewing as a tool to understand human processes. For one thing, we can understand interviews as a dialogic construction of text in a "purposefully situated" (Douglas 22) interview rather than believe that there are objective measures of a language-based experience such as reading.

THE INTERVIEWS IN THIS BOOK

The narrations of story-meaning I have presented and interpreted are self-consciously coconstructed narratives between interviewer and interviewees. No study can really measure the reading experience itself, just as no one can report on the experience of a dream and be dreaming at the same time. The girls' stories of reading and seeing texts are products of self-reflection in the interview situation, layered upon meanings that they have refined over time and that are subject to the usual conditions of memory and narrated history. Even if readers were queried *as* they were actually reading, the questioning would disrupt the experience and nothing would be gained. The girls' words were taken as a kind of textual evidence, with the assumption that "every word . . . is a microcosm of [a person's] consciousness" (Seidman 1).

QUESTIONS OF VALIDITY

The purpose of qualitative interviewing is to describe and specify people's life worlds, giving vivid accounts of a complex phenomenon such as reading and viewing stories. Although in my project I caution critics who make assertions about readers in history or from published texts without looking for evidence of reader response, the value of qualitative research lies not in generalizability (Seidman 45), but in its ability to raise theoretical questions (Coffrey and Atkinson 156), which is what I have tried to do here.

The validity of an interviewing project stems from consistency across individual cases (Rubin and Rubin 90) and its ability to uncover depth, detail, vividness, and nuance (76). Unlike other theorists, Herbert and Irene

Rubin believe that qualitative research can be generalizable, depending on its completeness and its applicability to different geographical locations. They recommend that for completeness, researchers add more interviews until they are satisfied that they understand a complex cultural process and feel that they have reached "saturation point" (72), called "saturation of information" by Seidman (48), the point at which the researcher is hearing the same patterns repeat and learning little new information. In qualitative research, there is generally a trade-off between depth and sample size. Researchers are hesitant to name a specific number for an ideal project, but Douglas says that if he had to give a number he would say twenty-five. Kvale says that interview projects typically include fifteen people, plus or minus ten. Rubin and Rubin recommend that the researcher test the sample's generalizability by conducting interviews in a different site, which is why I interviewed girls in two different geographical locations, California and New Jersey.

THE SELECTION OF INTERVIEWEES

I made every effort to interview as diverse a sample as possible. Speaking to a total of thirty-three girls, I spoke to eighteen girls in the Bay Area and fifteen in the Philadelphia area, from a wide range of communities. I visited homes in urban Oakland and suburban Walnut Creek, the poorer communities of Richmond and wealthier communities of Orinda. I visited girls in South Jersey tract homes, in the dilapidated neighborhoods of Pennsauken, in suburban Cherry Hill, and in country homes in Tabernacle. Roughly half the girls felt a particular racial or ethnic identity to be part of self-understanding, and roughly half the girls did not. Of the former, the sample included African American readers, Irish American readers, Eastern European American readers, an Asian American reader, an Hispanic reader, a Swedish American (second generation) reader, and an Italian American reader. Of those who did not self-identify as anything other than White, I encountered a mix of more subtle cultural and religious heritages, such as Jewish, Mormon, Christian fundamentalist (two who were also home-schooled), and Catholic. Income levels varied, but income levels of the California and New Jersey residents did not reflect the same living circumstances. Only a few of the girls were avid readers.

THE QUESTIONS

I used primarily open-ended questions, but I also combined unstructured, semistructured, and structured questions. The questions could be described as searching ones (Mishler 97, citing Paget), the style of which come from my years of assisting social scientist Cindy Clark in her qualitative-research firm. My understanding of what the girls told me largely depended upon follow-up and probing questions (see Rubin and Rubin for descriptions of different kinds), restatements, and pauses or acknowledgments. I followed the flow of the girls' spontaneously presented issues rather than my discussion guide, often taking notes on issues to pursue later in the interview. The order of my major topics, however, remained the same in each interview:

1. girls' own self-understanding
2. stories that matter and produce self-understanding
3. questions about girlhood, womanhood, and the female body

I wanted to get a sense of the girls' personal identity themes before learning which stories mattered and why.

My discussion guide reveals the influence of Merton, Fiske, and Kendall's *The Focused Interview*, which involves continually refocusing respondents on a specific stimulus that they have all experienced—in my case, the story of each girl's life and the stories that matter to her. Merton recommends that questions refer to the process of retrospection and to the specific stimulus: for example, "Thinking back to reading that story, what were you imagining while you were reading it?" Although an interview cannot capture the actual experience of reading a story as it occurs in time, I sought to have the girl imagine how she had experienced a story. For example, I might say, "I want to imagine that I'm you, reading that story. Am I feeling what Martin is? Am I imagining what Martin imagines? Or not?" or "I've never read *Harry Potter*. I know nothing about *Harry Potter*. Tell me that story. What's good about that story? Why does that story matter?" I often had the girl pretend to be reading or seeing a story and asked her to tell me her thoughts during the process. The focused interview strives for a range of affective responses, depth, specificity, and personal context.

Treating the interviewee as a cocreator and seeking to check my evolving theories about their readings (Briggs 108–9, Rubin and Rubin 154), I would often ask deliberately leading questions to see if I was correctly understanding them, or even to point out contradictions in their experiences of texts. For example, I might say, "You said that when reading the Mary Kate and Ashley Olsen mystery story, you're going around looking for clues. But isn't the detective going around looking for clues? So aren't you like the detective? Why not?" Or I'd point out a contradiction and ask the girl to explain: for example, "I don't understand something. When you're watching the news, you're imagining what would happen if that story happened to you. But when you're reading that mystery novel, you're not imagining what would happen if that story happened to you. Why not?" Or I would point out discrepancies between life and literary narratives and ask the girl to explain the discrepancies: "You said that you like to play dolls because you like to make up conversations for them. But you said that you don't play stories that you have read. Couldn't you make up conversations for your dolls from stories that you've read? Why wouldn't you do that? Why wouldn't *The Fairy Rebel* [Banks] be a good story for your dolls to pretend? What might be a good story for you to make up for your dolls? Let's pretend one."

A useful technique recommended by Merton, Fiske, and Kendall is to ask the interviewee to parallel an experience by comparing one experience to another. For example, I would ask a girl to tell me of an experience that felt the same as when she was reading *The Godfather* (Puzo). If a particular girl told me early in the interview that she liked certain activities, I would ask if seeing/reading her favorite story was at all like an activity: "You said that you like going out on a raft in the ocean with your cousin because you like the feeling of floating; is reading *Amelia's Notebooks* (Moss) more like the feeling of being on a raft in the ocean or like going to your cousin's wedding? Why is it more like going to a wedding?" Asking respondents to compare or contrast a parallel experience is particularly useful in interviewing children, because discussions of affective and emotional experience are easier when they involve specific, concrete circumstances.

Interviews with children as research subjects look a bit different from interviews with adults, as Clark discusses of her interviews with children on the subject of imaginal figures: "There was great variation from child to child in the kinds of discourse strategies that worked best to draw out and explore the child's world. But there was a clear and distinct difference between the conduct of adult interviews, via question and answer, and the conduct of child interviews, which were filled with role-playing, picture drawing, prop use, and other gamelike strategies for communication" (121). Some girls could "take off" after being asked one question, and some needed constant probing to determine why a particular story was meaningful. With younger girls, I often played dolls, games, and pretend to further understand the girls' experience of a story. As Briggs stresses, the norms of the interview situation are not always shared, and the research has to adapt to "native metacommunication" (46); though several girls were comfortable with the intimate girl talk of the interview situation, many were not.

While I stressed to the girls the fact that they were "teaching me today" and that "there are no right and wrong answers as there often are at school," a prefatory method taught to me by Clark, I also remained conscious of the role they ascribed to me as an adult. The issue is particularly problematic if interviews are conducted in an educational setting, so I chose to interview the girls in the privacy of their bedrooms, the access to which I was given because I was perceived as an unthreatening young woman. As Briggs and Foddy point out, the interviewee is always anticipating what the researcher is looking for, a challenge that I met with many vocal reminders of how "only you know the answer to this." Many girls thought I was a writer for children, although I was up-front about who I was and told them that my purpose was to understand what stories matter to them and why. None of the girls seemed to group me with English teachers, for they were quick to critique the practices of English teachers (I did not remind them that I was, in fact, in an English department). Many of the girls seemed more interested in the fact that I was a new mother than in my profession; I used my pager to time the interviews and I always explained that I had a pager so that the babysitter could reach me if there was any problem, since I had a very little infant who was newly left in someone else's care. With the older girls, it was quite clear that I had taken on a big-sister role; although I had mentioned my age and the fact that "I haven't been your age in a while," the girls often remembered my age incorrectly by the end of the interview and thought I was just slightly older than they.

At the end of every interview I asked the girls to sort a pile of pictures and match them to "the mood of being a girl" and "the mood of being a woman." Many of the girls insisted on a middle pile that they defined as a teen girl or as both girl and woman. Although few of the girls showed an interest in literary themes of femininity and struggle for self, the eleven- to sixteen-year-old girls certainly demonstrated a struggle for self when they discussed their narrations of themselves in a social context. Traditional struggles against heterosexual social roles, however, were curiously absent. The girls imagined womanhood in the context of a career and independent living; ironically, they were resistant to growing up, because growing up meant being out of relationships and "on your own," representing quite a different future from that of being a wife or mother (though these are the roles they played with their dolls). Many girls pictured living with roommates and girlfriends as a consolation for growing into adulthood, and some hazily pictured a family life "maybe sometime in my thirties or forties," after securing a professional life. The picture sort made it clear that the girls equated girlhood with freedom and womanhood with constriction, but not because of social roles under patriarchy. Rather, constriction stemmed from the responsibilities that come with independence—and the stark vision of being alone, explaining the fact that growing up is not an appealing subject. Since the narratives of the girls' lives revolve around relationships and the novel of manners, adult independence was the point beyond which the story could not go.

ANALYZING THE TRANSCRIPTS

Analysis and data gathering are inseparable, argue Coffey and Atkinson, as do Glesne and Peshkin. Organizing and coding the transcripts are inherently processes of conceptualization (Coffey and Atkinson 31). Analysis of transcripts has to involve as much attention to the interviewing self as it does to the interview responses, a point that Taylor, Gilligan, and Sullivan make when they discuss their listening guide in *Between Voice and Silence*. My early efforts to code the data by clustering passages in themes often failed and I had to start again, at least fifteen times. I often coded the responses by putting passages in more than one cluster; for example, I put all the responses to horror texts together, but would often find that a passage on response to horror should also be categorized under a topic on narrative theory—for example, "the reader as transcendent viewer" or "the reader as genre decoder." I would cluster a passage describing fear of violence under both "themes about growing up" and "desire for literary utopia." Categorizing responses in multiple categories, I was left with numerous contradictions and pluralities. I thought, for about a year, that the contradictions I had found between life narratives and responses to literature meant that I had a meaningless project.

My first sensible organization of the data involved separating responses by "genre responded to" and the argument that generic forms give shape to fears and allow girls to work out the immense fears they have; this was essentially an argument about catharsis. The predominance of fear in my respondents had to do with an imbalance of power in a patriarchal culture and a sociological reality: the Columbine shooting had recently occurred and was foremost in their minds. The Columbine shooting was and will remain a defining moment for the generation studied here, changing the meaning of being a child. And, even as I write this, September 11 has forever changed the meaning of being an American child, so I suspect that youth will continue to seek ways in which to empower themselves through fantasy. It is lucky for all of us that *Harry Potter* burst on the scene of children's literature to revitalize fantasy, a form that helps children cope with violence, imagine other worlds, and structure or plot fear (the comic aspect also fulfills these goals, in different ways). The problem with a catharsis argument is that literature is only an escape rather than a social force, because catharsis leaves the audience emotionally cathected—and nothing changes in the real world. It was not until the actual writing of this project that I realized that genre was not the only organizing principle of response, but a manifestation of the larger issue of form as both organizing principle of response and motivation for story experience; form allows texts to have action in the world by developing the girls' imaginations.

The ways in which I categorized, analyzed, and recategorized the interviews to produce the argument of this book are, ultimately, the very same that I use to analyze passages of literature, except that I edited the words of the girls for ease of reading (editing many fillers and sentences that would not make sense to my reader). When the subject of a study is people's voices rather than published texts, the contradictions and slipperiness of the texts are heightened, but the method of close reading applies to the narrative analysis of people's voices just as it does to literary texts. Just as Gilligan pioneered an understanding of girls by showing how their responses refused to answer Kohlberg's research questions in the ways that the questions laid out moral issues, I too found that the reader responses here refused and critiqued my questions and, by doing so, raised issues about all kinds of assertions that literary critics make when they interrogate the meaning of texts based upon a sample size of one—themselves. Given the decline of literariness among the general public, the implications of my research for encouraging reading seem all the more urgent. At heart, I would like to see more people—not just children—read and appreciate the ways in which fiction can explore something "felt to be real" but in a new, and perceptive, way.

Notes

1. Some examples include critics such as Vigen Guroian, who believes that children's literature teaches values; Alison Lurie, who argues that much of classic children's literature is subversive, critical of adults and their institutions; and Jack Zipes, who believes that children's literature inculcates particular ideological viewpoints.

2. Many aspects of television inform their perceptions. First, they equate television with news. News is its primary purpose and news links them to the real world, even though many of them object to that linkage and would like to escape the usually depressing news. They have no language to critique the aesthetics of television, including the news, and no sense that the artfulness of television's design can be brought to consciousness—a major fissure in media education, argues Kathleen Tyner. Second, their responses to television parallel the way in which critics believe television content to directly affect children, as if that content were real. For example, Robert Leibert's title *The Early Window: The Effects of Television on Children and Youth* demonstrates the concept that television is a window into the larger world, introducing children to more of "the real (ugly) world" than they would have seen before the "intrusion" of home television. Television participates in this illusion by creating "reality television," magazine format, talk shows, commentaries, and direct address to the viewer, mirroring an oral mode of communication, argues Nick Lacey. Canned laughter and call-ins offer the strangest illusion that the audience is not impersonal at all.

In reality television shows, such as *Candid Camera*, MTV's *The Real World*, *Survivor*, *Joe Millionaire*, *The Bachelor*, *Married by America*, *Fear Factor*, *Worst-Case Scenario*, *Cops*, and *Taxi Cab Confessions*, viewers are asked to believe that television is filming real life as it actually occurs in time, even creating narrative situations for real people—the effects of which viewers can appreciate (and be glad it's not them). In watching *The Jerry Springer Show*, we are asked to conflate fiction and life through being told that the responses of those on the talk show are spontaneous responses to situations the network has devised (such as bringing in a longlost lover). Game shows also encourage the illusion of spontaneity in the medium. In response, films such as *The Truman Show* and *Ed TV* poke fun at this equation of reality and television by exploring the effects of lives that are completely mediated by television and created for show, just as they have also begun to question how we distinguish our reality from our virtuality, in films such as *Total Recall* and *The Matrix*. The "chapter" structure of digital films demonstrates the invigorating relationship between literature and film in the popular perception, but this arts alliance is not extended to the family room's world within the tiny tube.

The girls register a cultural moment of television, which Johnson describes as the radical growth of television commentary. He sees this growth as a sign of digital age culture, in which people are bombarded with surplus information. With the advent of the digital age, Johnson argues, television has become more a metareflection on the effects of image making itself. "Television commenting on television" is a "parasite" form that thrives "at those threshold points where the signals degenerate into noise, where the datasphere becomes too wild and overwrought to navigate alone" (Johnson 28–32). Television has left the novelistic behind. In its everyday "commentating" existence, it does not pretend to take the role of literature or film in people's live—to give them substantial Secondary Worlds or fantasies.

By contrast, film *does* claim to do so; there are numerous intertexts of reading in films; two that come to mind are *Harry Potter and the Chamber of Secrets* and *Treasure Planet*. In the former, the autobiography of Tom Riddle sucks Harry Potter in as reader and gives him an unseen presence in the story within a story, as he follows the characters of history. Books have magical powers in high fantasy; in the end, Harry has to kill the book to kill the villain. *Treasure Planet* opens with a scene in the sea of space, ships battling and flying, a very large child's head looking over the story. We learn that the young child Jim is actually reading the story, which comes to life like virtual reality when he picks up the book to continue. Film makes direct claims for constructing fantasy space in the vein of novelistic strategy. Some television shows for young children attempt to create fantasy spaces within them, through, for example, creatures (Elmo, Teletubbies) or people (introducing and watching the feature film with the viewer) who stand for television as liminal space between Primary and Secondary Worlds. However, the girls feel that television claims to provide them with information and assistance for navigating real life, even for buying products. This is not necessarily logical. What is logical about believing an actor's promotion of medicine, just because he says, "I'm not a doctor, but I play one on TV"?

3. We can understand the difference between experiencing visual and written text if we invoke the ideas of two psychoanalytic theorists, Jacques Lacan and D. W. Winnicott, who discuss the roots of imagination and language.

In her discussion of the extent to which readers develop mental images while reading, Ellen Esrock argues that critics use Lacan to assert that the reader misrecognizes him/herself in a literary character:

> Lacan, who has had considerable impact on film studies and literature, characterizes the mirror stage as a formative period in the preverbal development of the child. It is part of the process of forming the self through a series of identifications. . . . This Lacanian notion provides film theory with a model of a basic identificatory process, that of narcissism, in which the spectator can recognize and also misrecognize himself in the likeness of a particular character on the screen. The reader's acts of visualization could be understood to serve the same function. The reader can narcissistically visualize, finding his image in a fictional character other than self. (Esrock 142–43)

A psychoanalytic theorist who looks at how language and image shape the infant's earliest conception of self, Lacan theorizes that infants have a "mirror stage" in which they *visually* discover that they are separate from the mother and, consequently, begin to use language to express the fact that they "lack" or "desire"—and that they are not equal to the image in the mirror or to the mother, because they lack motor control. Some critics have interpreted this to mean that language functions as a kind of mirror or mental image for the self. However, because those who use language are lacking something—which is why they feel compelled to use language at all—language also embodies the gap between people. Language is a social tool and thus it speaks *through* individual people, never quite encapsulating their meaning. In Vanessa's description of reading, the music video functions as an "image" of the self—its *picture*—while the literature functions as a gap between self and self-image.

D. W. Winnicott also discusses early infant experience as the root of appreciation for cultural and artistic experience. Like Lacan, he argues that the infant enters symbolic life at the moment he/she discovers separateness from the mother; he/she resolves the crisis, however, not by formulating an image of self but by investing transitional objects (teddy bears, blankets, etc.) with symbolic meaning. Symbolic systems, language, and literature are based upon this early capacity to fill, with symbols, individual "lack" and gaps between self and other. Vanessa's assertion that "I don't see myself" in the text suggests that music videos fill "gaps" between girl and culture by supplying her an image, but that literature more closely resembles the transitional object that is more flexibly "created" and given symbolic meaning by the child, whose creation of meaning also reveals her power.

This power is the power to narrate self rather than be completely defined by a cultural image of self, which is perhaps only to lend support to what teachers have always felt—that reading literature allows more imagination than viewing visual media. I did not enter this project believing that written fiction requires more imaginative capacity than does visual fiction, thinking this to be an elitist point of view. However, I came to the understanding that literature allows more flexibility of perspective than does visual media. I further believe that psychoanalytic critics are useful for helping teachers to understand how individual imaginations interact with cultural stories to produce meaning and fantasy. If the role of language is to symbolize but not totalize the reader's self-conception, then flexible discussions of literature are preferable to comprehension tests. Nancy Chodorow, in "Gender as a Personal and Cultural Construction," discusses how people create personal fantasy from cultural material. For discussion of Lacanian theory in analyzing narrative texts, see *MLN* 98.5 (1983).

4. As Jane Tompkins ("Introduction") discusses in her collection of reader-response criticism, the critic will attribute power to the text or reader depending upon whether he/she feels that literary conventions lie within the text or within the interpretive community. As Schweickart articulates, "Does the text control the reader, or vice versa? For David Bleich, Norman Holland, and Stanley Fish, the reader holds controlling interest. . . . At the other pole are Michael Riffaterre, Georges Poulet, and Wolfgang Iser, who acknowledge the creative role of the reader, but ultimately take the text to be the dominant force. To read, from this point of view, is to create the text according to its own promptings" (529–31).

5. Bakhtin describes the characters as independent voices in the novel: "The language used by characters in the novel, how they speak, is verbally and semanti-

cally autonomous; each character's speech possesses its own belief system, since each is the speech of another in another's language; thus it may also refract authorial intentions and consequently may to a certain degree constitute a second language for the author" (315). Although his insights are formal, he is often used by critics to assert the primacy of sociological concerns, a usage that falls into the current fashion of stressing identity politics. As Hale puts it, "What do we call a subject who is both more and less than an individual and stronger and weaker than a free agent? For all of the authors I have quoted [Robert Stepto, *From Behind the Veil*, Houston Baker, *Blues, Ideology, and African-American Literature*, and Mary Helen Washington, "Foreword" to *Their Eyes Were Watching God*], and for many cultural critics over the past two decades, the answer is 'voice.' Voice has become the metaphor that best accommodates the conflicting desires of critics and theorists who want to have their cultural subject and de-essentialize it, too" (197).

6. Fiction in books, films, plays, and some narrative songs define a range of literature for these girls. Terry Eagleton argues that definitions of literature have more to do with values than with objective qualities of written texts. In *Literary Theory*, he gives the example that if someone came up to him and whispered, "Thou still unravished bride of quietness," he would know he was in the presence of the literary, even though he had not picked up a book (2). Not only do the girls feel that they are in the presence of the literary across the media of films, plays, and books (and songs if they attend to the words as poetry or narrative), but also, when experiencing many of these works, they take on aesthetic presence to differentiate their "center world" from "possible worlds" (Ryan 99).

7. Porter argues, in reference to certain figures in American literature, that "in the broadest sense, reification refers to a process in the course of which man becomes alienated from himself. . . . The effects of this process as Lukács describes them, however, are by no means limited to the experience of the laborer, but in fact infiltrate the consciousness of everyone living in a society driven by capitalist growth" (xi).

8. Even though the Lacanian decentering of the subject troubles psychological concepts of self (outside language), Jameson points out that concepts such as identification, empathy, and projection continue to inform critical understandings of the reader (153). Norman Holland asserts that the reader imposes his/her "identity theme" on the text, and thus identity determines meaning. The concept of identification defines the perspectives of many psychoanalytic critics of reading (Rollin and West) and bibliotherapists (Crago). The principle of identity politics assumes a more stable idea of identity than the act of reading merits. To assume that an African American reader has an inherent connection to an African American character implies an "always already" understanding of identity, in conflict with theoretical suggestions that the subject is always being reconstituted and reconstituting the self in language. Judith Butler, for example, argues this point in *Bodies That Matter*.

9. Lily's discussion of *Clueless* also suggests that films have a more inherent relationship to realism because of their visual (iconic) and aural (vocal/music media) component. This echoes C. S. Pierce's distinction between iconic and symbolic sign systems, the former a representation of a particular object and the latter a representation of all objects to which the word refers (W. T. J. Mitchell). The distinction, however, is less within the sign itself as it is within the reading of the sign.

10. The girls' immersion in animal fantasy suggests that power lies in escaping the form of the female body. Cultural critics of female development emphasize the issue that cultural constructions of the female body equate it with disgust, marketing to girls and women a host of products designed to contain the female body and its products (blood, milk, sweat, pimples, hair, etc.) (Brumberg, Blackford). Kristeva argues that the female body represents the abject because it transgresses the body's boundaries, through body fluids such as blood, milk, and tears. Such critics as Wolf, Bordo, and Chernin argue that girls' anxieties about the female body find expression in illnesses, among them anorexia and bulimia, and obsessive control of the body through diet, exercise, and consumer products. Bordo argues that the possession of a female body and all it signifies in the larger culture prevents women from feeling that they are full participants of culture (5). Emily Martin's empirical research with women reveals that women feel alienated from their biological processes. I was continually struck by the fact that when I asked the girls direct questions about growing up in a female body, they had a complete lack of affect, seeming to have internalized what Michelle Fine terms "the missing discourse of desire" in health education, which stresses scientific discourse to describe the body. The alienating effect of this discourse contrasts with the rhetoric of pleasure that the girls voice in discussing becoming omniscient in fiction or living through animals in their imagination, both ways of transcending the real human body that demands more and more attention but does not inspire their imagination.

Works Cited

Aesop. *Aesop's Fables*. Ed. Jerry Pinkney. New York: SeaStar, 2000.

Alcott, Louisa May. *Little Women*. Ed. Elaine Showalter. New York: Penguin, 1989.

Allen, Marjorie. *What Are Little Girls Made Of? A Guide to Female Role Models in Children's Books*. New York: Facts on File, 1999.

Alvarez, Julia. *How the Garcia Girls Lost Their Accents*. New York: Plume, 1992.

———. *In the Time of the Butterflies*. Chapel Hill, NC: Algonquin Books of Chapel Hill, 1994.

American Association of University Women. *Shortchanging Girls, Shortchanging America*. Washington, DC: AAUW Educational Foundation, 1994.

Amistad. Dir. Steven Spielberg. 1997. DVD. Dreamworks, 2003.

Anderson, Benedict. *Imagined Communities: Reflections on the Origin and Spread of Nationalism*. New York: Verso, 1991.

Andrews, V. C. *Flowers in the Attic*. New York: Pocket, 1990.

Applebee, Arthur. *The Child's Concept of Story: Ages Two to Seventeen*. Chicago: U of Chicago P, 1989.

Arac, Jonathan. *Huckleberry Finn as Idol and Target: The Functions of Criticism in Our Time*. Madison: U of Wisconsin P, 1997.

Aristotle. *Aristotle's Poetics*. Trans. S. H. Butcher. New York: Hill and Wang, 1991.

Armageddon. Dir. Michael Bay. 1998. DVD. Touchstone Video, 2003.

Armstrong, Nancy. *Desire and Domestic Fiction: A Political History of the Novel*. New York: Oxford UP, 1987.

Atwood, Margaret. *Alias Grace*. New York: Doubleday, 1997.

———. *The Blind Assassin*. New York: Anchor, 2001.

———. *Bluebeard's Egg*. New York: Anchor, 1998.

———. *Cat's Eye*. New York: Anchor, 1998.

———. *The Edible Woman*. New York: Anchor, 1998.

———. *The Handmaid's Tale*. New York: Anchor, 1998.

———. *Lady Oracle*. New York: Doubleday, 1998.

———. *The Robber Bride*. New York: Anchor, 1998.

———. *Surfacing*. New York: Doubleday, 1998.

Austen, Jane. *Emma*. Ed. Alistair M. Duckworth. Boston: Bedford/St. Martin's, 2002.

Austin Powers—The Spy Who Shagged Me. Dir. Jay Roach. 1999. DVD. New Line Home Entertainment, 1999.

Avery, Gillian. *Behold the Child: American Children and Their Books, 1621–1922.* Baltimore: Johns Hopkins UP, 1994.

The Bachelor. Prod. Mike Fleiss. TV series. ABC, ongoing.

Bakhtin, Mikhail M. *The Dialogic Imagination.* Ed. Michael Holquist. Trans. Caryl Emerson and Michael Holquist. Austin: U of Texas P, 1981.

Bal, Mieke. *Narratology: Introduction to the Theory of Narrative.* Toronto: U of Toronto P, 1997.

Banks, Lynne Reid. *The Fairy Rebel.* New York: Avon Camelot, 1989.

Barrie, J. M. *Peter Pan: The Complete and Unabridged Text.* Viking, 1991.

Basic. Dir. John McTiernan. 2003. VHS. Columbia Tristar Home Video, 2003.

Bauer, Dale. "Gender in Bakhtin's Carnival." *Feminisms. An Anthology of Literary Theory and Criticism.* Ed. Robyn Warhol and Diane Price Herndl. New Brunswick: Rutgers UP, 1993. 671–84.

Bauermeister, Erica, and Holly Smith. *Let's Hear It for the Girls: 375 Great Books for Readers 2–14.* New York: Penguin, 1997.

Baum, L. Frank. *The Wonderful Wizard of Oz.* New York: New American Library, 1984.

Baym, Nina. *Novels, Readers, and Reviewers: Responses to Fiction in Antebellum America.* Ithaca: Cornell UP, 1984.

Benton, Michael. "Reader-Response Criticism." Hunt 71–88.

———. *Secondary Worlds: Literature Teaching and the Visual Arts.* Buckingham, PA: Open UP, 1992.

———. *Studies in the Spectator Role: Literature, Painting and Pedagogy.* New York: Routledge, 2000.

Berenstein, Rhona. *Attack of the Leading Ladies: Gender, Sexuality, and Spectatorship in Classic Horror Cinema.* New York: Columbia UP, 1996.

Bettelheim, Bruno. *The Uses of Enchantment: The Meaning and Importance of Fairy Tales.* New York: Vintage, 1989.

Blackford, Holly. Preface. *Moon Days: Creative Writings About Menstruation.* Ed. Cassie Premo Steele. Columbia, SC: Summerhouse, 1999. 12–23.

The Blair Witch Project. Dir. Eduardo Sánchez II and Daniel Myrick. 1999. DVD. Artisan Entertainment, 2001.

Bleich, David. *Subjective Criticism.* Baltimore: Johns Hopkins UP, 1978.

Blume, Judy. *Are You There, God? It's Me, Margaret.* New York: Yearling, 1970.

———. *Summer Sisters: A Novel.* New York: Dell, 1999.

Bordo, Susan. *Unbearable Weight: Feminism, Western Culture, and the Body.* Berkeley: U of California P, 1993.

Bourgeois, Paulette. *Franklin in the Dark.* New York: Scholastic, 1987.

Bradley, Marion Zimmer. *The Mists of Avalon.* New York: Del Rey, 1982.

Briggs, Charles. *Learning How to Ask: A Sociolinguistic Appraisal of the Role of the Interview in Social Science Research.* New York: Cambridge UP, 1986.

Brodhead, Richard. *Cultures of Letters: Scenes of Reading and Writing in Nineteenth Century America.* Chicago: U of Chicago P, 1993.

Brontë, Charlotte. *Jane Eyre.* 3rd ed. Ed. Richard J. Dunn. New York: Norton, 2000.

Brontë, Emily. *Wuthering Heights.* New York: Bantam, 1983.

Brooks, Peter. *Reading for the Plot: Design and Intention in Narrative.* Cambridge: Harvard UP, 1984.

Brownstein, Rachel. *Becoming a Heroine: Reading About Women in Novels.* New York: Viking, 1982.

Brumberg, Joan. *The Body Project: An Intimate History of American Girls.* New York: Random, 1997.

Burke, Edmund. *Reflections on the Revolution in France.* New York: Viking, 1982.

Burnett, Frances Hodgson. *A Little Princess.* New York: HarperTrophy, 1987.

———. *The Secret Garden.* New York: Oxford UP, 1987.

Butler, Judith. *Bodies That Matter: On the Discursive Limits of "Sex."* New York: Routledge, 1993.

———. *Gender Trouble: Feminism and the Subversion of Identity.* New York: Routledge, 1999.

Candid Camera. Creator Allen Funt. TV series. CBS, 1996–2000. PAX, ongoing.

Canfield, Jack, Mark Victor Hansen, and Kimberly Kirberger. *Chicken Soup for the Teenage Soul.* Deerfield Beach, FL: Health Communications, 1997.

Carter, Angela. *The Bloody Chamber and Other Stories.* New York: Penguin, 1990.

Cather, Willa. *My Ántonia.* Boston: Mariner, 1995.

Cats: The Musical. Dir. David Mallet. VHS. Music Andrew Lloyd Webber. Universal Studios, 2001.

Cherland, Meredith. *Private Practices: Girls Reading Fiction and Constructing Identity.* London: Taylor and Francis, 1994.

Chernin, Kim. *The Hungry Self: Women, Eating and Identity.* New York: HarperPerennial, 1994.

Child's Play. Dir. Tom Holland 1988. VHS. MGM/UA Studios, 1997.

Childress, Alice. *Rainbow Jordan.* New York: Avon, 1982.

Chodorow, Nancy. "Gender as a Personal and Cultural Construction." *Signs* 20.3 (1995): 516–44.

———. *The Reproduction of Mothering: Psychoanalysis and the Sociology of Gender.* Berkeley: U of California P, 1978.

Christ, Carol. "Black Beauty." *Lecture Notes: English X75 Classics of Children's Literature.* Berkeley: UC Regents, 1997. 31–34.

———. "The Wind in the Willows." *Lecture Notes: English X75 Classics of Children's Literature.* Berkeley: UC Regents, 1997. 35–38.

Christian, Barbara. "Trajectories of Self-Definition: Placing Contemporary Afro-American Women's Fiction." *Feminisms: An Anthology of Literary Theory and Criticism.* Ed. Robyn Warhol and Diane Price Herndl. New Brunswick: Rutgers UP, 1993. 316–32.

Cixous, Hélène. "The Laugh of the Medusa." *Feminisms: An Anthology of Literary Theory and Criticism.* Ed. Robyn Warhol and Diane Price Herndl. New Brunswick: Rutgers UP, 1993, 334–49.

Clark, Cindy Dell. *Flights of Fancy, Leaps of Faith: Children's Myths in Contemporary America.* Chicago: U of Chicago P, 1995.

Clueless. Dir. Amy Heckerling. 1995. DVD. Paramount Studio, 2003.

Coe, Richard, Lorelei Lingard, and Tatiana Teslenko. "Genre as Action, Strategy, and *Différence*: An Introduction." *The Rhetoric and Ideology of Genre: Strategies for Stability and Change*. Cresskill, NJ: Hampton, 2002. 1–10.

Coffey, Amanda, and Paul Atkinson. *Making Sense of Qualitative Data: Complementary Research Strategies*. Thousand Oaks, CA: Sage, 1996.

Collodi, Carlo. *Pinocchio*. New York: Puffin, 1974.

The Company of Wolves. Dir. Neil Jordan. 1985. DVD. Hens Tooth Video, 2002.

Cooper, James Fennimore. *The Last of the Mohicans*. Laurel, NY: Lightyear, 1984.

Cops. Creator Paul Stojanovich. TV series. Fox, 1989–2002.

Courage under Fire. Dir. Edward Zwick. 1996. VHS. Twentieth Century Fox, 2001.

The Craft. Dir. Andrew Fleming. 1996. VHS. Columbia/Tristar Studios, 1999.

Crago, Hugh. "Bibliotherapy and Psychology." Hunt 634–43.

Culler, Jonathan. "Reading as a Woman." *Feminisms: An Anthology of Literary Theory and Criticism*. Ed. Robyn Warhol and Diane Price Herndl. New Brunswick: Rutgers UP, 1993. 509–24.

Dances with Wolves. Dir. Kevin Costner. 1990. DVD. MGM/UA Studios, 2003.

Dante. *The Divine Comedy*. Trans. C. H. Sisson. New York: Oxford UP, 1998.

Darrieussecq, Marie. *Pig Tales: A Novel of Lust and Transformation*. Trans. Linda Coverdale. New York: New, 1997.

D'Aulaire, Ingri. *D'Aulaires' Book of Greek Myths*. New York: Picture Yearling, 1992.

Davidson, Cathy. *Revolution and the Word: The Rise of the Novel in America*. New York: Oxford UP, 1986.

Davies, Bronwyn. *Shards of Glass: Children Reading and Writing Beyond Gendered Identities*. Cresskill, NJ: Hampton, 1993.

Dawson's Creek. Creator Kevin Williamson. Prods. Paul Stupin, Tom Kapinos, Greg Prange. Prod. Sony Pictures Television. WB Network, ongoing.

DeBerry, Virginia, and Donna Grant. *Tryin' to Sleep in the Bed You Made*. New York: St. Martin's, 1997.

Deep Impact. Dir. Mimi Leder. 1998. VHS. Paramount Studio, 2001.

Dellasega, Cheryl. *Surviving Ophelia: Mothers Share Their Wisdom in Navigating the Tumultuous Teenage Years*. Cambridge: Perseus, 2001.

Die Hard. Dir. John McTiernan. 1988. VHS. Twentieth Century Fox, 2003.

Diamant, Anita. *The Red Tent*. New York: Picador, 1997.

Dinnerstein, Dorothy. *The Mermaid and the Minatour: Sexual Arrangements and Human Malaise*. New York: Harper, 1976.

Dodson, Shireen. *100 Books for Girls to Grow On*. New York: HarperPerennial, 1998.

———. *The Mother-Daughter Book Club*. New York: Harper, 1990.

Dora the Explorer. Creators Chris Gifford, Valerie Walsh, and Eric Weiner. TV series. Nick Jr., ongoing.

Douglas, Jack D. *Creative Interviewing*. Beverly Hills, CA: Sage, 1985.

Dresang, Eliza. *Radical Change: Books for Youth in a Digital Age*. New York: Wilson, 1999.

Drowning Mona. Dir. Nick Gomaz. 2000. DVD. Columbia/Tristar Studios, 2000.

Dumas, Alexander. *The Count of Monte Cristo*. Ed. David Coward. London: Oxford UP, 1998.

Dumbo. Dir. Ben Sharpsteen. 1941. Walt Disney Studios, 2001.

Duncan, Lois. *Killing Mr. Griffin.* New York: Dell, 1990.

Eagleton, Terry. *Literary Theory: An Introduction.* Minneapolis: U of Minnesota P, 1983.

EdTV. Dir. Ron Howard. 1999. DVD. Universal Studios, 2003.

Edwards, Julie. *Mandy.* New York: HarperTrophy, 1989.

Eliot, T. S. *Old Possom's Book of Practical Cats.* New York: Harcourt, 1982.

———. "Tradition and the Individual Talent." *The Norton Anthology of English Literature.* Vol. 2. 6th ed. Ed. M. H. Abrams. New York: Norton, 1992. 2170–75.

Elliott, Kamilla. Lectures on the history of film. University of California, Berkeley. Fall 1996.

Emerson, Ralph Waldo. *Nature and Other Writings.* Ed. Peter Turner. Boston: Shambhala, 1994.

Emshwiller, Carol. *Carmen Dog.* San Francisco: Mercury House, 1990.

Esquivel, Laura. *Like Water for Chocolate: A Novel in Monthly Installments, with Recipes, Romances and Home Remedies.* Trans. Carol Christensen and Thomas Christensen. New York: Anchor, 1994.

Esrock, Ellen. *The Reader's Eye: Visual Imaging as Reader Response.* Baltimore: Johns Hopkins UP, 1994.

Ever After: A Cinderella Story. Dir. Andy Tennant. 1998. DVD. Twentieth Century Fox, 2003.

The Faculty. Dir. Robert Rodriguez. 1998. VHS. Dimension Home Video, 2003.

Fear Factor. Prod. John De Mol and Matt Kunitz. TV series. NBC, ongoing.

Feminists on Children's Media. *Little Miss Muffet Fights Back: Recommended Non-Sexist Books About Girls for Young Readers.* New York: Feminists on Children's Media, 1974.

Ferris Bueller's Day Off. Dir. John Hughes. 1986. VHS. Paramount Studios, 1998.

Fetterley, Judith. "Introduction: On the Politics of Literature." *Feminisms: An Anthology of Literary Theory and Criticism.* Ed. Robyn Warhol and Diane Price Herndl. New Brunswick: Rutgers UP, 1993. 492–501.

Fiedler, Leslie. *Love and Death in the American Novel.* New York: Anchor, 1992.

Field of Dreams. Dir. Phil Alden Robinson. 1989. VHS. Universal Studios, 1999.

Fine, Michelle. *Disruptive Voices: The Possibilities of Feminist Research.* Ann Arbor: U of Michigan P, 1992.

Fish, Stanley. *Is There a Text in This Class? The Authority of Interpretive Communities.* Cambridge: Harvard UP, 1980.

Fitzgerald, F. Scott. *The Great Gatsby.* New York: Scribner, 1925.

Foddy, William. *Constructing Questions for Interviews and Questionnaires: Theory and Practice in Social Research.* New York: Cambridge UP, 1994.

Follett, Ken. *The Pillars of the Earth.* New York: Plume, 1999.

Foucault, Michel. *Discipline and Punish: The Birth of the Prison.* Trans. Alan Sheridan. New York: Vintage, 1979.

Frank, Anne. *The Diary of a Young Girl.* Ed. Otto Frank and Mirjam Pressler. Trans. Susan Massotty. New York: Bantam, 1995.

Franklin, Aretha. "A Rose Is Still a Rose." *A Rose Is Still a Rose.* Audio CD. Arista, 1998.

Freud, Sigmund. "The Interpretation of Dreams." *The Standard Edition of the Complete Psychological Works of Sigmund Freud.* Ed. and Trans. James Strachey. London: Hogarth, 1953. 1–713.

———. "The Uncanny." *The Standard Edition.* Vol. 17. 219–52.

Frye, Northrop. *Anatomy of Criticism: Four Essays.* Princeton: Princeton UP, 1957.

Full House. Prod. Jeff Franklin, Thomas L. Miller, Robert L. Boyett, Marc Warren, and Dennis Rinsler. TV series. ABC, 1987–95.

Gardner, John Champlin. *Grendel.* New York: Vintage, 1989.

Gates, Henry Louis, Jr. *The Signifying Monkey: A Theory of Afro-American Literary Criticism.* New York: Oxford UP, 1988.

Genette, Gerard. *Narrative Discourse Revisited.* Trans. Jane E. Lewin. Ithaca: Cornell UP, 1988.

Ghosts of Mississippi. Dir. Rob Reiner. 1996. VHS. Castle Rock, 2002.

Gilligan, Carol. *In a Different Voice: Psychological Theory and Women's Development.* Cambridge: Harvard UP, 1982.

Gilman, Charlotte Perkins. *The Yellow Wallpaper and Other Writings.* New York: Modern Library, 2000.

Glesne, Corrine, and Alan Peshkin. *Becoming Qualitative Researchers: An Introduction.* New York: Longman, 1992.

Goines, Donald. *Black Girl Lost.* Los Angeles: Holloway House, 1973.

Golding, William Gerald. *Lord of the Flies.* New York: Perigee, 1954.

Grahame, Kenneth. *The Wind in the Willows.* New York: Aladdin, 1989.

Greenblatt, Stephen. "Racial Memory and Literary History." *PMLA* 116.1 (2001): 48–63.

Guroian, Vigen. *Tending the Heart of Virtue: How Classic Stories Awaken a Child's Moral Imagination.* New York: Oxford UP, 1998.

Hale, Dorothy. *Social Formalism: The Novel in Theory from Henry James to the Present.* Stanford: Stanford UP, 1998.

Harry Potter and the Chamber of Secrets. Dir. C. Columbus. 2002. DVD. Warner Home Video, 2003.

Harshman, Terry. *Porcupine's Pajama Party.* New York: Harper, 1988.

The Haunting. Dir. Jan de Bont. 1999. VHS. Universal Studios, 2001.

Hawthorne, Nathaniel. *The Scarlet Letter.* New York: Bantam Classics, 1981.

———Preface. *The House of the Seven Gables.* New York: Bantam, 1981. vii–viii.

———. *Selected Tales and Sketches.* New York: Penguin, 1987.

Heaney, Seamus, ed. *Beowulf.* New York: Norton, 2001.

Heartburn. Dir. Mike Nichols. 1986. VHS. Paramount Studio, 1995.

Heath, Shirley Brice. *The Braid of Literature: Children's Worlds of Reading.* Cambridge: Harvard UP, 1992.

Hemingway, Ernest. *The Old Man and the Sea.* New York: Scribner, 1995.

High Fidelity. Dir. Stephen Frears. 2000. VHS. Walt Disney Home Video, 2002.

Hinton, S. E. *That Was Then, This Is Now.* New York: Penguin, 1998.

Hitchcock, Alfred. *Hitchcock on Hitchcock: Selected Writings and Interviews.* Berkeley: U of California P, 1995.

Hoffmann, E. T. A. *The Golden Pot, and Other Tales.* Trans. and ed. Ritchie Robertson. New York: Oxford UP, 1992.

Holland, Norman. "UNITY IDENTITY TEXT SELF." *Reader-Response Criticism: From Formalism to Post-structuralism*. Ed. Jane Tompkins. Baltimore: Johns Hopkins UP, 1980. 118–33.

Hubler, Angela. "Can Anne Shirley Help 'Revive Ophelia'? Listening to Girl Readers." *Delinquents and Debutantes: Twentieth-Century American Girls' Cultures*. Ed. Sherrie A. Inness. New York: New York UP, 1998. 266–84.

Hunt, Peter, ed. *International Companion Encyclopedia of Children's Literature*. New York: Routledge, 1996.

Hurston, Zora Neale. *Their Eyes Were Watching God*. San Bernardino, CA: Borgo, 1991.

Independence Day. Dir. Roland Emmerich. 1996. DVD. Twentieth Century Fox Home Video, 2002.

Indiana Jones and the Temple of Doom. Dir. Steven Spielberg. Paramount Studios, 1984.

Iron Eagle. Dir. Sidney J. Furie. 1986. DVD. Columbia/Tristar Studios, 2001.

The Iron Giant. Dir. Brad Bird. 1999. DVD. Warner Home Video, 1999.

Irving, Washington. *Rip Van Winkle*. New York: Grosset, 1997.

Iser, Wolfgang. *The Act of Reading: A Theory of Aesthetic Response*. Baltimore: Johns Hopkins UP, 1978.

Jackson, Shirley. *The Haunting of Hill House*. New York: Penguin, 1984.

Jacobs, Harriet. *Incidents in the Life of a Slave Girl: Written by Herself*. Ed. Jean Fagan Yellin. Cambridge: Harvard UP, 1987.

Jacques, Brian. *Redwall*. New York: Ace, 1986.

James, Henry. Preface to the New York Edition (1908). *The Portrait of a Lady*. New York: Norton, 1995. 3–15.

Jameson, Fredric. *The Political Unconscious: Narrative as a Socially Symbolic Act*. Ithaca, NY: Cornell UP, 1981.

Jauss, Hans Robert. *Toward an Aesthetic of Reception*. Trans. Timothy Bahti. Minneapolis: U of Minnesota P, 1982.

Jekyll and Hyde: The Gothic Musical Thriller. Music by Frank Wildhorn. Lyrics by Leslie Briscusse. Dir. Gregory Boyd. Audio CD. Atlantic, 1995.

The Jerry Springer Show. Prod. Richard Dominick. Syndicated series. Universal Domestic Television, ongoing.

Joe Millionaire. Prod. Jean-Michel Michenaud and Chris Cowan. TV series. Rocket Science Laboratories Production Co. Fox, ongoing.

Johnson, Steven. *Interface Culture: How New Technology Transforms the Way We Create and Communicate*. San Francisco: HarperEdge, 1997.

Jumanji. Dir. Joe Johnston. 1995. VHS. Columbia/Tristar Studios, 2001.

Karate Kid. Dir. John Avildsen. 1984. VHS. Columbia/Tristar Studios, 2001.

Kay, Susan. *Phantom*. New York: Island, 1991.

Keane, Carolyn. *The Secret of the Old Clock*. (Nancy Drew Series 1). New York: Price Stern Sloan, 1930.

Kincaid, Jamaica. *Annie John*. New York: Farrar, 2001.

King, Stephen. *The Stand: Complete and Uncut*. New York: Signet, 1991.

King-Smith, Dick. *Babe: The Gallant Pig*. New York: Random, 1997.

Kipling, Rudyard. *The Jungle Books*. New York: New American Library, 1995.

Kiss Me, Kate. Music and lyrics by Cole Porter. Book by Sam and Bella Spewack. New York: Harms, 1967.

Knowles, John. *A Separate Peace.* New York: Bantam, 1985.

Kristeva, Julia. *Powers of Horror: An Essay on Abjection.* Trans. Leon S. Roudiez. New York: Columbia UP, 1982.

Kvale, Steinar. *InterViews: An Introduction to Qualitative Research Interviewing.* Thousand Oaks, CA: Sage, 1996.

Lacan, Jacques. *Écrits: A Selection.* Trans. Alan Sheridan. New York: Norton, 1977.

Lacey, Nick. *Narrative and Genre: Key Concepts in Media Studies.* New York: St. Martin's, 2000.

The Last Unicorn. Dir. Jules Bass and Arthur Rankin, Jr. 1982. VHS. Family Home Entertainment, 1994.

Latham, Robert A. "Some Thoughts on Modernism and Science Fiction (Suggested by Robert Silverberg's *Downward to the Earth*)." *The Celebration of the Fantastic: Selected Papers from the Tenth Anniversary International Conference on the Fantastic in the Arts.* Ed. Donald E. Morse, Marshall B. Tymn, and Csilla Bertha. Westport, CT: Greenwood, 1992. 49–59.

A League of Their Own. Dir. Penny Marshall. 1992. VHS. Columbia/Tristar Studios, 2002.

Lee, Harper. *To Kill a Mockingbird.* New York: Harper, 1999.

The Legend of Bagger Vance. Dir. Robert Redford. 2000. VHS. Dreamworks, 2002.

Le Guin, Ursula. *Tehanu: The Earthsea Cycle.* New York: Simon Pulse, 2001.

Leibert, Robert. *The Early Window: The Effects of Television on Children and Youth.* New York: Pergamon, 1988.

Lesnik-Oberstein, Karin. *Children's Literature: Criticism and the Fictional Child.* New York: Oxford UP, 1994.

Lethal Weapon. Dir. Richard Donner. 1987. VHS. Warner Studios, 1998.

Lévi-Strauss, Claude. *Structural Anthropology.* Trans. Claire Jacobson and Brooke Grundfest Schoepf. New York: Anchor, 1967.

Lewis, C. S. *The Lion, the Witch and the Wardrobe. The Chronicles of Narnia.* Vol 2. New York: Harper, 1994.

Lightfoot, Cynthia. *The Culture of Adolescent Risk-Taking.* New York: Guilford, 1997.

Like Water for Chocolate. Dir. Alfonso Arau. 1993. VHS. Miramax, 2002.

The Lion King. Dir. Rob Minkoff and Roger Allers. 1994. DVD. Disney Home Video, 2003.

The Little Mermaid. Dir. Ron Clements and John Musker. 1989. DVD. Disney Home Video, 1999.

Little Women. Dir. Gillian Armstrong. 1994. DVD. Columbia/Tristar Studios, 2003.

London, Jack. *The Call of the Wild.* New York: Dover, 1991.

Lurie, Alison. *Don't Tell the Grown-Ups: Subversive Children's Literature.* Boston: Little, 1990.

Mann, Judy. *The Difference: Discovering the Hidden Ways We Silence Girls: Finding Alternatives That Can Give Them a Voice.* New York: Warner, 1996.

Mannequin. Dir. Michael Gottlieb. 1987. VHS. Anchor Bay Entertainment, 1990.

Married by America. Prod. Ted Haines. TV series. Fox, ongoing.

Martin, Ann Matthews. Baby-Sitters Club Series. Scholastic Paperbacks, ongoing.

Martin, Emily. *The Woman in the Body: A Cultural Analysis of Reproduction*. Boston: Beacon, 1992.

Martin, Karin. *Puberty, Sexuality, and Self: Boys and Girls at Adolescence*. New York: Routledge, 1996.

Martin, Wallace. *Recent Theories of Narrative*. Ithaca: Cornell UP, 1986.

Marx, Leo. *The Machine in the Garden: Technology and the Pastoral Ideal in America*. New York: Oxford UP, 2000.

Masse, Michelle. *In the Name of Love: Women, Masochism, and the Gothic*. Ithaca: Cornell UP, 1992.

The Matrix. Dir. Andy Wachowski and Larry Wachowski. 1999. DVD. Warner Studios, 1999.

Maverick. Dir. Richard Donner. 1994. DVD. Warner Studios, 1997.

May, Jill P. *Children's Literature and Critical Theory: Reading and Writing for Understanding*. New York: Oxford UP, 1995.

May, R. L. *Rudolph the Red-Nosed Reindeer*. Booklet. Chicago: Montgomery Ward, 1939.

McCaffrey, Anne. *The Chronicles of Pern: First Fall (The Dragonriders of Pern)*. New York: Ballantine, 1993.

———. *Crystal Singer*. New York: Ballantine, 1982.

Melville, Herman. *Moby-Dick; Or, The Whale*. New York: Penguin, 1992.

Men in Black. Dir. Barry Sonnenfeld. 1997. DVD. Columbia/Tristar Studios, 2003.

Merton, Robert K., Marjorie Fiske, and Patricia L. Kendall. *The Focused Interview: A Manual of Problems and Procedures*. Glencoe, IL: Free, 1956.

Message in a Bottle. Dir. Luis Mandoki. 1999. DVD. Warner Studios, 2003.

Metz, Christian. *The Imaginary Signifier: Psychoanalysis and the Cinema*. Trans. Celia Britton, Annwyl Williams, Ben Brewster, and Alfred Guzzetti. Bloomington: Indiana UP, 1982.

Miller, D. A. *The Novel and the Police*. Berkeley: U of California P, 1988.

Milne, A. A. *The Complete Tales of Winnie-the-Pooh*. New York: Penguin, 1996.

Mishler, Elliot G. *Research Interviewing: Context and Narrative*. Cambridge: Harvard UP, 1986.

Mitchell, Margaret. *Gone with the Wind*. New York: Macmillan, 1969.

Mitchell, W. T. J. *Iconology: Image, Text, Ideology*. Chicago: U of Chicago P, 1987.

Monaco, James. *How to Read a Film: The World of Movies, Media, and Multimedia: Language, History, Theory*. New York: Oxford UP, 2000.

Montgomery, Lucy Maud. *Anne of Green Gables*. New York: New American Library, 1991.

Moore, Lorrie. *Who Will Run the Frog Hospital?* New York: Warner, 1995.

Morrison, Toni. *Beloved*. New York: Plume, 1998.

———. *The Bluest Eye*. New York: Penguin, 2000.

———. *Playing in the Dark: Whiteness and the Literary Imagination*. New York: Vintage, 1993.

Moss, Marissa. *Amelia's Notebook*. Minneapolis: Pleasant, 1999.

Mulvey, Laura. "Visual Pleasure and Narrative Cinema." *Feminisms: An Anthology of Literary Theory and Criticism*. Ed. Robyn Warhol and Diane Price Herndl. New Brunswick: Rutgers UP, 1993. 432–42.

My Fair Lady. Dir. George Cukor. 1964. DVD. Warner Studios, 1998.

Naslund, Sene Jeter. *Ahab's Wife; Or, The Star-Gazer: A Novel*. New York: Perennial, 2000.

The Negotiator. Dir. F. Gary Gray. 1998. DVD. Warner Studios, 2003.

Needle, Jan. *Wild Wood*. Rockport, TX: Magner, 1993.

Nell, Victor. *Lost in a Book: The Psychology of Reading for Pleasure*. New Haven: Yale UP, 1988.

Newman, Joan E. *Girls Are People Too! A Bibliography of Nontraditional Female Roles in Children's Books*. Metuchen, NJ: Scarecrow, 1982.

Nikolajeva, Maria. "Beyond the Grammar of Story, or How Can Children's Literature Criticism Benefit from Narrative Theory?" *Children's Literature Association Quarterly* 28.1 (2003): 5–16.

Now and Then. Dir. Lesli Linka Glatter. 1995. VHS. New Line Studios, 1997.

The Nutcracker, George Balanchine's. Dir. Emile Ardolino. 1993. VHS. Warner Studios, 2003.

Oates, Joyce Carol. *Black Water*. New York: Plume, 1993.

Odean, Kathleen. *Great Books for Girls: More than 600 Books to Inspire Today's Girls and Tomorrow's Women*. New York: Ballantine, 1997.

An Officer and a Gentleman. Dir. Taylor Hackford. 1982. DVD. Paramount Studio, 2002.

Olsen, Mary-Kate and Ashley. New Adventures of Mary-Kate and Ashley Series. New York: Harper, ongoing.

Orenstein, Peggy. *School Girls: Young Women, Self-Esteem, and the Confidence Gap*. New York: Doubleday, 1994.

Ortner, Sherry. *Making Gender: The Politics and Erotics of Culture*. Boston: Beacon, 1996.

Orwell, George. *Animal Farm: A Fairy Story*. New York: Harcourt, 1996.

The Phantom of the Opera. Music by Andrew Lloyd Webber. 1986. Audio CD. Polygram Records, 2001.

Pipher, Mary. *Reviving Ophelia: Saving the Selves of Adolescent Girls*. New York: Putnam, 1994.

Poe, Edgar Allen. *The Narrative of Arthur Gordon Pym of Nantucket*. New York: Penguin, 1999.

Porter, Carolyn. *Seeing and Being: The Plight of the Participant Observer in Emerson, James, Adams, and Faulkner*. Middletown: Wesleyan UP, 1981.

Postman, Neil. *The Disappearance of Childhood*. New York: Vintage, 1994.

Poulet, Georges. "Criticism and the Experience of Interiority." *Reader-Response Criticism: From Formalism to Post-structuralism*. Ed. Jane Tompkins. Baltimore: Johns Hopkins UP, 1980. 41–49.

Power, Brenda Miller, Jeffrey D. Wilhelm, and Kelly Chandler. *Reading Stephen King: Issues of Censorship, Student Choice, and Popular Literature*. Urbana, IL: National Council of Teachers of English, 1997.

PowerPuff Girls. Creator Craig McCracken. TV series. Cartoon Network, ongoing.

Propp, Vladimir. *Morphology of the Russian Folk Tale.* 2nd ed. Trans. Laurence Scott. Austin: U of Texas P, 1968.

Pugh, Sharon L. "Teaching Children to Appreciate Literature." 1988. *ERIC Digests* 1. ERIC Information Analysis Products (IAPs) (071). ERIC Clearinghouse on Reading and Communication Skills, Bloomington, IN. 28 October 2003. http://ericfacility.net/databases/ERIC_Digests/ed292108.html

Puzo, Mario. *The Godfather.* New York: Putnam, 1969.

Radcliffe, Ann. *A Sicilian Romance.* New York: Oxford UP, 1998.

Radway, Janice. *Reading the Romance: Women, Patriarchy, and Popular Literature.* Chapel Hill: U of North Carolina P, 1991.

Randall, Alice. *The Wind Done Gone.* Boston: Houghton, 2001.

The Real World. Creators Jonathan Murray and Mary-Ellis Bunim. TV series. MTV, ongoing.

Rent. Writer Jonathan Larson. Dir. Michael Greif. New York: Nederlander Theater, 1996.

Return to Never Land. Dir. Robin Budd II and Donovan Cook. 2002. DVD. Walt Disney Home Video, 2002.

Rigoletto. Dir. Leo D. Paur. 1993. VHS. Tapeworm, 1995.

Robin Hood. Dir. Wolfgang Reitherman. 1973. VHS. Walt Disney Home Video, 2000.

Robin Hood—Prince of Thieves. Dir. Kevin Reynolds. 1991. VHS. Warner Home Video, 2003.

The Rock. Dir. Michael Bay. 1996. DVD. Hollywood Pictures, 2002.

The Rocky Horror Picture Show. Dir. Jim Sharman. 1975. DVD. Twentieth Century Fox Home Video, 2000.

Rollin, Lucy, and Mark West. *Psychoanalytic Responses to Children's Literature.* Jefferson, NC: McFarland, 1999.

Rose, Jacqueline. *The Case of Peter Pan; Or, The Impossibility of Children's Fiction.* London: Macmillan, 1984.

Rosenblatt, Louise. *The Reader, the Text, the Poem: The Transactional Theory of the Literary Work.* Carbondale: Southern Illinois UP, 1978.

Rowling, J. K. *Harry Potter and the Sorcerer's Stone.* New York: Scholastic, 1997.

Rubin, Herbert J., and Irene S. Rubin. *Qualitative Interviewing: The Art of Hearing Data.* Thousand Oaks, CA: Sage, 1995.

Runaway Bride. Dir. Garry Marshall. 1999. VHS. Paramount Studio, 2001.

Ryan, Marie-Laure. *Narrative as Virtual Reality: Immersion and Interactivity in Literature and Electronic Media.* Baltimore: Johns Hopkins UP, 2001.

Sabrina the Teenage Witch. Prod. Paula Hart and David Babcock. TV series. Prod. Hartbreak Films and Viacom. WB Network, ongoing.

Salinger, J. D. *The Catcher in the Rye.* New York: Bantam, 1964.

Schreiber, Flora Rheta. *Sybil.* New York: Warner, 1995.

Schweickart, Patrocinio. "Reading Ourselves: Toward a Feminist Theory of Reading." *Feminisms: An Anthology of Literary Theory and Criticism.* Ed. Robyn Warhol and Diane Price Herndl. New Brunswick: Rutgers UP, 1993. 525–50.

Seidman, Irving. *Interviewing as Qualitative Research: A Guide for Researchers in Education and the Social Sciences.* 2nd ed. New York: Teachers College P, 1998.

Sewell, Anna. *Black Beauty*. Dover, 1999.

Sexton, Anne. *Transformations*. New York: Mariner, 2001.

Shakespeare, William. *Hamlet*. New York: Penguin, 1994.

———. *The Taming of the Shrew*. New York: Cambridge UP, 2002.

Shakur, Tupac. "Changes." *2Pac Greatest Hits Disc 2*. Audio CD. Interscope, 1998.

Shandler, Nina, and Sara Shandler. *Ophelia's Mom: Loving and Letting Go of Your Adolescent Daughter*. New York: Three Rivers, 2003.

Shandler, Sara. *Ophelia Speaks: Adolescent Girls Write About Their Search for Self*. New York: HarperPerennial, 1999.

Shavit, Zohar. *The Poetics of Children's Literature*. Athens: U of Georgia P, 1986.

Shaw, George Bernard. *Pygmalion* and *My Fair Lady*. New York: New American Library, 1994.

Shaw, Janet. *Kirsten: An American Girl*. Minneapolis: Pleasant, 1990.

She's All That. Dir. Robert Iscove. 1999. DVD. Miramax Home Entertainment, 2003.

Shelley, Mary. *Frankenstein*. 2nd ed. Ed. Johanna M. Smith. Boston: Bedford/ St. Martin's, 2000.

Showalter, Elaine. *A Literature of Their Own: British Women Novelists from Brontë to Lessing*. Princeton: Princeton UP, 1977.

———. "Toward a Feminist Poetics." *Women's Writing and Writing About Women*. Ed. Mary Jacobus. London: Croom Helm, 1979. 22–41.

Sister, Sister. Creators Fred Shafferman, Kim Bass, and Gary Gilbert. TV series. ABC, 1994–95. WB, 1995–99.

The Sixth Sense. Dir. M. Night Shyamalan. 1999. VHS. Walt Disney Home Video, 2000.

Smith, Louisa. "Real Gardens with Imaginary Toads: Domestic Fantasy." Hunt 295–302.

Smith, Michael, and Jeffrey Wilhelm. *"Reading Don't Fix No Chevys": Literacy in the Lives of Young Men*. Portsmouth, NH: Heinemann, 2002.

Sophocles. *Oedipus Rex*. New York: Dover, 1993.

Spirit—Stallion of the Cimarron. Dir. Lorna Cook and Kelly Asbury. 2002. DVD. Universal Studios, 2002.

Sprague, Marsha, and Kara Keeling. "A Library for Ophelia." *Journal of Adolescent and Adult Literacy* 43.7 (2000): 640–47.

Spyri, Johanna. *Heidi*. New York: Random, 1998.

Stacey, Jacquelyn. *Star Gazing: Hollywood Cinema and Female Spectatorship*. New York: Routledge, 1994.

Star Trek V—The Final Frontier. Dir. William Shatner. 1989. DVD. Paramount Studio, 2003.

Star Wars. Dir. George Lucas. 1977. VHS. Twentieth Century Fox, 1996.

Stepmom. Dir. Chris Columbus. 1998. VHS. Columbia/Tristar Studios, 2001.

Steiber, Ellen. *Empathy: A Novelization*. X-Files 5. New York: HarperTrophy, 1997.

Stevenson, Robert Louis. *The Strange Case of Dr. Jekyll and Mr. Hyde*. Dover, 1991.

Stine, R. L. Goosebumps Series. Scholastic, ongoing.

Stoker, Bram. *Dracula*. New York: Signet, 1997.

Styron, William. *Sophie's Choice*. New York: Vintage, 1992.

Sullivan, C. W., III. "High Fantasy." Hunt 303–13.

Survivor. Prod. Mark Burnett. TV series. CBS, ongoing.

Taxi Cab Confessions. Dir. and prod. Rob Goodman. TV series. CBS, ongoing.

Tapscott, Dan. *Growing Up Digital: The Rise of the Net Generation*. New York: McGraw-Hill, 1998.

Taylor, Jill McLean, Carol Gilligan, and Amy M. Sullivan. *Between Voice and Silence: Women and Girls, Race and Relationship*. Cambridge: Harvard UP, 1995.

Teaching Mrs. Tingle. Dir. Kevin Williamson. 1999. VHS. Dimension Home Video, 2003.

Ten Things I Hate about You. Dir. Gil Junger. 1999. VHS. Touchstone Video, 2002.

Terminator 2—Judgment Day. Dir. James Cameron. 1991. DVD. Artisan Entertainment, 2001.

A Time To Kill. Dir. Joel Schumacher. 1996. DVD. Warner Studios, 2003.

Titanic. Dir. James Cameron. 1997. DVD. Paramount Studios, 1999.

Todorov, Tzvetan. *Introduction to Poetics*. Trans. Richard Howard. Minneapolis: U of Minnesota P, 1981.

Tolkien, J. R. R. *The Hobbit and The Lord of the Rings*. Boston: Houghton, 1994.

Tompkins, Jane. "An Introduction to Reader Response Criticism." *Reader-Response Criticism: From Formalism to Post-structuralism*. Ed. Tompkins. Baltimore: Johns Hopkins UP, 1980. ix–xxvi.

———. *Sensational Designs: The Cultural Work of American Fiction, 1790–1860*. New York: Oxford UP, 1985.

Total Recall. Dir. Paul Verhoeven. DVD. Artisan-Fox Video, 1990.

Treasure Planet. Dir. John Musker and Ron Clements. DVD. Walt Disney Home Video, 2002.

Trites, Roberta. *Disturbing the Universe: Power and Repression in Adolescent Literature*. Iowa City: U of Iowa P, 2000.

———. *Waking Sleeping Beauty: Feminist Voices in Children's Novels*. Iowa City: U of Iowa P, 1997.

The Truman Show. Dir. Peter Weir. DVD. Paramount Studio, 1998.

Turkle, Sherry. *Life on the Screen: Identity in the Age of the Internet*. New York: Simon, 1997.

Twain, Mark. *The Adventures of Huckleberry Finn*. New York: Bantam, 1981.

———. *Puddn'head Wilson*. New York: Bantam, 1994.

Tyner, Kathleen. *Literacy in a Digital World: Teaching and Learning in the Age of Information*. Mahwah, NJ: Erlbaum, 1998.

Van Draanen, Wendelin. *How I Survived Being a Girl*. New York: HarperTrophy, 1998.

Walker, Alice. *The Color Purple*. New York: Pocket, 1990.

Walkerdine, Valerie. *Daddy's Girl: Young Girls and Popular Culture*. Cambridge: Harvard UP, 1997

Walpole, Horace. *The Castle of Otranto*. In *Three Gothic Novels*. Ed. Peter Fairclough. New York: Penguin, 1968. 37–148.

Watt, Ian P. *The Rise of the Novel: Studies in Defoe, Richardson, and Fielding*. Berkeley: U of California P, 2001.

Weston, Carol. *Girltalk: All the Stuff Your Sister Never Told You*. New York: HarperPerennial Library, 1997.

White, Barbara. *Growing Up Female: Adolescent Girlhood in American Fiction.* Westport, CT: Greenwood, 1985.

White, E. B. *Charlotte's Web.* New York: Harper, 1999.

Weird Science. Dir. John Hughes. 1997. VHS. Universal Studios, 1997.

The Wild Wild West. Dir. Barry Sonnenfeld. 1999. VHS. Warner Studios, 1999.

Wilder, Laura Ingalls. *Little House in the Big Woods.* New York: HarperTrophy, 1971.

Wilhelm, Jeffrey. *"You Gotta* BE *the Book": Teaching Engaged and Reflective Reading with Adolescents.* New York: Teachers College P, 1997.

Williams, Margery. *The Velveteen Rabbit.* Garden City, NY: Doubleday, 1922.

Winnicott, D. W. *Playing and Reality.* London: Tavistock, 1971.

Wolf, Naomi. *The Beauty Myth: How Images of Beauty Are Used Against Women.* New York: Anchor, 1991.

Worst-Case Scenario. Prod. Craig Peligian. TV series. SONY Pictures Television. WB, ongoing.

Wyss, Johann David. *The Swiss Family Robinson.* New York: Yearling, 1999.

Yalom, Marilyn. *A History of the Wife.* New York: Harper, 2001.

Zipes, Jack. *Fairy Tales and the Art of Subversion: The Classical Genre for Children and the Process of Civilization.* New York: Methuen, 1988.

Index

About the Author

HOLLY BLACKFORD is an assistant professor of English at Rutgers University, Camden, where she teaches and researches literature and readers. She received her PhD in English from UC Berkeley and has published critical articles on nineteenth- and twentieth-century American literature, children's literature, film, pedagogy, women's culture, and coming of age. She is also an associate at the Center for Children and Childhood Studies, and director of the Reading and Writing Program at Rutgers, Camden. She lives in South Jersey with her husband and two daughters.